D1001773

THE LETTERS OF THOMAS GAINSBOROUGH

Thomas Gainsborough Self-Portrait, 1787
Royal Academy of Arts, London

THE LETTERS OF THOMAS GAINSBOROUGH

EDITED BY

JOHN HAYES

PUBLISHED FOR THE PAUL MELLON CENTRE FOR STUDIES IN BRITISH ART

BY

YALE UNIVERSITY PRESS

2001

Designed in Adobe Garamond by Guilland Sutherland.
Printed in Great Britain by BAS Printers Limited, Over Wallop, Hampshire

Library of Congress Catalog Card Number 00-111790
ISBN 0-300-08732-2

A catalogue record for this book is available from the British Library.

CONTENTS

LIST OF ILLUSTRATIONS

ACKNOWLEDGMENTS

Gainsborough's letters were first collected and edited nearly forty years ago by Dr Mary Woodall. They were published in handsome private press editions by the Lion and Unicorn Press at the Royal College of Art, London (1st edition containing 91 Gainsborough letters, limited to 400 subscribers, 1961) and the Cupid Press, Woodbridge (2nd revised and slightly expanded edition, with 96 Gainsborough letters, 1963). Since then 13 hitherto unknown letters, of which 3 are only fragmentary, have come to light; while all known instructions from Gainsborough to his bankers, and receipts for payments from his clients, are included in the present edition (6 of the former and 3 of the latter were published in Woodall).

In the course of assembling the present edition, and preparing the explanatory notes, I have been helped by a great many people, whom it is a pleasure to thank here. Two Gainsborough scholars have supported my work over a period of years, providing much valuable information and patiently answering a stream of questions: Hugh Belsey, Curator of Gainsborough's House, and Susan Sloman, who has recently completed a study of late-eighteenth-century Bath for a doctorate at Bristol University under the supervision of Michael Liversidge. I am greatly indebted to them both. For particular help and advice I thank also Dr Brian Allen; the late John Bensusan-Butt; John Blatchly; Polly Bowen, at Maggs Bros.; Jane Cunningham, Photographic Survey Librarian, Courtauld Institute of Art; Dr Oliver Davies, of the Royal College of Music; Dr Andrew Fisher, Archivist at Drumlanrig Castle; Dr Chris Fletcher, of the Department of Manuscripts at the British Library; Mireille Galinou, until recently Curator of Paintings, Prints and Drawings at the Museum of London; Cynthia Gibbons, of Art Placement International; John Ingamells; Ingrid Lackajis, Area Librarian, Royal Borough of Kensington and Chelsea; Iain Mackintosh; Mark Pomeroy, Archivist of the Royal Academy of Arts; Roger Pringle and Dr Robert Smallwood, of the Shakespeare Birthplace Trust, Stratford-upon-Avon; Professor Michael Rosenthal; Jacob Simon; Lindsay Stainton; Steven Tomlinson, at the Bodleian Library; and David Tyler. Others are acknowledged in specific places in the notes.

I am most grateful, as always, to the Librarians and their colleagues, of the different departments of the British Library; the Guildhall Library; the London Library; the Paul Mellon Centre for Studies in British Art; the National Portrait Gallery; and the Witt Library, Courtauld Institute of Art; and to successive Keepers, and their colleagues, of the Department of Prints and Drawings at the British Museum. The standard biographical reference works used in the notes, such as Burke's *Peerage*, *The Dictionary of National Biography* and *The History of Parliament* are gratefully acknowledged.

Brian Allen, Director of the Paul Mellon Centre, which commissioned this publication by Yale University Press, and John Nicoll, my publisher, have both kept a watchful eye on progress. Also at the Mellon Centre I owe an immense debt to Emma Lauze for gathering the photographs for the illustrations, obtaining permissions and other essential tasks; while Guilland Sutherland has brought her customary sympathetic understanding and exceptional skills as an editor to the exacting work of preparing the volume for the press. More personally, Morag Timbury has been a constant source of encouragement throughout.

Above all, I am deeply grateful to the public and private owners of the letters and other documents for their kindness in agreeing to their publication.

John Hayes
November 2000

CHRONOLOGY

1727 Baptized 14 May at the Independent meeting house in Friar's Street, Sudbury, fifth child and youngest son of John Gainsborough, a shroud-maker, and Mary Burrough.

c.1740 Sent up to London and became a pupil of Hubert François Gravelot, the French draughtsman and engraver, who taught at the St. Martin's Lane Academy. Strongly influenced by Francis Hayman, who also taught at the Academy, and collaborated with him on various occasions over the next decade or so, notably in some of his decorative painting for the supper boxes at Vauxhall gardens; in turn Hayman was also influenced by Gainsborough's style as it developed in later years.

c.1743/4 Established his own studio in London, renting rooms in Hatton Garden, Clerkenwell, the centre of the jewellers' and watchmakers' trades.

1746 Married Margaret Burr, natural daughter of Henry, 1st Duke of Beaufort—who had settled an annuity of £200 a year on her—on 15 July at Dr Keith's Mayfair Chapel, London, well known for the celebration of clandestine weddings. They moved to a house with a fair-sized garden in Hatton Garden.

1748 'Mary Gainsborough of Hatton Garden' was buried at St Andrew's' Holborn on 1 March (this was probably the Gainsboroughs' first child). Presented a view of the Charterhouse as one of a series of eight roundels of London hospitals for the embellishment of the Court Room of the Foundling Hospital.

1749 Left London in the early part of the year and returned to settle in Sudbury.

1750 Birth of his elder daughter, Mary, baptized at All Saints, Sudbury, on 3 February.

1751 Birth of his younger daughter, Margaret, baptized at St Gregory's, Sudbury, on 22 August.

1752 Moved to Ipswich, where he leased a house opposite the Shire Hall.

1753 Met his future biographer, Philip Thicknesse, who commissioned a view of Landguard Fort as an overmantel.

1755 Completed two overmantels for John, 4th Duke of Bedford (redecoration was then in progress both at Bedford House, London, and Woburn Abbey).

1758-59 Spent a season in Bath from October 1758 until possibly April or May 1759.

1759 Sold his household goods, together with a number of paintings and drawings, in Ipswich in October. Subsequently moved to Bath, where he leased a large house in Abbey Street, making an income from letting rooms to lodgers. The lease ran for seven years from 24 June 1760, and was renewed for a further seven. Painted his first masterpiece in full-length portraiture, the portrait of the beautiful amateur musician Ann Ford, soon to marry Philip Thicknesse.

1761 First exhibited at the Society of Artists, London.

1763 Seriously ill in September/October, largely from overwork, and subsequently took a house outside Bath, in Lansdown Road, from where he could ride on Lansdown.

1766 Moved to a house in the newly built Circus, Bath, using the house in Abbey Street solely for lettings.

1768 Invited to become a founder-member of the Royal Academy, of which Joshua Reynolds had been appointed President.

1769 First exhibited at the Royal Academy. The spectacular full-length of Lady Molyneux, later Countess of Sefton, was his *chef d'oeuvre*.

1772 Took as a formal apprentice his nephew, Gainsborough Dupont (1754-97). Dupont was his only recorded pupil and assistant.

1773 Quarrelled with the Royal Academy over the hanging of his pictures, which resulted in his not contributing to the annual exhibition again until 1777.

1774 Left Bath to settle in London, taking a tenancy of the west wing of Schomberg House, Pall Mall, from midsummer 1774 until his death.

1777 Exhibited *The Watering Place* and the magnificent full-length of the Hon. Mrs Graham at the Royal Academy.

1780 Marriage of his daughter Mary to the oboeist Johann Christian Fischer on 21 February (the couple were soon to separate; his younger daughter Margaret never married). Exhibited a series of masterpieces at the Royal Academy, including full-lengths of Sir Henry Bate-Dudley, his son-in-law Fischer, and six landscapes said to 'beggar description', notably *The Country Churchyard* and *The Cottage Door.*

1781 Exhibited full-lengths of George III and Queen Charlotte at the Royal Academy, and thereafter received numerous royal commissions, virtually becoming court painter. Also exhibited the first of his fancy pictures, *A Shepherd Boy.*

c.1781-82 Constructed his peep-show box in which he displayed transparencies.

1783 Made a tour of the Lake District in the summer with his old friend, Samuel Kilderbee. His only documented Continental trip, to Antwerp, took place in October.

1784 Quarrelled again with the Royal Academy over the hanging of his pictures and never again exhibited there. Started a series of annual exhibitions at his own showrooms at Schomberg House.

1788 Died on 2 August and was buried in Kew Churchyard.

EXPLANATION AND ABBREVIATIONS

SELECTION

All known letters are included, even if only fragments survive. The order is chronological. Other notes and documents written and signed by Gainsborough (for example, receipts for payments made by his clients) are printed, also in chronological order, following the main series of letters. The numbering is consecutive.

No letters written to Gainsborough are included. In the few cases where letters from Gainsborough are replies to known letters from his correspondent, these are noted in footnotes.

EDITING

The owners of those letters that are known in manuscript are noted at the top of the letter. The text is reproduced as faithfully as possible. Capitalization, punctuation or the lack of it, misspellings, strike-throughs, amendments and insertions are preserved. The symbol < > denotes an insertion; [ ] encloses illegible or deleted word(s) or indicates lacunae as a result of the manuscript being damaged; [*sic*] is not introduced after misspellings—for example, Gainsborough, like Reynolds, consistently wrote 'immediatly'. Valedictions and addresses follow the style of Gainsborough's own text.

Where letters remain untraced the source or sources of the text printed are indicated at the top of the letter. References are not otherwise made to previous owners or places of publication.

Addresses, postmarks and other stamps employed by the postal services are noticed. Where they are not given it may be assumed that they are missing or else never used in the letter concerned, perhaps because of hand delivery. Endorsements by recipients are not noted.

APPENDICES

A Biographical Register gives a brief account of recipients or persons mentioned whose names occur three time or more. Others are identified in footnotes. An index of recipients precedes the general index.

ABBREVIATIONS

Fulcher
: George Williams Fulcher, *Life of Thomas Gainsborough, R.A.*, 2nd ed., revised, London, 1856

Hayes
: John Hayes, *The Landscape Paintings of Thomas Gainsborough*, 2 vols., London, 1982

Waterhouse
: Ellis Waterhouse, *Gainsborough*, London, 1958

Whitley
: William T. Whitley, *Thomas Gainsborough*, London, 1915

Woodall
: Mary Woodall, *The Letters of Thomas Gainsborough*, 2nd ed. revised, Cupid Press, 1963

THE LETTERS OF THOMAS GAINSBOROUGH

Johan Zoffany (1733-1810). *Thomas Gainsborough*
Canvas, 19.4 x 16.8. c.1772
Tate Gallery (on loan to the National Portrait Gallery)

INTRODUCTION

'Brilliant but eccentric . . . too licentious to be published.' So one bundle of Gainsborough's letters, which appears later to have been destroyed, was described in the early part of the nineteenth century. 'For a letter to an intimate friend, he had few equals, and no superior', was another, more sympathetic, comment. 'It was like his conversation gay, lively and fluttering round subjects which he just touched and away to another—expressing his thoughts with so little reserve that his correspondents, considering the letter as part of their friend had never the heart to burn it'. Thus William Jackson, the composer, recipient of some of Gainsborough's most eloquent and original letters, and whose descendants, fortunately, were as discerning as he.

Neither description is, however, characteristic of the typical cultivated eighteenth-century letter-writer, who was informative, elegant in expression, often wise, often witty, with felicitous turns of phrase, but rarely eccentric, inconsequential or unrestrained. Even Horace Walpole, perhaps the most celebrated letter-writer of the age, is not an exception to this rule. Sometimes, to be sure, his words do seem to pour out in something of a torrent: 'Stay, Madam; my letter is not got on horseback yet'; or the whimsy of his comment catches one unawares: 'I have danced three country-dances with a whole set, forty-years younger than myself! Shall you not think I have been chopped to shreds and boiled in Medea's kettle?' Undoubtedly

William Jackson (1730–1803)
Canvas, 78.2 x 56.1. RA 1770
Private Collection, Scotland

his letters sparkle; he was brilliantly amusing, outrageous, malicious, cynical, never less than sharply observant; but for all that he was fastidious in literary composition, wrote with clarity and point, and settled in to a subject or an anecdote. He was neither mercurial nor episodic, nor was he revealing about himself in any deep sense. Decorously brought up in the age of Pope, Walpole was too much the Augustan, the civilized man of the world and arbiter of taste, ever to have been a man of feeling, as Gainsborough was: he would have found abhorrent the self-indulgent outpourings of Rousseau, the arch-priest of the new age of *sensibilité*. If there are elements in common between the writings of the two, they are occasional, and the most convincing comparison to be made between Gainsborough and any of this contemporaries — the only one which rings consistently true — is, as Jackson pointed out, with Sterne.

Laurence Sterne, whose *Tristram Shandy* came out in pairs of volumes between 1760 and 1765, achieving for its author an instantaneous literary success and personal celebrity (Reynolds's famous portrait dates from 1760), was not unlike James Joyce in his total transformation of the literary idiom of his day. To start with, the physical extent of his world was small, bounded indeed by the grounds of Shandy Hall; his concern was with the feelings and responses of his characters within the confines of domestic life and incident. Thus he was intimate, spoke from the heart, and wrote as people talk (his style was formed on long experience of sermon-writing); his pages flow on, darting from subject to subject, without apparent focus, punctuated by dashes which signify the pauses, nods and gestures of normal converse. He was also original and inventive in his use of language—a pedagogue, for instance, is neatly hit off as a 'gerund-grinder' in Walter Shandy's catalogue of the 'husk and shell ...which grows up with learning'.

Gainsborough was an original in much the same way; his phrases are equally striking and apposite, equally to be savoured. Thus to Garrick (incidentally also a correspondent of Sterne's), criticizing the excesses of the great actor's stage lighting: 'When the streets are paved with Brilliants, and the Skies made of Rainbows I suppose you'l be contented, and satisfied with Red blue & yellow'. To Edward Stratford, after much procrastination with a commission: 'if I disapoint you of *seeing* your Pictures hung in their Places *with my own Eyes*, I'll give you leave to boil me down for Painters Drying oil, and shiver my Bones into Pencil = Sticks'. Or to Jackson, about the mind of the distinguished lawyer, John Dunning: 'his Store=Room seems cleared of all french Ornaments and gingerbread Work . . . no disorder or confusion in the *furniture* as if he was going to remove'. Occasionally, there is a telling transmutation of a word, as when, after an admonishment to the talented but socially ambitious Jackson, ' 'tis mighty pretty to be sure to stand and admire another man hop upon one leg, and forget the use of *two damnd long ones* . . . you underthimble me'. And, of course, there was what the nineteenth century censured as licentious, an easy freedom in expression, again characteristically to the strait-laced Jackson: 'I'll not *take* any thing for it [*a harp*] but give [it] to you to twang upon when you can't twang upon Mrs Jackson', or 'What can a Man say pent up in a corner thus; if you was a Lady I would say what I have often said in a corner by way of making the most of the last Inch. yours up to the hilt'. One recalls Sir Francis Bourgeois's reminiscence that Gainsborough said 'he talked bawdy to the King, & morality to the Prince of Wales'.

Gainsborough's letters are no less fluent and brilliant than Sterne's prose, and are similarly punctuated with dashes—pauses that arrest for a brief moment the rapid motions of his agile brain. Sometimes, too, there are abrupt changes of mood or pace, as at the conclusion of some remarks to James Unwin about his brother: 'I think he does not meet Eyes quite so steadily as yourself, but don't you tell him what I say. Oh, my poor Head. Don't you think a Jackass three quarters asleep upon the ridge of a Bank undermined and mouldring away is very expressive of the happiness of not seeing danger?' Again like Sterne, he was not concerned with the wide world. His correspondence was almost entirely personal in content, stimulated by his painting or other interests, his domestic affairs or those of his friends. He may have been intimate with Ralph Allen, and Garrick, and Shelburne, but he never commented upon literature, the theatre or politics except very occasionally in relation to advice given to a friend. Even social comment, the very stuff of contemporary letter-writing, is rare, and then subordinated to wit: 'new Buildings are extending in all points from the old center of Bath, the Pump Rooms—We almost reach Landsdown & Cleverton=down, north & south, but not quite to Bristol & London for East & West. I think verily the End of some of our *Master* Builders will be to meet some of their Marylebone Friends near a certain Ditch. It does not appear to me that many of the new Houses are occupied by Genteal Families newly residing in Bath, but only that the Lodging-House *Cats* are endeavouring to draw more Talons upon us, by having Houses in all quarters'.

Dr Wolcot, the satirist and poet, said that he 'had supposed Gainsborough to be an illiterate man, till He saw a letter from Gainsborough to Lord Lansdown, which displays a powerful talent for writing'. Gainsborough's close friend and admirer, Sir Henry Bate-Dudley, proprietor and editor of the *Morning Herald*, went a good deal further when he wrote shortly after the artist's death that his correspondence 'possessed the ease of *Swift*, and the nervous force of *Bolingbroke*', adding that 'a selection of his letters would offer to the world as much originality and beauty, as is ever to be traced in his PAINTING!' Gainsborough clearly was as ready with his pen as with his brush, and would dash off, between sittings, even a longish letter to a friend. Nonetheless, hardly a hundred letters survive today out of what must have surely been a voluminous correspondence; and of the letters received by Gainsborough from his many friends, sadly there remain none (except in the case where an official, such as the agent

The Revd Sir Henry Bate-Dudley (1745–1824)
Canvas, 72.4 x 57.8. c.1780
Burton Trustees (on loan to the Tate Gallery)

to the Duke of Bedford, retained a file copy). It is in keeping with the artist's impulsive character that he seems never to have kept letters, as he seems not to have preserved his account and sitter books; for no records of any kind have come down to us from Gainsborough or his descendants.

Who were Gainsborough's principal correspondents, as we know them? Apart from Garrick, they were not, on the whole, well-known people. Samuel Kilderbee, the letters to whom were those described as 'too licentious to be published', was an attorney at Ipswich who became a lifelong friend and was appointed his executor; little, however, is known of their 'long and uninterrupted friendship' save Gainsborough's references to his family going to stay with him in 1777 and to their travelling together to the Lake District in 1783. James Unwin was a financial adviser and banker from early days with whom Gainsborough was able to share the problems of his private life: 'My Regard for you was originally built upon such a foundation that you know no time can shake'. William Jackson, whom he met in the 1760s, perhaps through the Linleys, but from whom he is said to have become estranged in later life, he corresponded with about music and painting: each learnt much

Samuel Kilderbee (1725–1813)
Canvas, 125.1 x 100 c.1755
Fine Arts Museums of San Francisco, Gift of the M. H. de Young Endowment Fund

from the other about their respective arts (Gainsborough often said that he thought he was born to be a musician). There were his children, in whose case, again, no letters survive, for we are told that Margaret Gainsborough 'regretted much having lost many letters which he wrote to her and her sister while they were at Blacklands School, containing instructions for drawing'. And Mary Gibbon, his sister, was a trusted confidante in family matters. With his wife he seems never to have corresponded, though a long letter to her composed by a modern faker was published as his in the *Essex and Suffolk News*, 25 July 1908. Series of letters are extant to three of his patrons: Lord Dartmouth, Richard Stevens and Edward Stratford. Otherwise only single, or at most two, letters survive to particular correspondents. Curiously, three of Gainsborough's main correspondents — Unwin, 'a brisk little man', Jackson, conservative and genteel, and his sister, a pious Methodist — were quite opposed to him in temperament. Not that this in the least affected his manner of writing to them: 'you being all regularity & Judgment', he told Jackson, 'I own provoke me the more to break loose'. No letters survive, save a brief official one, to Joshua Kirby, father of the evangelical writer, Sarah

Trimmer, another person of great piety and rectitude who was a close friend from youth and next to whose grave he desired to be buried. Nor, strangely, do any letters exist to his intimate friend, Karl Friedrich Abel; only two to Bate-Dudley and one to Philip Thicknesse. A tally of Gainsborough's friends and principal patrons is the measure of our loss.

The bulk of Gainsborough's extant correspondence dates from his middle years. No more than a handful of letters survives from before he turned thirty-five — and none, sadly, prior to the age of twenty-five, so that nothing is to be gleaned from his own writings, except occasionally in retrospect, concerning his ambitions or state of mind as a young man. About a quarter of the letters were written in the last decade of his life. From the beginning Gainsborough wrote with fluency; there are few corrections. However, his handwriting changed significantly over the years. In the 1750s it was tight and neat. In the early 1760s it was somewhat looser, but still very regular, the lines as though traced out carefully with a ruler. By the latter part of the decade it had become much more flowing and authoritative. Not until the last months of his life did his hand show signs of irresolution: his last pathetic letter to Reynolds, written shortly before he died, was a much corrected scrawl.

What a man writes to his friends and acquaintances is (or at least it was when a letter was the principal means of communication) the surest guide to his character, beliefs and approach to life when that person is no longer alive. Reynolds's letters are lucid and businesslike, carefully, but unimaginatively, expressed — he worried about his style — and inclined to be pompous or effusive, according to the recipient. They are singularly unrevealing; though, in that very fact, informative about Reynolds. Spontaneous and idiosyncratic letters such as Gainsborough wrote are, by contrast, unusually revealing, but inevitably disclose greater psychological complexities. Gainsborough was, in any case, a creature of moods, who wondered at Reynolds's relentless regularity: 'I am the most inconsistent, changable being, so full of fitts and starts'.

Partly owing to the incompatibility of his wife — 'My Dear Good Wife', whom he loved dearly, but who was 'never much formed to humour my Happiness', and was frugal and unwelcoming to his friends — Gainsborough often rebelled against domesticity and lapsed into conviviality or worse, which prevented him from working: 'I have done nothing but fiddle since I came from London, so much was I unsettled by the continual run of Pleasure which my Friend Giardini and the rest of you engaged me in'. He had an immense capacity for enjoyment: 'do but recollect how many hard featured fellows there are in the world that frown in the midst of enjoyment, chew with unthankfulness, and seem to swallow with pain instead of pleasure'. He was warm-hearted as well as sociable and as incurably generous as his wife was mean; the son of his friend and patron, the Revd Robert Hingeston, who lived near Southwold, recalled that he had 'seen the aged features of the peasantry lit up with a grateful recollection of his many acts of kindness and benevolence. . . . Many houses in Suffolk, as well as in the neighbouring county, were always open to him, and their owners thought it an honour to entertain him'. Yet, Thicknesse asserted, he was 'of a modest, shy, reserved disposition, which continued with him till his death'; in a letter to John Cooke describing a visit they had both made to Lord Bateman at Shobdon Court Thicknesse complained that their host might have seen that he was 'a shy bashful man, that he could have opened *him* with a bottle of Champaigne at dinner and another at supper'.

Gainsborough 'had two faces, his studious & Domestic' as well as 'His Convivial one', his daughter Margaret told the diarist, Joseph Farington. 'As to his common acquaintance he was sprightly and agreeable, so to his intimate friends he was serious and honest'. He could be candid, but, since he disliked talking 'like old square toes', he was gently or wittily so. 'Whatever so great a Genius as Mr Garrick may say or do to support our false Taste, He must feel the truth of what I am now saying.' Or to Jackson: 'ever since I have been quite clear in your being a real Genius, so long have I been of Opinion that you are dayly throwing your Gift away upon *Gentlemen* & only studying how you shall become the *Gentleman* too'. He hated humbug and deceit, and was determined to have what he called 'truth and Day light' in everything. In his last illness he told Kilderbee that he greatly regretted his own faults, adding, however: 'They must take me altogether, liberal, thoughtless, and discipated [*sic*]'. He was a God-fearing man: 'I trust if I do my best, all will be well through the merits of Him who hath promised to make good our failings if we trust sincerely'. And his friends helped. 'That you know the worst of me', he wrote to Unwin, 'I am not sorry for, because I know you have good sense & Good nature to place things in their proper light. . . . I always think one cannot be too open to sensible people nor too reserved to fools'. He was worldly wise as well as raffish and precipitate.

The liveliness of Gainsborough's conversation was much admired, so Bate-Dudley tells us, by wits as brilliant as Sheridan and Richard Tickell. 'The swallow . . . never skimmed a surface so light as Gainsborough touched all subjects . . . his favourite subjects were music and painting; which he treated in a manner peculiarly his own. The common topics, or any of a superior cast, he thoroughly hated, and always interrupted by some stroke of wit and humour'. Garrick is said to have pronounced that 'His cranium is so crammed with genius of every kind that it is in danger of bursting upon you, like a steam-engine overcharged'. His eye was as sharp as his imagination was vivid, and Reynolds tells us how 'He had a habit of continually remarking to those who happened to be about him, whatever peculiarity of countenance, whatever accidental combination of figures, or happy effects of light and shadow, occurred in prospects, in the sky, in walking the streets, or in company. . . . He neglected nothing which could keep his faculties in exercise'. Gainsborough's acute visual sense and devotion to his art were matched by his craft and his professionalism, and it is, above all, of course, for his views on matters connected with his painting that Gainsborough's letters are especially valuable.

THE POSTAL SERVICE IN GAINSBOROUGH'S TIME

The modern British postal service was founded by William Dockwra in 1680. Hundreds of receiving offices, where letters might be lodged, were opened in London; messengers called every hour to take the mail to the seven London sorting offices for distribution in the metropolis, which happened within the hour, and to the General Post Office in Lombard Street for dispatch to the country, which took place on Tuesdays, Thursdays and Saturdays. The country post roads were divided into sections, or stages, each presided over by a postmaster, usually also an inn-keeper. At first all country mail was routed through London; the earliest cross-country service, from Exeter to Bristol, was established in 1696. It was the postmaster's responsibility to collect the penny postage and postmark the letters, and to distribute the mail. Ralph Allen was appointed postmaster for Bath in 1720, and was succeeded by John Palmer the younger (see Biographical Register), who ran an office of one clerk and three letter-carriers (for whom uniform was introduced in 1792). It was Palmer who persuaded the postmaster-general to introduce the mail-coach service; the first of these ran from Bristol to London in 1784, taking seventeen hours and thus halving the journey time; in 1792 sixteen mail-coaches left London every day.

Since houses were mostly unnumbered, addresses had to be descriptive; Gainsborough was unusually precise in his letter to Kirby (see Letter 37). With someone as famous as Garrick, just London was apparently sufficient, and Gainsborough often put no more than Exeter on his letters to William Jackson. Members of Parliament did not have to pay postage, hence Gainsborough's addition of M.P. on his letters to Richard Stevens. Envelopes were not always used; letters were folded and sealed, the address being written on the outer fold. Letters to particular towns were made into packets for carriage. If Palmer went off to London on business, the Exeter service suffered; Gainsborough did not receive a letter from Jackson for nearly a month 'after it arrived shut up in a Music Book at Mr Palmer's'. Not all towns had a mail service, and an early postmaster of Sudbury (where Gainsborough's father was postmaster from the time of his bankruptcy in 1733 until his death in

John Palmer (1742–1818)
Canvas, 76.2 x 63.8. c.1775
Philadelphia Museum of Art
(William L. Elkins Collection)

1748) was obliged himself to carry the letters to Braintree and back, a distance of thirty-two miles, three times a week. Within a town letters were, of course, very often hand-delivered; an example is Gainsborough's note to the Royal Academy Hanging Committee (Letter 97), written on a Saturday evening and presumably taken round immediately.

John Gainsborough (1683-1748), the artist's father
Canvas, 61.2 x 51.1. c.1746–48
Corcoran Gallery of Art (Edward C. and Mary Walker Collection), Washington, DC

THE LETTERS OF THOMAS GAINSBOROUGH

Gainsborough was born in Sudbury, a small market town in Suffolk — a county then and in Constable's day deeply proud of its agricultural innovativeness and prosperity — and was baptized in May 1727 in the Independent meeting house in Friar's Street. He came of Dissenting stock, reflecting that independence of temper characteristic of the Eastern counties; and many of the Gainsboroughs had been associated with, or supported, the Friar's Street chapel. His forbears had long been connected with the woollen industry in East Anglia, and Gainsborough's father, John, was a prosperous cloth merchant until his business fell on hard times in the early 1730s. There were nine children, five sons and four daughters, of whom Thomas was the youngest. 'All', so Thicknesse, who was the artist's earliest biographer, reported, 'were wonderfully ingenious'. Gainsborough took to sketching from an early age and later told Thicknesse that 'during his Boy-hood, *though he had no idea of becoming a Painter then, yet there was not a Picturesque clump of Trees, nor even a single Tree of beauty, no, nor hedge row, stone or post, at the corner of the Lanes, for some miles round about the place of his nativity, that he had not . . . perfectly in his* mind's eye'.

At the age of thirteen, that is to say in 1740 or 1741, he persuaded his parents to let him go up to London as an art student, and he worked for four or five years in the studio of the distinguished French draughtsman, Hubert Gravelot, the person who was chiefly responsible for introducing and disseminating in England the rococo style in design, the style we associate with Chippendale furniture, Chelsea porcelain and the silver of Paul de Lamerie. Through Gravelot he would have met most of the avant-garde artists and craftsmen of the day, and through Gravelot, too, he is said to have studied at 'the old academy of the arts, in St. Martin's Lane', where Francis Hayman, whose portraits-in-little and conversation pieces with landscape settings were an undoubted influence on early Gainsborough, is reputed to have taught him.

In about 1743 or 1744 he set up on his own, renting rooms in Hatton Garden, Clerkenwell. From this moment he seems to have left the world of Gravelot and the decorative arts firmly behind him, for 'his first efforts were small landscapes, which he frequently sold to the dealers at trifling prices'; these works were largely the product of his study, in the London salerooms, of the techniques and compositions of such seventeenth-century Dutch naturalist painters as Ruisdael, Hobbema and Wijnants. He also executed at this period a number of portraits-in-little. In 1748 he was invited to contribute one of the eight roundels of London hospitals which were to form part of the decoration of the Court Room of the Foundling Hospital; his own picture was of the Charterhouse, an enchanting canvas, original in concept and design, which George Vertue, the art chronicler of the day, informs us was 'tho't the best & masterly manner'.

On 15 July 1746, at Dr Keith's Mayfair Chapel, a venue for the celebration of clandestine weddings, Gainsborough married Margaret Burr, a beautiful Scots girl a year or so younger than himself, who was, as their daughter later told Farington, 'a natural daughter of Henry, Duke of Beaufort, who settled £200 a yr. upon Her'. According to Fulcher, a Sudbury printer who was the first serious biographer of Gainsborough, she was the sister of a commercial traveller employed by the artist's father. Margaret may have been pregnant at the time of her wedding (their child christened Mary died in infancy), which would account for the secrecy of the marriage; no doubt, too, Gainsborough's parents would have objected to her because she was illegitimate.

In October 1748, Gainsborough's father died, and early in the following year he decided to return to Sudbury. His elder daughter, also called Mary, was born there in 1750. In spite of the réclame *attached to his view of the Charterhouse, 'he had not formed any high Ideas of his own powers, but rather considered himself as one, among a crowd of Artists, who might be able in a country town (by turning his hand to every kind of painting)* [to] *pick up a decent livelihood'. It was an unusual step, for, then as now, London was the centre of artistic patronage, but Gainsborough was not one of those who enjoyed the schemings and jostle for place characteristic of the art world; he kept well clear, in later life, of the politics of the Royal Academy.*

One of the works he painted soon after his return home was a masterpiece, exquisite in touch and colour and fresh and true in its rendering of the Suffolk countryside. This was the celebrated double portrait, now in the National Gallery, of Robert Andrews of Auberies and his wife Frances, which shows the young couple set against the broad acres of their modern and well-tended estate. But such commissions were rare, and the going was hard; as he said later, 'the truth is . . . I suffered some hardships in the first part of my Voyage'. In view of his wife's not insubstantial income, it is puzzling that he should have been in financial straits; nevertheless we know that, in November 1751, a few months after the birth of his younger daughter, Margaret, he was seeking a loan of four hundred pounds. In 1752 Gainsborough moved to Ipswich, a larger and more thriving town which was also a social, political and cultural centre of some consequence in East Anglia. The house he rented, of a fair size, with garden and stable, was close to the harbour, in Foundation Street, opposite the Shire Hall.

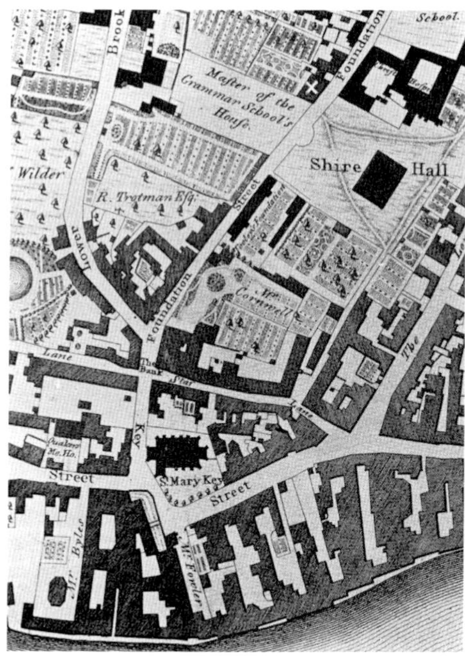

The parish of St. Mary Key, Ipswich, 1778, showing Gainsborough's house (marked with a white cross) north of the schoolmaster's house.
From Pennington's map of 1778

Admiral Edward Vernon (1684–1757)
Canvas, 124 x 99.5. 1753
With Richard Green, London

1

TO ELIZABETH RASSE[1] [1753]

MS. Yale Center for British Art, New Haven (Paul Mellon Collection)

Madam

I call'd yesterday upon a Friend in hopes of borrowing money to pay you, but was disapointed & as I shall finish the Admirals picture[2] in a Week you shall have it when I go to Nacton will call & pay you at your new abode

I'm sorry it happen's so but you know I can't make money any more than yourself & when ['you' *crossed out*] I receive it you shall surely have it before anybody

Who am

Mad^{m}. yours to Com^{d}.

Tho Gainsborough

Thursday Morning

1 The letter is endorsed 'To Mrs Rasse', who was presumably the wife of the Ipswich grocer, Thomas Rasse, who was Gainsborough's landlord.

2 The portrait of Admiral Edward Vernon (1684–1757), of Nacton, Suffolk, Member of Parliament for Ipswich 1741–57, was formerly in the Dashwood collection (Haussner Family Limited Partnership sale, Sotheby's, 22 March 2000, Lot 63 repr. col., and col. cover detail, bt. Richard Green; unknown to Waterhouse). The picture in the National Portrait Gallery (881) (Waterhouse No. 692, pl.45), long regarded as the original, is clearly a version. An excellent seaman and commander, Vernon became a national hero after the capture in 1740 of Porto Bello in the Spanish West Indies. He later cultivated a parliamentary connection in Ipswich 'at an immense expense and unspeakable trouble.'

2

TO MR HARRIS[1] 7 MAY 1756

MS. Whereabouts unknown

M^{r}. Harris

I dont pretend to say but my Debt is of too long standing, & I believe I could borrow the money, tho' with this Inconvenience that nobody lends a painter [*word crossed out*] without picture Int. Now as I am already Indebted to you for waiting so long, Why won't you stay till I can pay you, & let me give you a picture: this I assure you I shall willingly do, for I'm neither so ungrateful or Ignorant as to think you wrong in what you

'a little Canvas the size of M^{r}. Barry's'

Lambe Barry (1704–68)
Canvas, 33 x 30. c.1756
Private Collection, England

wrote me, so far from it, that what I'm obliged to do in the picture way, ['in' *crossed out*] <to end> this affair I had much rather do for you, than another who might lend me the money; for besides the disagreeable Jobb of asking, take my word that no one does me services of that nature without a picture. Excepting one Man & he is far from home. these are truths but [*word crossed out*] yet secrets, therefore trust that you'l not let this Letter be seen. What I propose to you is this, if you'l stay till Mid Sum^{r}. for the Money (for which if you desire good security shall have it) I will then paint you any thing you like, either Landskip, or if you will yourself upon a little Canvas the size of M^{r}. Barry's;[2] which I'll shew you whenever you'l call. Give me your answer by John Davis[3]

Which will oblige
Sir your hum^{e}. Servt.
Tho: Gainsborough

Fryday May 7th. 1756
P.S. I have but 3 Debts standing against me one of them is 6 pounds odd, to Olliver[4] Who instead of writing like a Gentleman as you have done,

got into a way of sending an old Crooked Woman every Day or two: She I got rid off by threatning to Draw her picture. Now tho' I don't threaten you, yet I hope to get rid of you by [*word crossed out*] means of the pencel. [*drawing of a hand with a pointing forefinger*] if you have a girl that you'd rather have drawn than yourself tis Equal to me

[*Addr.*] To Mr Harris

1 Possibly Josiah Harris (died 1783), an Ipswich cabinet-maker and auctioneer (see also Letter 34), or Charles Harris, a churchwarden of St. Mary Key in 1759.
2 Probably the three-quarter-length portrait in little (13 x 12 in.; 33 x 30 cm.) of Lambe Barry (1704–68) (Private Collection, England: Waterhouse No. 40, pl.32).
3 John Davis has not been identified.
4 Olliver has not been identified.

3

TO JAMES HATLEY[1] [C.MID TO LATE 1750S]

MS. Gainsborough's House, Sudbury (1994.070)

[unintelligible fragment of letter mutilated to preserve the two portrait sketches on the reverse of the sheet. The two portrait sketches are of John Wood and Captain Clarke:][2]

with regard / was agreed [*two letters illegible*] / . . . ke them away / thing, and the / opportunity of / that take the [*two letters illegible*] / I shall [*letter illegible*] / which is all I [*letter illegible*] / [*letter illegible*] & take a Rec . . . / [*two words illegible*] how

John Wood (1718–83) and Capt. Abraham Clerke (1718–82).
Pen and ink sketches drawn in Letter 3

1 James Hatley (c.1721–87), of Ipswich, was a cultivated amateur who subscribed to the publication of a number of volumes of music and other works. He is not known to have sat to Gainsborough.

2 The identities of the sitters (and of the recipient of the letter) are established by an inscription fixed to the back of the frame when the drawings were cut from the letter: 'These two Caricatures were done by Mr Gainsborough scratched with his pen in a letter to James Hatley [Esq] [*word illegible*] Jack Wood—and to—Capt Clarke [*word illegible*] Wood was a dancing Master well k[nown] in Suffolk, played ['a good' *crossed out*] an <excellent> second Fiddle, and was a good musician; the above three Gentlemen being all distractedly fond of Music, Mr Wood [and] family made one in all their musical meetings, [and] [con]stantly assisted [a]t their convivial [par]ties—Capt Clarke was an Officer of great Merit, and Respectability'. Both John Wood and Captain Abraham Clerke featured in Gainsborough's lost painting of the musical society at Ipswich, described by its mid-nineteenth-century owner, Mr Strutt, as 'exceedingly spirited . . . Immediately in front of the spectator are the portraits of Gainsborough himself, and his friend Captain Clarke, who is leaning familiarly on the Painter's shoulder. The heads of both are turned towards Wood, a dancing master, who is playing on the violin' (Fulcher, p.56). John Wood (1718–83) was the son of Isaac Wood, a dancing master at Bury St Edmunds; by 1740 he was teaching dancing at Ipswich (he was a subscriber to William Boyce's *Twelve Sonatas*, 1747, and other sets of music). Abraham Clerke (1718–72), also a subscriber to several sets of music, was first apprenticed to an attorney, joined the 7th Marines where he rose to the rank of captain before the unit's disbandment in 1748, and was later a lieutenant in the Eastern Battalion of the Suffolk Militia. (I am very grateful to Hugh Belsey for kindly sending me the typescript of his forthcoming article *Gainsborough and caricature: two new pieces of evidence*).

Gainsborough's principal love was always for landscape, and at Ipswich he developed an attractive style which was a fusion of his love for nature, the influence of the more naturalistic Dutch landscapists of the seventeenth century, and his schooling in the French rococo. When Thicknesse first visited his studio in 1753 he was captivated by these works, and commissioned a view of Landguard Point and Fort (of which he was Lieutenant-Governor), 'of the size of a pannel over my chimney piece'. Overmantels were positions in which it was customary to hang landscapes, and two such were ordered by the Duke of Bedford in 1755. But the demand was limited, and Gainsborough depended upon portraiture for his living. His clientèle was largely among the local gentry, the clergy and professional classes, whose requirements were usually a simple and inexpensive likeness: head and shoulders and a plain background, for which, by 1758, the price had risen from five to presumably eight guineas (a half-length then being fifteen). Gainsborough's technique, at first smooth and bland, in the manner with which the cognoscenti would have been familiar from the fashionable face painting of Thomas Hudson and Allan Ramsay, became more vigorous and more painterly towards the end of the decade. Although often in debt, he seems not to have been demanding about his own bills.

4

TO WILLIAM MAYHEW[1] 24 FEBRUARY 175[8][2]

Untraced (Fulcher 1856, p.50)

Sir,

I am favored with your obliging letter, and shall finish your picture in two or three days at farthest, and send to Colchester according to your order, with a frame. I thank you, Sir, for your kind intention of procuring me a few Heads to paint when I come over, which I purpose doing as soon as some of those are finished which I have in hand. I should be glad [*if*] you'd place your picture as far from the light as possible; observing to let the light fall from the left. Favor me with a faithful account of what is generally thought of it; and as to my bill, it will be time enough when I see you,

Who am Sir

Your most obed^{t} hum^{e} serv^{t}

Tho Gainsborough

Ipswich Feb 24th 1757

1 William Mayhew (1706–64) was first identified as the recipient of this and the following letter by John Bensusan-Butt (*Thomas Gainsborough in his Twenties*, 3rd ed., 1993, pp.16–19). Mayhew, the son of a Chelmsford haberdasher, was a prosperous attorney in Colchester; he acted there for Gainsborough's sister, Mary Gibbon. His head-and-shoulders portrait, inscribed on the back 'Gainsborough de Ipswich pinxit 1757', is now in the Western Australian Art Gallery at Perth (Waterhouse No.474a).

2 This letter, like the following one, almost certainly dates from 1758. Either Gainsborough misdated it 1757, as so often happens at the beginning of the year (especially then, when the change to the calendar year beginning in January rather than in April had only taken place in 1752); or Fulcher transcribed it wrongly (see John Bensusan-Butt, *Thomas Gainsborough in his Twenties*, privately published, Colchester, 3rd ed., 1993, p.14). Certainly it would be strange if the sitter had waited for over a year to give Gainsborough the 'faithful account' of what was thought of his portrait that the artist had asked for, an account to which the latter refers in his letter to Mayhew of 13 March 1758. Moreover, Gainsborough mentions his intention of coming over to Colchester as soon as as he had finished work in hand; in the second letter he writes: 'I thought I should have been at Colchester by this time'.

William Mayhew (1706–64)
Canvas, 76.2 x 63.5. 1757
Art Gallery of Western Australia, Perth

5

TO WILLIAM MAYHEW 13 MARCH 1758

Untraced (Fulcher 1856, pp.51–52)

Sir,

I am favor'd with your obliging letter, and return you many thanks for your kind intention; I thought I should have been at Colchester by this time, as I promis'd my sister I would the first opportunity,[1] but business comes in, and being chiefly in the Face way, I'm afraid to put people off when they are in the mind to sit. You please me much by saying that no other fault is found in your picture than the roughness of the surface, for that part being of use in giving force to the effect at a proper distance, and what a judge of painting knows an original from a copy by; in short being the touch of the pencil, which is harder to preserve than smoothness, I am much better pleas'd that they should spy out things of that kind, than to see an eye half an inch out of its place, or a nose out of drawing when viewed at a proper distance. I don't think it would be more ridiculous for

The Revd John Clubbe (1702–73)
Canvas, 76.2 x 63.5. Late 1750s
Private Collection, England
(detail). Before restoration.

a person to put his nose close to the canvas and say the colours smell offensive, than to say how rough the paint lies; for one is just as material as the other with regard to hurting the effect and drawing of a picture. Sir Godfrey Kneller used to tell them that pictures were not made to smell of;[2] and what made his pictures more valuable than others with the connoisseurs was his pencil or touch. I hope, Sir, you'll pardon this dissertation upon pencil and touch, for if I gain no better point than to make you and Mr. Clubb[3] laugh when you next meet at the sign of the Tankard,[4] I shall be very well contented. I'm sure I could not paint his picture for laughing, he gave such a description of eating and drinking at that place. I little thought you were a Lawyer when I said, not one in ten was worth hanging. I told Clubb of that, and he seemed [*to*] think I was lucky that I did not say one in a hundred. It's too late to ask your pardon now, but really, Sir, I never saw one of your profession look so honest in my life, and that's the reason I concluded you were in the wool trade. Sir Jaspar Wood[5] was so kind [*as*] to set me right, otherwise perhaps I should have made more blunders.

I am,

Sir, your most obed[t] & obliged hum. serv[t],

Tho. Gainsborough

Ipswich, Mar. 13th 1758.

[*Addr.*] . . . ey at Law, in Colchester

1 Gainsborough's eldest sister, Mary (see Biographical Register) had married the Revd Christopher Gibbon, then curate of All Saints, Colchester.
2 A saying of Rembrandt, Kneller's first teacher.
3 The Revd John Clubbe (1703–73), rector of St. Margaret's, Whatfield, some ten miles west of Ipswich; Clubbe was well-known as a humorous writer. Gainsborough's portrait of him was last recorded in an Anon. Sale, Sotheby's, 11 July 1990, lot 36 (repr. col.).
4 The Tankard, a picturesque Tudor hostelry, stood in Tacket Street, next to the theatre.
5 No Sir Jaspar Wood is known, and John Bensusan-Butt sensibly suggested that this might have been a misreading for Joseph Wood, the engraver (letter to the compiler, 12 September 1982).

In 1758–59 Gainsborough spent a season in Bath in his search for fresh patronage. 'We have a painter here', wrote William Whitehead, 'who takes the most exact likenesses I ever saw. His painting is coarse and slight, but has ease and spirit.' He needed little inducement now to leave Ipswich, and Thicknesse, who had a house in Bath, where he lived during the winter, may have had some hand, as he certainly claimed, in Gainsborough's decision to try his fortune in the smart West Country spa where the conjunction of wealth and enforced idleness made the visit to a portrait painter part of the routine if not the cure and where the principal practitioner was then William Hoare, well paid and highly respected, but a mediocre talent. The move took place in the autumn of 1759. Gainsborough leased a large house in Abbey Street, in the very heart of the city—premises which he inspected with Thicknesse, and part of which he could let as lodgings. With his studio in this prime site 'business came in so fast' that within five years, by 1764, he was able to raise his prices from eight to twenty guineas for a head and from fifteen, then twenty guineas, to forty guineas for a half-length; his charge for a full-length, a challenge comparatively new to him (Mrs Delany was disturbed by the eccentric originality of his first work at Bath on this scale, a portrait of Thicknesse's wife-to-be, when she saw it in the studio in October 1760), was sixty guineas. His relationships with the aristocracy were as easy and natural as they had been with his friends who met at The Tankard. And Gainsborough was never spoiled by success. He continued to give careful and personal attention to matters of framing, packing and transport, papering up a picture, if necessary, 'to secure the dust from lodging on the surface'.

James Blackamore, *South East View of the Abbey Church of Bath*, showing Gainsborough's house in Abbey Street. Pencil, ink and wash, 36 x 56.7. 1785
Victoria Art Gallery, Bath City Council (detail)

6

TO CAPTAIN HENRY TOWNSHEND[1] 22 APRIL 1762

Untraced (transcribed by H. Isherwood Kay from the original at that time owned by H. S. Marsham-Townshend)

Sir,

I am sorry that from the nature of my damn'd Business, the Time of my coming to Town remains yet uncertain. But you may depend upon it, when I do, will wait on your sister & make the alterations She shall think necessary in your Picture. I would not have you trouble yourself to pay Gossett,[2] but let it alone till your return; I assure you, Sir, that's the least of my thoughts, since if I had never heard your Name, your Countenance I should think security for more than I shall ever get by Painting.

I am Sir

Your most obedient humble servant

Tho Gainsborough

Bath, April 22nd 1762

[*Addr.*] To Capt. Townshend / at Thomas Townshend's Esq[r]. in / Old Burlington Street, London
[*Postmark*] 24 AP BATH

1 Captain Henry Townshend (1737–62), who was promoted Lieutenant-Colonel in the 1st Foot Guards in 1762, was killed in action at Wilhelmstahl near Kassel on 24 June that year. Lord Granby, to whom he had been an ADC, wrote to the Duke of Newcastle: 'My Corps was very warmly engaged. I am sorry to acquaint your Grace that I have lost poor Harry Townshend'. It is clear from Gainsborough's letter that Townshend was about to embark for Germany for service during this last victorious phase of the Seven Years War (Granby sailed from Harwich on 28 May). Gainsborough's portrait of Townshend (Waterhouse, No.670) was last recorded in the possession of William K. Beatty, Florida, in 1984. Townshend was also painted by Reynolds; in this portrait he is depicted in uniform, with a bust of his brilliant commander, Lieutenant-General the Marquis of Granby, beside him.

2 Isaac Gosset (1713–99), the French Huguenot wax modeller and frame maker, also employed by William Hoare. Gainsborough paid him £15 on 14 September 1762 through his account at Hoare's Bank.

7

TO PHILIP, VISCOUNT ROYSTON, LATER 2ND EARL OF HARDWICKE[1] 21 JULY 1763

MS. British Library Add. MS.35350, fo.9r, 10r

Bath July 21st. 1763

My Lord

I should have answer'd your Lordship's Obliging Letter sooner but was from home when it came and return'd but yesterday. I am now about your Lordship's Picture and shall spare no pains to make it as good a Picture as I possibly can; but for fear I should not be able to compleat it time enough for Lord Hardwick to have it into the Country when His Lordship leaves Town, I should be much Obliged if Your Lordship would be pleased to give orders that it may not be open'd in London, but forwarded immediatly on its arrival, into the Country as I shall paper it up to secure the dust from lodging on the surface of the Picture. The payment of the remainder of the Money would be soon enough when your Lordship comes again to Bath; But if your Lordship should be uneasey 'til the Debt is discharged, M[r]. Hoare Banker at Temple Bar will give a proper Receipt in my Name.[2]

His Grace The Duke of Devonshire[3] left Bath about 3 weeks since, and M[r]. Quin[4] told me he <himself> was going to Chatsworth to stay a few

Philip Yorke, 2nd Earl of Hardwicke (1720–90)
Canvas, 127 x 101.6. c.1763
Whereabouts unknown

weeks. Dr Moisy[5] has had a severe fit of the Ague, and (as I am told) says he should make himself very easey with the loss of his Money if he could get rid of the Ague; But whether the loss of the Money might not bring on a shaking fit that form'd itself into an Ague I must leave.[6]

I am your Lordship's most Obedient &
most Obliged humble Servant
Tho Gainsborough

1 Philip Yorke, 2nd Earl of Hardwicke (1720–90), son of the Lord Chancellor, was Member of Parliament for Reigate, 1741–47, and Cambridge, 1747–64. He held the courtesy title of Viscount Royston from 1754, and succeeded his father in 1764. The portrait, a three-quarter length, was last recorded in the William E. Klein, Jr., sale, Sotheby's, 28 November 1973, lot 51 (repr.), bt. P. Collins (Waterhouse, No.350, pl.74). Hardwicke made his final half-payment for it (£21) through Gainsborough's account at Hoare's Bank on 28 August 1764.

2 Gainsborough opened his account with Henry Hoare, of 37 Fleet Street, in 1762. This account, which was closed in 1785, was chiefly concerned with the payment of Mrs Gainsborough's annuity of £200 from Henry, 3rd Duke of Beaufort, previously the responsibility of James Unwin (see Biographical Register). Gainsborough gave six of his drawings to the chief accountant, Charles Wray.

3 William Cavendish, 4th Duke of Devonshire (1720–64), who served as First Lord of the Treasury, 1756–57, when William Pitt was first appointed Prime Minister.

4 James Quin (1693–1766), the distinguished actor, of whom Gainsborough painted a full length (National Gallery of Ireland, Dublin: Waterhouse No. 567, pl.69), exhibited at the Society of Artists in 1763.

5 Dr Abel Moysey, a prominent Bath physician (see Biographical Register).

6 Dr Moysey had a reputation for being mercenary.

8

[TO AN UNKNOWN RECIPIENT] 28 JULY 1763

MS. (last recorded in the R.E.D. Rawlins sale, Sotheby's, 2/4 June 1980, 3rd Day, lot 985, bt. Garber)

[*some two-thirds of page torn off*] of something better. I have sent you two bottles of Varnish, of my own making, so that if you like it I can either give you more of the same or a Rec^t how to make it you are to lay on [*some two-thirds of second page torn off*] for you, the first I did, which I shew to M^r. Bold[ry][1] when he call'd. pray favor me with a Line & believe me [*some two-thirds of the third page torn off: on the remaining fragment are two small landscape sketches in pencil*][2]

dear Sir yours most sincerely
Tho Gainsborough

Bath July 28th. 1763

1 Probably Andrew Baldry, whom Gainsborough knew in Suffolk; he became a partner in Joshua Kirby's house and coach painting business in Ipswich in 1755, and took over the business in 1759.

Gainsborough, though wholly professional and full of common sense, was also highly strung, and his constitution was far from being as robust, nor his nervous system as resilient, as those of his irritatingly equable rival, Reynolds. His daughter Margaret later told Farington that her father 'had not strong health and frequently complained'; he 'always dined at 3 o Clock, began to paint abt. eleven o Clock and was generally exhausted by dinner time', while 'towards the latter part of his life when He thought he did not sleep so well after having applied to drawing in the evening not being able to divest himself of the ideas which occupied his mind, He therefore amused himself with Music'. He was easily seduced, moreover, by his loose-living friends; thus he 'often exceeded the bounds of temperance & his Health suffered from it, being occasionally unable to work for a week afterwards'. On top of this, he adored attractive women and found it difficult to curb his impulses — which was not without danger, as he knew full well, in the streets and taverns of London. In 1763, mentally and physically exhausted by the unaccustomed strain of a practice which had become only too fashionable, he succumbed to nervous fatigue, partly induced by venereal anxiety; indeed, so seriously ill was he known to be that in October the Bath Journal *erroneously announced his demise. He was no more than thirty-six.*

9

TO JAMES UNWIN[1] 24 JULY 1763

MS. British Library Add. MS.48964, fo.7r, 8r

Dear Sir

You must think me very unworthy of the sincere regard which your kind Letter proves you to have for me to let it remain so long unanswer'd; and such I should certainly think myself, had not my Absence from home been the cause of it. I had an unexpected call to London from whence I am but just return'd. I had the pleasure of seeing your Brother for 5 minutes and fully intended to have spent a grave Evening with him; but such is the Nature of that D— place, or such that of this T.G that I declare I never made a Journey to London th[at] I ever did what I intended. 'tis a shocking place for that and I wonder amongst the number of things [*word scratched out in a different ink*] I leave undone which should be done, that I don't do many more which ought not to be done. I am going to settle in prodigeously hard to work, and

James Unwin (1717–76)
Canvas, 73.7 x 61. Late 1750s
Private Collection

if you will be so good to divert Capt. Saumarez in the most ingenious way you can so that he will not ['think' *crossed out*] fancy the time long before he has M^rs. Saumarez's Picture,[2] I will endeavour in the mean time to make the same in reallity as short as possible.

But My Dear Friend how shall I continue with you concerning M^rs. Unwin's Picture[3] I pray Sir, could not you divert yourself with the original for one week longer? I hope M^rs. Unwin is not so round but that you can bring that about.[4] Pray make our Joint Compliments to Her. Molly is better I think than ever she was, & the Captain the same[5]

I am

Dear Sir

Your most Affectionate

Obliged humble Servant

Tho Gainsborough

Bath July 24th. 1763

P.S. I am much Obliged for your care of my Note; are you sure it was paid?

Mrs James Unwin (dates unknown)
Canvas, 125.7 x 106.7
Finished 1771
Private Collection

1 Unwin was Gainsborough's attorney and banker until about 1760 (see Biographical Register).
2 Captain Thomas Saumarez married Miss Mount Stephens. Gainsborough began her portrait in 1760; its whereabouts are unknown, if indeed it was ever completed.
3 A portrait begun in about 1761–62, shortly after the Unwins' marriage; it was eventually completed in 1771 (Gainsborough had painted Unwin's own portrait in the late 1750s; this was last recorded in an anon.(=Unwin) sale, Sotheby's, 26 July 1950, lot 173, bt. Bellesi: Waterhouse, No.687). A three-quarter-length seated beside a table, it is in a Private Collection in Canada, by descent from A.J. Nesbitt, Montreal (Waterhouse, No.688).
4 Mrs Unwin was shortly to give birth to a son.
5 Gainsborough's nickname for his younger daughter, Margaret; it perhaps reflected her tendency to be bossy.

10

TO JAMES UNWIN 15 SEPTEMBER 1763

MS. Holburne of Menstrie Museum, Bath

My Dear Friend

This is the first time I have been able to hold a pen since I wrote to you before I have had a most terrible attack of a Nervous Fever so that for

Dr Rice Charlton (1710–89)
Canvas, 228.6 x 152.4. SA 1770
Holburne Museum of Art, Bath (Ernest E. Cook Bequest)

whole nights together I have thought it impossible that I could last 'til the Morning. But Thank God I am greatly recover'd by the ['great' *crossed out*] care & tenderness of Doctor Charlton[1] Who apply'd the Bark & Saline Draughts[2] so properly & cautiously that they have done wonders, 'tho. I must not forget a prescription of My Sisters (who you know is a Woman of Corage) of six Glasses of good, old Port which she made me swallow one Evening when I should have thought two or 3 must have knock me off the Stage. The truth is, I have apply'd a little too close for these last 5 years, That both my Doctors & Friends really think. I have got a Horse which I had of my good Friend Sir William S^{t}. Quintin[3] not handsom but perfectly sure footed & steady upon the Road, and what I purpose is to be as indolent as possible in every thing but Observing the exact quantity of food & Exercise best for me, and to stick to the 6 glasses of Port at Night. By this means I shall Weather the Point,[4] and live to see you at Bath & M^{rs}. Unwin who we should rejoyce to hear is well.

But all this time what is to be said about the Picture! I think I'll defer that til my Next, for my Head throbs a little with writing

so my Dear Friend Adieu for the present
and believe me yours most sincerely
and Affectionately
Tho Gainsborough

Bath Sepr. 15th. 1763

1 Dr Rice Charlton was one of Gainsborough's most trusted doctors (see Biographical Register).
2 Probably doses of quinine (found in cinchona bark) and magnesium.
3 Sir William St. Quintin (?1699–1770), 4th Bt., of Harpham, near Burton Agnes, in the East Riding of Yorkshire; a member of an ancient and prominent Yorkshire family, he served in his youth as Member of Parliament for Thirsk, 1722–27. Gainsborough had painted him soon after his move to Bath (Private Collection, England: Waterhouse, No.595, pl.59).
4 A nautical expresssion for sailing into calmer waters; Gainsborough had lived for many years in a seaport, indeed quite close to the harbour, and it would be surprising if he had no experience of sailing.

Dr Abel Moysey (1715–80)
Canvas, 127 x 101.6. c.1764
Private Collection, England
(on loan to the Holburne
Museum of Art, Bath)

II

TO JAMES UNWIN 25 OCTOBER 1763

MS. British Library Add. MS.48964, fo.9r, 10r

My Dear Friend

Excuse my Answering your Letter a little longer, for I am but just able to hold a Pen, and not able to know well what I say to you. I have kept my Bed 5 weeks to morrow excepting two hours sitting up for the last 3 Days of a most terrible Fever. It has been all upon my spirits from the first, that is from a single trip I made in London, as you guessd;[1] and occasiond by the uncertainty which followed the foolish Act. I was safe in the Opinion of two of the best Men in their way, but possess'd in my Mind that I was ruin'd. O my Dear Friend nobody can think what I have suffer'd for a Moments Gratification My Life was dispaird of by Doctor Charleton after he had tried all his skill, and by his own desire Dr Moisey was call'd in when in three days my faintings left me and I got strength.

I am now what they call out of Danger; I wish my Dear Friend I could sleep refreshing sleeps, then all would be well again. You shall hear from me again soon. My Dear Good Wife has sat up every night til within a few and has given me all the Comfort that was in her power. I shall never be a quarter good enough for her if I mend a hundred degrees.[2]

Keep my secret, but remember me kindly to good Mrs Unwin and believe me

y^rs^ most Affectionately
til Death
Tho Gainsborough

Bath 25th Octo^r^
1763

1 Presumably from Gainsborough's remarks about the temptations of London in Letter 9.

2 Gainsborough and his wife may have been incompatible, but Margaret was a good wife and housekeeper, and there is no doubt that Gainsborough felt warmly towards her.

12

TO JAMES UNWIN 30 DECEMBER 1763

Untraced (published in Sydney E. Harrison, 'New Light on a Gainsborough Mystery: Important Discovery of Original Documents', *Connoisseur*, vol.62, January 1922, p.10). The text of Gainsborough's first page, from the beginning of the letter to 'Am I right to ease myself of as much ...' is taken from the original manuscript reproduced in Catalogue 608, Maggs Bros., Summer 1935 (340, pl.IV.)

My Dear Friend

My Head is so extreemly bad still, that 'tho' I have intended Writing to you every day almost since the receipt of your last kind Letter, I have not been able to sit down 'til now. I have so many returns of my Nervous complaint in the back part of my Head that I almost dispair of getting the better of it: I am really a Weather Cock; more so now than what you always took me for. All my hopes are built upon what the spring may do in throwing out the humour[1] that yet seems playing about me. My Spirits are at times so low, but damn it, I won't entertain you with any more of my misfortunes — We are sincerely glad that Mrs Unwin is well, and wish you Joy of your Son. I have taken a House about three quarters of a Mile in the Landsdown Road.[2] 'tis sweetly situated and I have every convenience I could wish for; I pay 30 pounds p^r^ Year; and so let off all my House in the Smoake[3] except my Painting Room

'my dear Girls'
Mary (1750–1826) and Margaret (1751–1820) Gainsborough
Canvas, 40.6 x 62.2. Late 1750s
Victoria and Albert Museum

and best parlour to show Pictures in. Am I right to ease myself of as much Painting work as the Lodgings will bring in. I think the scheeme a good one. I Ride every minute in the Day unless it rains pouring; and do intend when I can, to be down from eleven to one o'clock, in my office, but not a moment longer for the King. I think I shall do yet my Friend. Pray have you any thoughts of paying us a visit this year? I long to see you more than all my Relations, for not one of them knows what you do. I always thought you extreemly clever; but whether I have not made you more knowing than you could have been had I been a close cunning fellow, that I must leave. I always think one cannot be too open to sensible people nor too reserved to fools; nay I believe I should have blush'd to have confess'd that to an Ass, which I did to you, and so much for secrets. Don't be revengeful now and not let me hear from you of a Month; for I promise upon the little honour I have left in your esteem, to be punctual in answering your Letters for the future.

My wife and my dear Girls beg to be remembered to yourself and Mrs. Unwin. They are thank God charmingly well, and what's more (tho' I say it), good in grain.

Adieu my dear Friend, and believe me,
Yours most Affectionately
Tho: Gainsborough

P.S.—I fully intend to mention something about Mrs. Unwin's Picture in my next. I had a Letter with nobody's Name to it, desiring his Wife's Picture might be finish'd and sent as soon as possible; sure it could not be honest Saumarez.[4] I think when I recollect the way that he wears his Hat in, it may possibly come from him. How does your Brother? I pay'd him an exceeding short Visit when I was in Town; sure he could not smoake what was the matter with me by my down looks: he has a quick eye, I can tell you, as well as somebody else, 'tho not so perfectly the command of it; I think he does meet Eyes quite so steadily as yourself, but don't you tell him what I say. Oh, my poor Head.

Don't you think a Jackass three quarters asleep upon the ridge of a Bank undermined and mouldring away is very expressive of the happiness of not seeing danger?[5]

Dec: 30th 1763.

1 State of mind, without any obvious reason for it (OED).
2 A recently built road ascending to Lansdown, a plateau between the hills north of Bath.
3 The house in Abbey Street right in the middle of town which Gainsborough leased when he settled in Bath in 1760.
4 See Letter 9, note 2.
5 Gainsborough frequently used donkeys or jackasses as staffage in his landscapes, chiefly in the Ipswich period, and there is one in which a jackass is shown asleep (Hayes *Landscape Paintings*, No.58), but there is none in which he uses the more expressive image of the foolish animal contentedly sleeping on a mouldering bank, without a care in the world, described here.

13

TO JAMES UNWIN 1 MARCH 1764

MS. British Library Add. MS.48964, fo.11r, 11v, 12r

Dear Sir

I received yours with very <great> pleasure as I really began to fear that your Nerves were bad too, not hearing from you. come I hope we shall do very well yet, I never had better spirits in all my life than I have now. I'm certainly reprieved for this time & have got a new Lease. It has been of service to me my Friend; I think better, and will act better for the future.[1] You have my sincerest thanks for your kind offer and intention in regard to Molly; but you must know I'm upon a scheeme of learning them both to paint Landscape; and that somewhat above the common Fan-mount stile. I think them capable of it, if taken in time, and with proper pains bestow'd. I don't mean to make them only Miss Fords in the Art, to be partly admired & partly laugh-'d at at every Tea Table;[2] but in case of an Accident that they may do something for Bread. You know it will be an Employment not so apt to lay snares in their way as Portrait or Miniature Painting, because they may be retired.[3] I think (and indeed always did myself) that I had better do this than make fine trumpery of them, and let them be led away with Vanity, and ever subject to disapointment in the wild Goose chace. I've mark'd the end of it sufficiently.[4] I'm in earnest and shall set about it in good earnest.

My House, my Dear Sir, brings me in the Rent, with the expence I have been at in Furniature; so make yourself easey, and you'l see this affair[5] has been <only> the wag of a Dogs tail out of the strait Road: I may say I have already more than recoverd the expences of it,[6] having painted a Whole length, three half lengths and seven Heads, exclusive of a full length of Doctor Charleton [*word scratched out in a different ink*], and a half length of Doctor Moysey's son.[7] This is true my Friend 'tho: I am so well known at Baddow.[8] They know my Faults, but ask them <u>who</u> knows any of my Virtues. ah! that a Jack Ass should be so foolish.[9]

you give us pleasure in the account of Mrs. Unwin and your self being well, and your intention of seeing Bath next Winter but you say nothing of your Son, so we conclude He is well too.

May we all continue so til we have the pleasure of seeing you here; you'l find me happy with Old Margt I hope,[10] and [*word scratched out in a different ink*] much yours

Tho Gainsborough

Landsdown Road ['Bath' *crossed out*][11] March 1st. 1764.

I hope you are happily & pleasantly situated in the House you mention, which my Wife knows extreemly well.[12] Remember me kindly as the Country folks say to Mrs. Itchener[13] she is a good little Woman as ever existed to my certain knowledge

Adieu I'm going down to Bath

Zouns, I forgot Mrs. Unwins & Capt Saumarezs Picture I shall work upon them soon depend on't.[14] that's enough.

Ann Ford, later Mrs Philip Thicknesse (1732–1824)
Canvas, 197.1 x 135. 1760
Cincinnati Art Museum (Bequest of Mary M. Emery)

1 Gainsborough's serious illness the previous year (see his earlier letters to Unwin) had had a profound effect on him.
2 Ann Ford (1732–1824), now the third Mrs Philip Thicknesse, of whom Gainsborough painted a magnificent and highly original, indeed provocative, full length in 1760 was a talented amateur musician, who gave public recitals in London, both as a singer and as an instrumentalist, playing the viola da gamba and the guitar. She was also an amateur fan-painter, but was evidently less gifted in this direction.
3 Work in solitude.
4 Bath was a city given up to leisure where mothers had greater expectations of finding husbands for their unmarried daughters. Gainsborough had seen how often this ended in tears.
5 His illness, venereally caused.
6 The expense caused by incapacity to work.
7 Exclusive because they were painted not for profit but as presents to his two doctors (see Biographical Register).
8 The Unwins lived at Great Baddow, a village in the environs of Chelmsford, Essex, where the more prosperous citizens of that town had houses.
9 A third reference to his dangerous illness, which preyed on his mind. Like a jack ass he had been oblivious of danger (see Letter 12, note 5) at the time of 'the foolish Act' in London.
10 Gainsborough referred to his wife as 'Old Margaret' more than once in his letters, but only to Unwin. This pejorative expression, like 'Ma' So-and-So, is indicative of being hen-pecked.
11 'Bath' has been crossed out and, as is evident from the postscript, Gainsborough regarded his house close to Lansdown as a country retreat above and out of Bath, remote from the smoke of the city — not only the coal smoke but the steam which rose from the baths.
12 It is not known where Unwin lived in Great Baddow, or why Mrs Gainsborough should have known the house 'extreemly well'. John Bensusan-Butt, in a letter to Mrs Gloria Harris dated 2 January 1997 (kindly communicated to me by Hugh Belsey), made what he called 'a wild guess' that the teen-age Margaret had been brought up by Mrs Itchener (see note 13 below), but Mrs Itchener, who married in 1748, may not have been much, if any, older than Mrs Gainsborough. Clearly, however, as is apparent from the postscript to his letter to Unwin, Gainsborough himself both knew and respected Mrs Itchener.
13 Mrs Itchener was the vicar's wife. Elizabeth Murvell married George Itchener, Vicar of Great Baddow, 1741/2–67, at Ingatestone by licence on 16 March 1748 (John Bensusan-Butt papers, Essex University Library: kindly transmitted by Hugh Belsey).
14 It is increasingly clear that neither was a priority; certainly the first was not to be paid for.

14

TO JAMES UNWIN 10 JULY [1764]

MS. British Library Add. MS.48964, fo.13r, 14r, 14v

Dear Sir

I was very agreeably favour'd with yours at my return from Wilton[1] where I have been about a Week, partly for my Amusement, and partly to make a Drawing from a fine Horse of L^d. Pembroke's, on which I am going to set General Honeywood, as large as life.[2]

We are extreemly glad to hear you & Mrs Unwin are pretty well. My Wife says you goe on briskly, I tell her you was always a brisk little man.

Thank God I have got the better of all my Complaints both real & imaginary; I don't remember to have enjoy'd better health & spirits any part of my life than at present. With regard to your Baddow Friends, when you hear them touch my Character, you may assure yourself that they attempt a thing as ridiculous to the full, as if I undertook to draw their Pictures without ever having seen them, for they know nothing of me. That you know the worst of me, I am not sorry for, because I know you have good sense & Good nature to place things in their proper light; that they have either of those blessings, who held me up to be view'd by you & Mrs Unwin (who, for ought they knew might have been strangers to me) is not quite so clear. however, My Wifes Compliments attend Mrs Itch in here

The Beauties of Mrs Unwins drapery li(ke) our Virtues have laid conceal'd for some time only to flash out the more suddenly, and to surprize those who least expect them.[3] God bless you—

I shall rejoyce to see you again at Bath—and am most sincerely

Yours

Tho Gainsborough

My Wife, Molly & The Capt desire their respectful Compts to you & Mrs Unwin

[*Addr.*] To / James Unwin Esqr / at Baddow near / Chelmsford / Essex.
[*Postmark*] IO JY BATH

1 Wilton House, near Salisbury, the seat of the Earls of Pembroke. Gainsborough painted a large copy of Van Dyck's celebrated group portrait of the Pembroke family (Compton Wynyates, Marquess of Northampton: Waterhouse No. 1015) 'by Memory, after having seen the original at Wilton'.

2 His portrait of Lieutenant-General Philip Honywood (1710–85) was exhibited at the Society of Artists in 1765 (33) (John and Mable Ringling Museum, Sarasota, Florida: Waterhouse No. 375, repr. pl.83).

3 A teasing reference to possible progress on the portrait.

In the autumn of 1764 Gainsborough sent his daughters, then aged fourteen and thirteen respectively, to Blacklands School in Chelsea, partly to learn drawing. Apart from music, no doubt increasingly important to him with his children away, Gainsborough's chief relaxation from the pressures of society portraiture was sketching from nature, both in chalks and watercolours, and painting landscapes from his imagination, assisted by his sketches and by models he constructed consisting of 'cork or coal for his foregrounds . . . middle grounds of sand and clay, bushes of mosses and lichens, and . . . distant woods of broccoli.' Ozias Humphry, the miniaturist, in the early 1760s a young student who had lodgings with Gainsborough's lively and talented musical friends, the Linleys, tells us that 'when the Summer advanced, and the luxuriance of Nature invited and admitted of it, he accompanied Mr Gainsborough in his Afternoon Rides on Horseback to the circumjacent Scenery, which was in many Parts, picturesque, and beautiful in a high Degree'; and Uvedale Price, later the theorist of 'the Picturesque', who was in his 'teens in the 1760s, also 'made frequent excursions with him into the country' at that time. It must seem paradoxical, in view of the scenery around Bath (and remembering that, in portraiture, he sought individuality, likeness and immediacy), that Gainsborough in his maturity subscribed to seventeenth- and eighteenth-century academic convention in the field of landscape painting, venerated Claude and Rubens, and concerned himself with idealization, effect and mood. Topography, the very staple of his contemporaries, he eschewed.

15

TO PHILIP, 2ND EARL OF HARDWICKE [DATE UNKNOWN][1]

MS. British Library Add. MS.35350, fo.11r

Mr Gainsborough presents his Humble respects to Lord Hardwicke; and shall always think it an honor to be employ'd in any thing for His Lordship; but with regard to real Views from Nature in this Country, he has never seen any Place that affords a Subject equal to the poorest imitations of Gaspar or Claude Paul Sanby is the only Man of Genius, he believes, who has employ'd his Pencil that Way[2] — Mr G. hopes Lord Hardwicke will not mistake his meaning, but if His Lordship wishes to have any thing tollerable of the name of G. the Subject altogether, as well <as> figures &c must be of his own Brain; otherwise Lord Hardwicke will only pay for Encouraging a Man out of his Way — and had much better buy a Picture of some of the good Old Masters.

Saturday Morng –

Mr Gainsborough presents his Humble respects
to Lord Hardwicke; and shall always think
it an honor to be employ'd in any thing for
His Lordship; but with regard to real Views
from Nature in this Country, he has never
seen any Place that affords a Subject equal
to the poorest imitations of Gaspar or Claude
Paul Sandby is the only Man of Genius, he
believes, who has employ'd his Pencil that
way — Mr G. hopes Lord Hardwicke will
not mistake his meaning, but if His Lordship
wishes to have any thing tollerable of the
name of G. the Subject altogether, as well as
figures &c must be of his own Brain; otherwise
Lord Hardwicke will only pay for Encouraging
a Man out of his way - and had much better
buy a Picture of some of the good old Masters.

Saturday Morn

Letter 15

1 The letter must date from after March 1764, when Philip Yorke succeeded his father as 2nd Earl of Hardwicke.

2 Paul Sandby is chiefly known nowadays for his watercolours and gouaches, but the quality (and indeed existence) of his work as a landscape painter in oils in the early 1760s has been revealed by Luke Herrmann (see his *Paul and Thomas Sandby*, London, 1986, pp.23–25). It is noteworthy, and perhaps surprising, that Gainsborough makes no mention of Richard Wilson.

Ozias Humphry (1742–1810)
Self-Portrait
Black and white chalks on buff paper, 47.6 x 36.2. c.1770
British Museum

16

TO OZIAS HUMPHRY[1] [DATE UNKNOWN]

MS. Historical Society of Pennsylvania (Dreer Collection)

Dear Sir

I should be glad to lend you any of my Landskips to copy, did it not affect the sale of new Pictures, to have any copies taken of them. for which reason I have often been obliged to refuse, when it would have given me pleasure to Oblige my friend

believe me

Dear Sir

your most Obedient

humble Servt –

Tho Gainsborough.

Friday m<u>or</u>n

[*Addr.*] Humphry Esq<u>re</u>

1 Ozias Humphry (1742–1810) made his career as a portrait miniaturist.

The press of business meant that, as with (but not so chronically as) Lawrence after him, Gainsborough was often dilatory in completing his commissions, and apologies accompanied by promises are a constant refrain in his letters. The problem was compounded by the need to have pictures ready in April for the annual exhibition of the Society of Artists (founded in 1760). But he seems to have kept his clients happy, in part by genuine consideration, in part by wit; Gainsborough was never deferential to his patrons, and he gave short shrift to the idle company which thronged Bath, but equally he was often ready to put himself out for the sake of 'future advantage': in this way he maintained an active professional relationship with the Duke of Bedford for twenty years.

17

TO PERCIVAL BEAUMONT[1] 7 JANUARY 1765

MS. Marquis of Tavistock and the Trustees of the Bedford Estate, Woburn MSS

Sir

Bath Jan 7th 1765

I received the favor of your Letter yesterday, and beg you will be so good to let Their Graces know that my not sending the Pictures sooner has been owing to some difficulty of pleasing myself in the two Copies of His Grace; but that they shall all be finished and sent next week without fail to Bedford House.[2]

I should be much Obligd if you would also acquaint The Dutchess that 'tho my Ill Health forbids my following Business in London (to which I have frequent invitations) Her Grace may nevertheless command me at any time to paint any of The Family there.[3]

I am Sir

your most Obedient humble

Servant

Tho Gainsborough

[*Addr.*] P. Beaumont Esqre

1 Percival Beaumont was the house steward of John, 4th Duke of Bedford (1710–71), at Bedford House in London.

2 Southampton House, Bloomsbury, which was inherited by the Bedfords through marriage following the death of the last Earl of Southampton in 1667, was known as Bedford House since 1734 (Bedford House in the Strand had been pulled down in 1705).

3 This second paragraph is in response to the Duchess's invitation to London communicated by Beaumont, whose letter of 4 January is published in Woodall (p.35).

‘The Duke of Bedford Whom you must know I made an exceeding like head of (tho’ I say it)’

John, 4th Duke of Bedford (1710–71)
Canvas, 76.2 x 63.5. 1764
The Marquess of Tavistock and Trustees of the Bedford Estates, Woburn Abbey

18

TO JAMES UNWIN 21 JANUARY 1765

MS. Institut Néerlandais, Paris

My Dear Friend

I have much against my Inclination suffer'd two posts to pass without thanking you for your last Obliging Letter. I am very busey now in preparing a large Picture for the Exhibition, and have been closely employ'd all this winter and thank God successfully, tho' so little deserving.

I am not without hopes of taking a trip to Baddow just to look at you, and to admire how you & Mrs Unwin goe on (which according to your Letter cannot but excite admiration in all Beholders if not a small matter of Imitation) it will depend upon a scheem taking place with The Duke of Bedford Whom you must know I made an exceeding like head of (tho' I say it) and also of The Dutchess & Lady Mary Fitzpatrick this winter in Bath,[1] and since that I had a Letter to inform me that more work was cutting out for me, and to know if I would goe to Town to do it. this came but the same post with your Letter, and I have answer'd that tho' I have refused frequent Invitations to undertake large Pictures in Town, on account of my Health, I cannot resist the honour of doing something for the Duke of Bedford productive of future advantage let the present Inconvenience be what it will to me. Am I right?

When I read your Letter to O[ld] Margaret, there said She, you find M^{r}. Unwin is so much of a Gentleman now, that he would not mention a Word to know if M^{rs}. Unwin's Picture was finished, and you so much of a scrubb that you'l not get it done for him. Says I My Dear, hem, My Dear He always was a Gentleman; you know from the first of our Acquaintance he was a Gentleman, but, but what you scrubb said She, have not you been as long about a Shaddow[2] as he have been in making three Substantial whole length figures.[3] no my Dear not three, but two. yes M^{r}. Do little I say three. pray did not M^{rs}. Unwin goe away big from Bath the Summer before your Illness, and did not <She> lay in when we came to live up the Hill, about this time, of her first Child, and then according to M^{r}. Unwin's Letter again in August; and now three months gone again; I say three you scrubb. pray is all this true or not, Sir?

Molly & The Capt. are out at School and have been these 5 Months otherwise they would most certainly join with Old Marg^{t} in best respects to you & M^{rs}. Unwin. I am afraid I was not quite in my Senses when I writ my last Letter to you. I beg My Comp^{ts}. to M^{rs}. Itchiner, & am, Dear Sir,

Yours most sincerely & Affec:

Tho Gainsborough

Bath Jan 21st. 1765.

[*Addr.*] To James Unwin Esq / at Baddow near / Chelmsford / Essex
[*Postmark*] 23 JA BATH

1 These three portraits are in the possession of the Marquess of Tavistock and the Trustees of the Bedford Estates, Woburn Abbey (Waterhouse Nos. 54 and 58) and the Earl of Ilchester, Melbury House, Dorset (Waterhouse No. 255).

2 A lay-in for the portrait.

3 A reference to the Unwins' two young children, and another on the way.

19

TO PERCIVAL BEAUMONT 27 JANUARY 1765

MS. Marquis of Tavistock and the Trustees of the Bedford Estate, Woburn MSS

Sir

I have pack'd up Their Graces Pictures to come by Wiltshire's flying Waggon,[1] which sets out from hence on Sunday Evening and arrives at the White Horse Cellar—Piccadilly on Wednesday Morning. I have directed them to be call'd for there by your Order, & beg the favor of you to send some careful Servant for Them.

The Copy of The Duke's Picture I have not been able to finish so as to send ['it' *crossed out*] along with the Original, and was afraid of Keeping them any longer after having orders to send them; But if M^{rs}. Fortiscue[2] is in Town, should be obliged if you will acquaint Her that ['they' *crossed out*] it shall be sent as soon as possible to Bedford House.

I am

Sir your most Obedient & Obliged humble
Servant
Tho Gainsborough

Bath <Saturday> Jan: 27th. 1765.

[*Addr.*] To Mr Beaumont

1 Walter Wiltshire (see Biographical Register) operated a carrying business from Bath.

2 Mrs Fortescue, presumably a member of the Duke of Bedford's household (see also Letter 135), has not been identified.

20

TO JAMES UNWIN 7 NOVEMBER 1765

Untraced ((published in Sydney E. Harrison, 'New Light on a Gainsborough Mystery: Important Discovery of Original Documents', *Connoisseur*, vol.62, February 1922, p.88)

Dear Sir,

To convince you that you have never said anything amiss in any one of your Letters, give me leave to assure you that it would never be in your power to offend me even by telling me the worst of my Faults, as I should esteem any correction as a favor from Mr. Unwin. Few Friends have regard enough to do so good an office, let their sincerity be what it will, and perhaps none of mine, except yourself, the judgment to apply the proper manner of doing it. I should think it a very bad sign was I capable of taking anything ill from a Person of your sense and good Qualities: it would be scorning to look at Vandyke whilst conscious of being yet but a dauber. No sir, I'm not quite so far gone neither.

My Health is better than ever, and everything goes on to my wishes, except Mrs Unwin's Picture and that stands still, still in my Painting Room, notwithstanding I have the greatest desire to finish it; I have no oftener promised myself the Pleasure of sitting down to it but some confounded ugly creature or other have pop'd their Heads in my way and hindred me: I do positively intend to lock myself up one day soon, and order myself to be gone a Journey through Essex to Harwich but what I will do it for you.

We are heartily glad you go on so merrily; you put me in mind of a little Fiddle that Giardini[1] pick'd up here at Bath, which nobody would think well of, because there was nobody who knew how to bring out the tone of, and which (though somewhat undersized) in his Hands produced the finest Music in the World: I believe Mrs Unwin has found out the exact place where to fix your sound-post.[2] Our best Compliments attend her.

I am, My Dear Friend,

most truly and sincerely yours

Tho. Gainsborough

Bath, Nov. 7th 1765.

P.S. — My dear Girls are at Chelsea.[3] I send you two Letters of theirs to see how prettily they can write.

1 Felice de' Giardini (see Biographical Register), the greatest violinist of his day.

2 The rock of their marital relationship. Technically, the peg of wood fixed inside a fiddle to counter the downward pressure of the bridge, its correct position affecting the tone of the instrument.

3 They were at Blacklands School, facing Chelsea Common, near what is now Sloane Square (Blacklands Terrace still exists, north of the King's Road). Both Chelsea Place and Blacklands House, properties of the Cheynes, had been 'let to French boarding-schools' by 1705. The extensive Blacklands estate was purchased by Sir Hans Sloane in 1712 and was later developed; Blacklands House seems to have remained a school until 1820; Boswell's daughter, Betsy, was a boarder there, 1789-94. It is not known why Gainsborough should have chosen to send his two daughters, of whom he was very fond, away to school in London; but, from the end of the seventeenth century, Chelsea had been celebrated for girls' schools. (Ms Ingrid Lackajis, of the Royal Borough of Kensington and Chelsea Public Libraries, kndly provided me with the available information about Blacklands School).

The annual exhibitions were not an unmixed blessing. They were important for sales, and for keeping one's name before the public, but they encouraged an unhealthy competitiveness in scale, effect and colour. Reynolds said they had 'a mischievous tendency, by seducing the Painter to an ambition of pleasing indiscriminately the mixed multitude of people who resort to them'. Nevertheless, in the mid-1760s Gainsborough continued to work in a restrained key, which owed much, in landscape, to the sombreness of Ruisdael. Late in 1766 he moved from the hill which led up to Lansdown, where in 1763 he had taken a house for the sake of his health, to the Circus, then newly built (1754–58) and also—part of its attraction for him—on the outskirts of Bath, though more expensive and more fashionable: one of the principal houses, indeed, was occupied by his patron and friend, the Duke of Bedford. In 1767 Gainsborough advertised the house in Lansdown Road as to let.

21

TO DAVID GARRICK[1] [MAY 1766]

Untraced (Anon. Sale, Puttick and Simpson, 3 June 1921, lot 196, bt. Maggs)

Don't think I am in the least angry with any of our friends at the Exhibition . . . I don't look upon the Exhibition, as it is conducted at present, to be calculated so much to bring out good Painters as bad ones. There is certainly a false taste and an impudent stile prevailing, which if Vandyke was living would put him out of countenance; & I think even his work would appear so, opposed to such a Glare. Nature is modest, and the Artist should be so in his addresses to her [*remainder unknown*][2]

1 David Garrick (see Biographical Register).

2 Whitley was allowed to examine this letter by Maggs (who bought it at auction in 1921) but not to copy it. The date of the letter (May 1766) and the first sentence are as remembered by Whitley; the rest is as published in the sale catalogue; of the remainder nothing is known. Whitley remembered that Gainsborough wrote that he had made more money in the previous year than ever before and that he would not let Garrick pay for Mrs Garrick's portrait, although he might pay Gosset for the frame (Whitley Papers, Dept. of Prints and Drawings, British Museum: Gainsborough box, Guard Book for 1745–1780, fo.12).

Gainsborough was a spontaneous artist, preferring to work out his portrait designs directly on the canvas rather than to make elaborate studies. In landscape, he subordinated his rustic and pastoral staffage to the trees and pictorial effects which were the true vehicles of his feelings gradually, however, allowing these figures to become, in Sir Lawrence Gowing's phrase, 'poetic expositors' of his pastoral intentions. For both these reasons he did not follow the example of his contemporary, Richard Wilson, who included subject-matter drawn from the classics in many of his landscapes, and he was praised for his good sense by Reynolds: 'As Gainsborough never attempted the heroick style, so neither did he destroy the character and uniformity of his own style, by the idle affectation of introducing mythological learning in any of his pictures'. History painting proper, as handed down from the age of Raphael and the High Renaissance, never appealed to Gainsborough because the complex interplay of character and incident required would have inhibited the flow of his brush: it is symptomatic that the one mythological subject he did attempt, and that was not until late in life, was of Diana and her nymphs surprised at their woodland bathing place by Actaeon.

22

TO WILLIAM JACKSON[1] 23 AUGUST [1767]

MS. Royal Academy of Arts

Bath Aug^st^. 23^d^.

My Dear Jackson

Will it (damn this Pen) will it seem as any apology for not answering your last obliging Letter, to inform you that I did not receive it of near a Month after it arrived shut up in a Music Book at M^r^. Palmer's –[2]

I admire your notions of most things and do agree with you that there might be exceeding pretty Pictures painted of the kind you mention But are you sure you don't mean instead of the flight into Egypt, my flight out of Bath! do you consider my dear Maggotty[3] Sir, what a deal of work history Pictures require to what little dirty subjects of Coal horses & Jack asses[4] and such figures as I fill up with; no you don't consider any thing about that part of the Story, you design faster than any man or any thousand men could Execute—There is but one flight I should like to paint and that's yours out of Exeter, for while your numerous & Polite Acquaintance encourage you to talk so cleverly, we shall have but few Productions, real & substantial Productions—But to be serious (as I know you love to be) do you really think that a regular Composition in the Landskip way should ever be fill'd with History, or any figures but such as fill a place (I won't say stop a Gap) or to create a little business for the Eye to be drawn <from> the Trees in order to return to them with more glee[5]—I did not know that you admired those tragi-comic Pictures, because some have thought that a regular History Picture may have too much ba[ck]ground, and the composition hurt by not considering what ought to be principal.

But I talk now like old square toes there is no rule of that kind says you

But then says I
damme you lie

If I had but roome & time before Palmer seals up his packet I'd trim[6] you—I have been riding out with him this Morng —I wish I had been with him in Devonshire –

Adieu

T G

[*Addr.*] To / Mr. Jackson

1 William Jackson (see Biographical Register), to whom Gainsborough wrote his most unbuttoned letters. Although this is the earliest of Gainsborough's many letters to Jackson of which we know, the first paragraph makes it clear that this is due only to the accident of survival.

2 John Palmer (see Biographical Register) controlled the postal service to and from Bath.

3 Whimsical.

4 Susan Sloman has stressed the importance of the local coalfields in the Bath economy and the omnipresence of colliers and their horses, quoting Josiah Wedgwood's reservations about the location of his first shop in the city: 'I do not quite like this situation. The street is full of Coal Carts, Coal horses and Asses' ('The Holloway Gainsborough: its subject re-examined', *Gainsborough's House Review*, 1997/8, p.50).

5 Gainsborough's advice was for Jackson. He himself had just exhibited *The Harvest Wagon* (Barber Institute of Fine Arts, Birmingham: Hayes *Landscape Paintings*, No.88), with its magnificent pyramid of figures.

6 Rebuke.

'to create a little business for the Eye to be drawn <from> the Trees in order to return to them with more glee'
Wooded Landscape with Horse Drinking, Flock of Sheep and Milkmaid Crossing a Bridge
Canvas, 146.1 x 157.5. c.1763
Worcester Art Museum, Mass.

23

TO WILLIAM JACKSON 2 SEPTEMBER 1767

MS. Royal Academy of Arts

My Dear Jackson

To show you that I can be as quick as yourself, 'tho: I shall never be half a quarter so clever, I am answering your Letter the very moment I received it from Mr Palmer — I shall not teaze you upon the subject of the flight, as we are now upon a better & that which of all others I have long wish'd to touch upon; because tho I'm a rogue in talking upon Painting & love to seem to take things wrong, I can be both serious & honest upon any subjects thoroughly pleasing to me: and such will ever be those wherin your happiness and our Friendship are concern'd — let me then throw aside that damn'd grinning trick[1] of mine for a moment & be as serious & stupid as a Horse

Mark then, that ever since I have been quite clear in your being a real Genius, so long have I been of Opinion that you are dayly throwing your Gift away upon Gentlemen & only studying how you shall become the Gentleman too — now damn Gentlemen, there is not such a set of Enemies, to a real Artist, in the World as they are, if not kept at a proper distance

They think (& so may you for a while) that they reward your merit by their Company & notice; but I, who blow away all the chaff & by G— in their Eyes too if they don't stand clear, know that they have but one part worth looking at, and that is their Purse; their Hearts are seldom near enough the right place to get a sight of it –

If any Gentleman comes to my House, my Man asks them if they want me (provided they don't seem satisfyed with seeing the Pictures and then he askes what they would please to want with me; if they say a Picture Sir please to walk this way and my Master will speak to you; but if they only want me to bow & compliment Sir my Master is walk'd out — and so my dear there I nick them. Now if a Lady a handsom Lady comes `tis as much as his Life is worth [to send] them away so — But this is [*several words torn*] as you knew this before — [*the rest of this page, three or four lines, has been torn off*]

I wish you lived a little nearer so that I could see you often, or a good deal nearer if you please — I have no Acquaintance now, nor will I 'til I can say within myself I approve my choice — there are but very few clever fellows worth hanging — and that consideration makes you the more worthy

Adieu for want of room I'll write
again very soon
T G –

Bath
Sep.^t 2.^d 1767

[*Addr.*] [M]^r. W^m. Jackson / Exeter

1 Disguising an attitude with grinning, as in 'grinning Infamy' in Thomas Gray's *Ode on a Distant Prospect of Eton College*, 1.74. Addison refers to mastery 'in the whole art of grinning' (OED).

24

TO WILLIAM JACKSON 14 SEPTEMBER [1767]

MS. Royal Academy of Arts

Bath Sep: 14th.

My Dear Jackson

Now you seem to lay too much stress upon me, and show yourself to be a serious fellow. I question if you could splice all my Letters together whether you would find more connection & sense in them than in [*word scratched out*] <many> Landskips join'd where half a Tree was to meet half a Church to make a principal Object—I should not think of my pretending to reproach you who are a regular System of Philosophy, a reasonable Creature & a particular[1] Fellow. If I meant any thing (which God knows if I did) it was this, that many a real Genius is lost in the fictitious Character of the Gentleman; and that as many of those Creatures are continually courting you, possibly you might forget, what I without any Merit to myself remember from meer Shyness. Namely, that they make no part of the Artist

depend upon it Jackson you have more sense in your little finger than I have in my whole Body & Head; I am the most inconsistent, changable being, so full of fitts & starts, that if you mind what I say, it will be shutting your Eyes to some purpose

I am only sensible of meaning, and of having once said, that I wish you lived nearer to me; but that this wish does not proceed from a Selfishness rather than any desire of correcting any Step of yours I much doubt—perhaps you can see that, though I cannot. I might add perhaps in my red hot way that damn me Exeter is no more a place for a Jackson, than Sudbury in Suffolk is for a G– But all the rest you know better than I can tell you I'm certain—You have one Fault which I must tell you of, you can Stop to gaze with wonder and astonishment upon such a fellow as H____y[2] and let slip all his merit of care, labour & prudent selfishness through your own fingers—'tis mighty <pretty> to be sure to stand and admire another man hop upon one Leg, and forget the use of two damnd long ones, think of that Backer Longo[3] think of that—Why Man you have as good a Stock of Haberdashery about you as any of them all, if you had but the same hungry Eyes to look about you—Well after all Bath is a lively Place—not but Lond[on] is above all =

you underthimble me [*word torn*] hope no offence — I look upon this Letter a[s] one of my most regular performances so don't let's have any of your Airs — I could say a deal more but what can a Man say pent up in a corner thus; if you was a Lady I would say what I have often said [*short word, perhaps* 'up', *crossed out*] in a corner by way of making the most of the last Inch. yours up to the hilt[4] –

T G –

[*Addr.*] To / William Shakespeare Jackson / Esqr / at / Exeter

1 Exact.
2 Conceivably the actor, Hartley, who performed in Bath.
3 The phrase 'Backer Longo' has not been explained. Trevor Fawcett has very plausibly suggested to Susan Sloman (her letter to the compiler, 26 February 1999) that it might be the name of a character in a burlesque.
4 This expression is not Gainsborough's, and may be found, for example, in John Cleland, *Fanny Hill: Memoirs of a Woman of Pleasure*, London, 1970 edition, p.43.

Like most good craftsmen Gainsborough was continually concerned about the quality and suitability of the materials he used. When he discovered a colour that was better than the pigment he had used up-to-date, he was impatient to obtain a supply: the indigo brought to his notice by the amateur, William Jackson, and mentioned in two of his letters, is a case in point. So with drawing paper. In his early pencil drawings Gainsborough often used the wiremarks to positive effect as an instrument of modelling. Such furrows, however, were an impediment to the flow of wash or watercolour, and it is in the context of his watercolours of the 1760s that his correspondence with Dodsley, bookseller brother of the publisher of Johnson and founder of the Annual Register, *may be understood.*

25

TO JAMES DODSLEY[1] 10 NOVEMBER 1767

MS. Gainsborough's House, Sudbury (1968.018)

Sir

I should take it as a particular favor if you would send me half a Doz^{n}. Quire of the same sort of Paper as the ['second' *crossed out*] <fifth> Edition of the new Bath Guide is printed on, it being what I have long been in search of for making wash'd Drawings upon; I shall be in Town about Xmas & will with thanks call to pay you for it. There is so little impression of the Wires, and those so very fine, that the surface is like Vellum; but lest I should give you more trouble than I am willing to do in so trifling an affair, I have inclosed a bit of it.

I beg the favor of you to direct it for me, and to order it to be delivered at the White Horse Cellar Piccadilly to come by Wiltshires Waggon[2] which will much Oblige

Sir your most Obedient
humble servant
Tho Gainsborough
Portrait Painter at Bath

Nov 10th 1767

P.S. I have some of your fine Writing Paper but this made for Printing is much superior for the use I want it on account of the substance & not having so much of the Glaze upon it—I could wish it to be of the very sort of the inclosed, as it really comes up to the Italian drawing Paper such as they made formerly.

[*Addr.*] To / Mr J. Dodsley / in Pall Mall / London
[*Postmark*] 15 NO BATH
[*Inscribed*] post pd double
[*Stamped*] POST PAID

1 James Dodsley (1724–97), bookseller and publisher, who in 1759 had succeeded his brother as owner of the firm of R. & J. Dodsley, Pall Mall.
2 See Biographical Register.

26

TO JAMES DODSLEY 26 NOVEMBER 1767

MS. Gainsborough's House, Sudbury (1968.019)

Sir

I beg you to accept my sincerest thanks for the favor you have done me concerning the Paper for Drawings; I had set my Heart upon getting some of it, as it is so compleatly what I have long been in search of: the mischief of that you were so kind to inclose, is not only the small Wires, but a large Cross Wire at about I I this distance, which the other has none of, nor hardly any of the impression of the smallest Wire. I wish Sir, that one of my Landskips, such as I could make you upon that paper, would prove a sufficient inducement for you to make still further enquiry I should think my time well bestow'd however little the Value you might <with reason> set upon it.

I am

Sir your much Obliged

& most Obedient humble Servant

Tho Gainsborough

Bath / 26th Nov 1767

P.S. I am this moment viewing the difference of that you send & the Bath Guide holding them Edgeways to the light, and could cry my Eyes out to see those furrows; upon my honor I would give a Guineas a Quire for a Dozn quire of it.

[*Addr.*] To / Mr Jas Dodsley / Pall Mall / London
[*Postmark*] 30 NO BATH
[*Inscribed*] post pd
[*Stamped*] POST PAID

The expenses of a larger establishment in the fashionable Circus and a determination not to lose ground financially meant that Gainsborough often neglected smaller canvases (see for example Letter 59, note 3) in favour of the more lucrative full-lengths required by wealthier clients. His wife managed his accounts, and to some extent no doubt controlled his work.

27

TO RICHARD STEVENS 13 SEPTEMBER 1767

MS. Koriyama City Museum of Art, Japan

Sir

The least I can do when told of my faults in a genteal and friendly manner, is to acknowledge them, and ask pardon: I was tempted to exceed the bounds of good manners in keeping Mrs Awse[1] so long as my situation now requires all the <u>sail</u> I can croud:[2] the truth is Sir, I suffered some hardships in the first part of my Voyage and fancying now that I see Land makes me forget myself. I will send it immediatly: and happy I shall be if you think the care & pains I have taken in the finishing part at all compensates for my faults in other respects.

I had the Frames made at the time I received your first Letter with the Drawing, and though doubtless there may appear some small difference upon immediate comparison with that it is design'd to match,[3] yet the dimensions being pretty exact, I hope it will pass, especially Sir whilst the Eyes of your Friends are employ'd in admiring the Excellence of my Performances. I wish I could make you laugh 'til you forget how deficient I have been in point of good manners.

I hope Sir the more I have punished you, the less pain you will suffer from the Gout, Methinks I could with pleasure bear a pinch in my Toe for you.

I am

(hoping M^{rs}. Awse is well)

Sir your Obedient humble Servt

Tho Gainsborough

Circus,
Bath, Sepr. 13th. 1767

P.S. I believe Sir it would astonish you to see how the new Buildings are extending <in> all points from the old center of Bath, The Pump Rooms—We amost reach Landsdown, & Cleverton = down, north & south, but not quite to Bristol & London for East & West. I think verily the End of some of our Master Builders will be to meet some of their Marylebone Friends near a certain Ditch.[4] It does not appear to me that many of the New Houses are occupied by Genteal Families newly residing in Bath, but only that the Lodging-House Cats are endeavoring to draw more Talons upon us, by having Houses in all Quarters.[5]

1 Mrs Awse was Richard Stevens's sister. The portrait was painted for Stevens, and is now in the Koriyama City Museum of Art, Japan (Waterhouse, No. 24).

2 Another nautical metaphor (see Letter 10, note 4), suggesting that Gainsborough may have done some sailing at Ipswich.

3 The portrait of Stevens, completed as long ago as April 1762 (last recorded in the Mrs Naylor sale, Christie's, 13 July 1951, Lot 72, bt. Davidge: Waterhouse, No. 634).

4 Perhaps the Thames.

5 Gainsborough himself profited quite considerably from the lodging house business, as did his sister, Mrs Gibbon (see Susan Legouix Sloman, 'Gainsborough and "the lodging-house way",' *Gainsborough's House Annual Report*, 1991/92, pp.34–35 and note 59).

Richard Stevens
(dates unknown)
Canvas, 76.2 x 63.5.
Finished 1762
Whereabouts unknown

28

TO RICHARD STEVENS 2 OCTOBER 1767

MS. Koriyama City Museum of Art, Japan

Sir,

I hope by this time you have received M^{rs}. Awse's Picture, and that it meets with your approbation. I this morning paid the Frame-maker, and am sorry to say that I think it a dear one, but he says the trouble he had in working after a limitted scale & pattern in drawing Occasion'd the additional charge; he set it at four Guineas, and for 3 Guineas & ½ I have the Burnishd Gold sort. However if you, Sir, think it dear too I shall be willing to become a fellow sufferer as My Profits in the Portrait way is a little upon Apothecary order[1] — I should be glad to hear it comes safe to hand, and suits pretty well with the other –

I am

Mrs Awse (dates unknown)
Canvas, 73.7 x 61
Finished 1767
Koriyama City Museum of Art, Japan.

Sir your most Obedient
Serv.[t]
Tho Gainsborough

Bath
Oct. 2.[d] 1767
I hope the Gout has left you & that M.[rs] Awse is well –
P.S. Packing Case cost me 7 Shillings which My Wife desires me always to remember and I often forget Voluntarily because I am ashamed to mention it.

[*Addr.*] To / Rich[d] Stevens Esq[re] / at Winscott near / Torrington / Devonshire / M:P:
[*Postmark*] BATH

1 In other words, they were not very high. While physicians were respected members of society, apothecaries were lower down on the social ladder and, of course, charged less; for this reason, many visitors to Bath used them as doctors (pointed out by Susan Sloman).

29

TO RICHARD STEVENS 28 JANUARY 1768

MS. Koriyama City Museum of Art, Japan

Sir

I have rec^{d} the favor of your inclosing a Bill Value £15 Which when p^{d} I acknowledge to be in full for M^{rs}. Awses Picture & Frame & all Demands.

I am sorry Sir I have not been so happy in M^{rs}. Awses Picture as to give satisfaction to yourself & Friends, but I believe nobody can always succeed alike at all times: I can only say it was not for want of either pains or Inclination: & as to the Frame it was done after the Drawing you sent, by the best frame maker at Bristol. If at any time you should have a convenience of bringing M^{rs}. Awse's Picture with you to Bath I shall very willingly make any alterations which you or M^{rs}. Awse may think proper, without any additional charge—and am

Sir

Your most Obedient & humble

Servant

Tho Gainsborough

Bath Jan 28th. 1768

P.S. I am extreemly sorry for your long conf[inement] but hope now you'l be free from the Gout [for] some years –

[*Addr*] To / Richd Stevens Esqre / at Winscott near Torrington / Devonshire / M:P:
[*Postmark*] BATH

In later life, increasing affluence meant that Gainsborough could afford to buy works of art. Though 'he was a universal admirer of fine pictures, and was not exclusively devoted to any one in particular,' over half of the fifty-odd pictures he acquired were landscapes, and it is clear that he bought less as a connoisseur than as a practising artist who liked to have around him examples of work he admired. The following letter is the first reference to an intended purchase by Gainsborough.

'a large Picture of Tommy Linley & his Sister'

Beggar Boy and Girl (Elizabeth and Thomas Linley)
Canvas, 71.1 x 63.5
Begun 1768
Sterling and Francine Clark Art Institute, Williamstown, Mass.

30

TO WILLIAM JACKSON 11 MAY 1768

MS. Royal Academy of Arts

My dear Jackson

I will suppose all you say about my Exhibition Pictures to be true because I have not tried to dispute it with you—I am much obliged to you, and wish I could spend a few days with you in Town; but I have began a large Picture of Tommy Linley & his Sister,[1] and I cannot come—I suppose you know the Boy is bound for Italy the first opportunity.[2] Pray do you remember carrying me to a Picture dealers somewhere by Hanover Square, and my being struck with the leaving and touch of a little bit of Tree; the whole Picture not above 8 or 10 Inches high & about a foot long—I wish if you have time that you'd enquire what it might be purchased for, and give me one line more whilst you are stay in Town—

If you can come this way home [*word torn: perhaps* 'that'] one may enjoy a day or two of your Company I shall be [*word scratched out*]

<heartily glad>. I can always make up one Bed for a Friend without any trouble and nobody has a better claim to that Title or a better title to that Claim than yourself—

believe me Dear Jackson
yours most sincerely
Tho Gainsborough

May 11th 1768

My Compliments attend all enquiring Friends and damn this Pen

[*Addr.*] To / Mr Jackson

1 The Linleys, a remarkable musical family, were amongst Gainsborough's closest friends in Bath; Thomas (1756–78), who died tragically young, was a child prodigy on the violin, and the beautiful Elizabeth (1754–92) was the leading soprano at the Three Choirs Festival and subsequently married Sheridan. The large picture of the two youngsters may have been cut down to form the picture acquired by the Duke of Dorset in 1784 (see Letter 146) as 'one sketch of a Begger Boy and Girl' (Sterling and Francine Clark Art Institute, Williamstown, Massachusetts: Waterhouse, No. 801), which was known from at least 1817 as *Miss Linley and her brother.*

2 The young Thomas was sent to Florence that year to study with Pietro Nardini, and there in 1770 he was befriended by the Mozarts, then travelling in Italy.

The pattern of Gainsborough's life at Bath was to a large extent dictated by the Season which, by this period, had expanded from two short periods in the autumn and spring, and by 1780 lasted from September until May. When the demand for portraits slackened Gainsborough planned trips to the country to see friends. Barton Grange, near Taunton, in Somerset, was one of the places he visited: fourteen of Gainsborough's drawings, gifts from the artist, remained in the family collection until 1913, and a brilliant oil sketch, at present on loan to Gainsborough's House, Sudbury, survives of a local lad who used to carry his paints.

31

TO JAMES UNWIN 25 MAY 1768

MS. British Library Add. MS.48964, fo.15r, 15v, 16r, 16v

My Dear Friend

If any of my sitters were to appear in half so bad a light as I'm certain I must do in your & Mrs Unwins Eyes, I should make the devil of them. Ingratitude how ugly — repeated neglects how unpardonable — and yet to Write to <me> so good naturedly; believe me my Dear Friend I'm most horridly ashamed of myself come to see you indeed what a sweet Irish Countenance you must suppose me to have — [*word scratched out in a different ink*] I should blush if I thought you could ever spy me through a Telescope within the distance of a whole County of you — If the People with their damnd Faces would but let me alone a little I believe I should soon appear in a more tolerable light but I have been plagued very much thank God I shall now shut myself up for the summer and not appear til september comes in — methinks I hear you say, ay, or suppose you hang yourself up for the summer and winter too — Shall I never mend o dear o dear I dont think Im a bit alterd since I lived in Hatton Garden only that I'm grey in the Poll — my Wife says I am not so good as I was then tho I take more pains. Well, I'm better settled tho' than ever I was in my Life — more settled more creditably settled and happier so who knows. You don't say whether you are better in your Health nor how Mrs Unwin does — now I blush again — The weather Sir, is settled in very fine in these Parts but rather too warm for Riding in the middle of the Day especially upon Lands-down where there is no shade

I suppose your Country is very woody — pray have you Rocks and Water-falls?[1] for I am as fond of Landskip as ever –

The Captain begs her Comp^{ts} only she is making a damnd Jangling upon the Harpsicord this moment — Molly and Mam: also desires their best respects — thank God they are all well and too Good for [*word or words torn*] but says you again why I know that [*word or words torn: one presumably* 'you'] do know a good deal I must confess but still I defye you to be certain how much I really am

Your Affectionate & sincere
Obed^{t} Servt
Tho Gainsborough

Bath May 25th 1768

God bless that good woman Mrs Somerez. don't you come to Bath this year? pray, let me hear from you soon. could I send a Case cross the Country to you, or best by London?

[*Addr.*] To / James Unwin Esqre / at Wooton Lodge near Ashburn / Derbyshire
[*Postmark*] 27 MA BATH

1 The Unwins were now living on the borders of Derbyshire. This and subsequent letters were addressed to 'Wooton Lodge near Ashburn' (Ashbourne), a fine, large but compact late Elizabethan or early Jacobean mansion.

Eighteenth-century politics were governed by the patronage system, and politicians accumulated power from the number of 'placemen' who owed them loyalty and the number of votes they could control. Many of the places, or jobs, at their disposal were sinecures, the post-holders employing subordinates to perform the duties. Although very independently minded, Gainsborough was no radical, and he accepted the system as he did the status quo in life generally: for example, though a deeply feeling man, he never questioned the penalty of hanging for robbery—it was 'richly deserved'. He was also very solicitous for his friends. But Jackson did not get the job for which he was lobbying.

32

TO JOHN, 4TH DUKE OF BEDFORD[1] 29 MAY 1768

MS. Marquis of Tavistock and the Trustees of the Bedford Estate, Woburn MSS

My Lord Duke

A most worthy honest Man, and one of the greatest Genius's for Musical Compositions England ever produced, is now in London, and has got two or three Members of Parliament along with him out of Devonshire to make application for one of the Receivers of the Land Tax for that County, now resign'd by a very old Man one Mr. Haddy—His Name is William Jackson, lives at Exeter, and for his plainness truth, and Ingenuity at the same time, is beloved as no Man ever was, your Grace has doubtless heard his Compositions but He is no Fiddler your Grace may take my word for it; He is extreemly clever and good, is a married Man with a young Family, and is qualified over and over for the Place; has got Friends of Fortune who will be bound for him in any sum, and they are all making application to His Grace The Duke of Grafton[2] to get him this Place—But my Lord Duke, I told him they could not do it without me, that I must write to your Grace about it.

He is at Mrs. Arnolds[3] in Norfolk Street in the Strand, and if your Grace would be pleased to think of it, I should be ever bound to Pray for your Grace—Your Grace knows that I am an Original and therefore I hope will be the more ready to pardon this monstrous freedom from

Your Graces
most dutiful most Grateful
& Obedient Servant
Tho Gainsborough

Bath May 29th 1768

1 John, 4th Duke of Bedford (see Biographical Register), a neighbour in the Circus at Bath, who had first patronized Gainsborough in 1755 and had become a friend.
2 Augustus, 3rd Duke of Grafton (1735–1811), had become Prime Minister after the Earl of Chatham retired in 1768. He strengthened his cabinet by the inclusion of the Duke of Bedford's party.
3 Isabella Arnold is listed in the ratebooks for 1768 for the parish of St Clement Danes as an owner or occupier of a house in Norfolk Street (there were then no street numbers) with a ratable value of £60 (Westminster City Archives). She was, therefore, a person of some substance.

33

TO WILLIAM JACKSON 29 MAY [1768]

Untraced (Sir Ian Malcolm of Poltalloch sale, Sotheby's, 28 February 1949, lot 157, bt. Myers). Whitley examined this letter when it was offered at Sotheby's, 3 May 1928, lot 889, and the present text follows his transcription (Whitley Papers, Dept. of Prints and Drawings, British Museum: Gainsborough box, Guard Book for 1745–1780, slip on fo.15).

Bath, May, 29

Dear Jackson,

I have outdone myself in a letter to the Duke of Bedford, the sketch of which perhaps you may see some time or other—I can draw a Character better than I thought for, & I reckon upon the whole I have been lucky in the style of the letter. If my single plumper will do anything you'l soon hear, for I have told the Duke where you lodge. Let me hear soon from you, & believe me

Yours ever sincerely
Tho Gainsborough

[*Addr.*] Mr. W. Jackson / Mrs. Arnolds / Norfolk Street, Strand

Gainsborough was not a bookish man and, unlike Reynolds,[1] *did not move in literary circles, though he certainly knew Ralph Allen, with whom Pope and Fielding had been intimate, and Allen's neighbour the poet Richard Graves,*

Rector of Claverton, who apostrophized Gainsborough in verse as early as 1762. His best friends were musicians—Giardini, Abel and J.C. Bach among them—and men of the theatre, notably Garrick. It was in 1768, the year in which Gainsborough was commissioned to paint a full length of Garrick with a bust of Shakespeare for the Shakespeare Bicentennial at Stratford-upon-Avon, that John Palmer persuaded George III to grant letters patent to his theatre in Orchard Street, Bath, which thus became the first Theatre Royal in the provinces. Gainsborough's letters to Garrick about his projected portrait of the great actor between Tragedy and Comedy illustrate his difficulties with the allusive type of portraiture that to Reynolds was meat and drink.

34

TO DAVID GARRICK [27 JULY 1768]

MS. Gainsborough's House, Sudbury (1998.024) (badly scorched at the edges). The present text is taken from the original, the missing parts being derived from Harry Colburn and Richard Bentley, *The Private Correspondence of David Garrick*, London, 1831, vol.1., p.308.

Dear Sir,

I, as well as the rest of the world, acknowledge your Riches & know your princely spirit, but all will not do for, as I told you before I am already overpaid for that shabby performance; and if you have a mind to make me happier than all the presents London can afford, you must do it by never thinking yourself at all in my Debt—I wished many years for the happiness of Mr. Garrick's acquaintance and pray dear Sir let me now enjoy it quietly, for sincerely and truly I shall not be easy if you give way to any of your Romantic Whimsies: besides damn it I thought you knew me too well, you who can read Hearts & Faces both at a View, and that at first sight too. Come, if you will not plague me any more upon this frightful subject, I will tell you a story about first sight. you must know Sir whilst I lived at Ipswich, there was <a> benefit Concert in which a new Song was to be introduced, and I being steward, went to the honest Cabinet=maker who was our Singer[1] instead of a better, and asked him if he could sing at sight, for that I had a new song with all the parts written out, yes Sir said he I can—upon which I order'd Mr. Giardini of Ipswich to begin the symphony and gave my Signal for the Attention of the Com-

Felice de Giardini (1716–96)
Canvas, 76.2 x 63.5
Early 1760s
Private Collection

pany; but behold a dead silence followed the symphony instead of the song; upon which I jumped up to the fellow: D—n ye Why don't you sing? did not you tell me you could sing at sight? Yes, please your honor I did say I could sing at sight, but not first sight—

I am

Dear Sir your most

Obedient humble

Serv—

Tho Gainsborough

P_S_ I beg Sir you'l leave the affair of Gossett[2] to me, I shall give him a Bill payable at first sight I assure you.

[Addr.] To / David Garrick Esq<u>re</u> / at Hampton. / near / London
[Postmark] 28 JY BATH

1 Josiah Harris (see Letter 2, note 1), a subscriber to at least one set of music. (He was identified by John Bensusan-Butt, *Gainsborough in his Twenties*, privately published, 1993, p.49).
2 Probably a reference to the frame-maker, Isaac Gosset (1713–99).

35

TO DAVID GARRICK [AUGUST 1768][1]

MS. Victoria and Albert Museum (Forster Bequest)

Dear Sir

I take particular notice of your friendly Anxiety for my recovery I do assure you, & thank you most Kindly for your Sharp thought but having had 12 oz: of Blood taken immediatly away, am perfectly recoverd, strong in <the> Back & able so make your sublime self easy—I suppose your Lett^{r}. to M^{r}. Sharp[2] was upon no other Business, so have inclosed it—But observe I thank you sincerely.

Shakespeare shall come forth forthwith[3] as the Lawyer says—damn the Original Picture of him[4] with your leave. for I think a Stupider Face I never beheld Except D—k's[5] I intend with your approbation, my dear Friend, to take the form from his Pictures & Statues just enough to preserve his likeness past the doubt of all blockheads, at first sight, and supply a Soul from his Works—it is impossible that such a Mind, and Ray of Heaven, could shine, with such a Face & pair of Eyes as that Picture has; so as I said before damn that

Im going to dinner, and after, I'll try a sketch—I shall leave the Price to you—[*part of word scratched out*] I don't care whether I have a farthing if you will but let me do it—to be sure I should never ask more than my Portrait price (which is 60 Guineas) but perhaps ought to ask less as there is no confinem^{t}. of Painting from [*two or three words crossed out*] < Life> but I say I leave it to you, promising to be contented

upon Honor—I could wish to you to call upon any pretence any day after next Wednesday at the Duke of Montagus because you^{d} see the Duke & Dutchess in my last manner;[6] but not as if you thought any thing of mine worth that trouble, only to see his <Grace's> Landskips of Rubens, and the 4 Vandykes whole length in his Graces dressing Room—.[7]

1 This letter endorsed by Garrick: 'a letter from Gainsborough about Shakespeare & my Picture 1768'. Letter 36, dated 22 August 1768, was evidently written shortly afterwards.

2 From the context, presumably Garrick's long-time friend, Samuel Sharpe (1700?–78), surgeon to Guy's Hospital, with whom he often kept company at the Queen's Arms, St. Paul's Churchyard (Carola Oman, *David Garrick*, London, 1958, pp.99 and 157).

3 Martin Postle ('Gainsborough's "lost" picture of Shakespeare,' *Apollo*, December 1991, pp. 374–79) has demonstrated that this paragraph and the bulk of Letter 35 refer to a

'the Dutchess in my last manner'

Mary, Duchess of Montagu (1711–75)
Canvas, 125.7 x 100.3. 1768
Duke of Buccleuch and Queensberry KT, Bowhill

full-length of *Shakespeare between Tragedy and Comedy* which Garrick had commissioned for himself, possibly with the intention of exhibiting it at the Shakespeare Bicentenary at Stratford-upon-Avon to be held in 1769. Gainsborough was unable to complete the picture to his satisfaction, indeed it caused him considerable frustration, but the unfinished work has been revealed by X-rays (Postle, *op.cit.*, repr. p.377) as lying beneath the well-known portrait of Gainsborough's son-in-law, Johann Christian Fischer (Royal Collection, Buckingham Palace: Waterhouse, No. 252, pl.216). The Corporation eventually asked Garrick (in December 1768) for a portrait of Shakespeare for the Jubilee, and he commissioned the requisite portrait from Benjamin Wilson.

4 Probably the widely known portrait now in the National Portrait Gallery (1), then owned by the Duke of Chandos, or the engraving by Droueshout which had first appeared in the folio edition of Shakespeare's works (Postle, *op.cit.*, note 21).

5 Samuel Derrick (1724–69), a minor poet, had succeeded Beau Nash as the Master of Ceremonies at Bath in 1761. Dr Johnson, on being asked whether Derrick or Smart was the better poet, caustically replied that there was 'no settling the point of precedency between a louse and a flea'.

6 Now Duke of Buccleuch, Bowhill (Waterhouse, Nos. 490 and 491, pls. 100 and 101).

7 There was only one Rubens landscape, the well-known The Watering Place (National Gallery, London). The four Van Dycks were portraits of James, 1st Duke of Hamilton; Henry, Earl of Holland; George, 2nd Marquis of Huntly; and James, Duke of Richmond and Lennox (all Duke of Buccleuch, Bowhill, Selkirk).

36

TO DAVID GARRICK 22 AUGUST 1768

MS. Victoria and Albert Museum (Forster Bequest)

Dear Sir

I doubt I stand accused (if not accursed) all this time for my neglect of not going to Stratford, and giving you a Line from thence as I promised; but, Lord, what can one do such Weather as this, continual Rains. My Genius is so dampt by it that I can do nothing to please me. I have been several days rubbing in & rubbing out my design for Shakespeare and damn me if I think I shall let it go or let you see it at last—I was willing like an Ass as I am, to expose myself a little, out of the simple Portrait way, and had a notion of shewing where that inimitable Poet had his Ideas from, by an immediate Ray darting <down> upon his Eye turn'd up for the purpose;[1] but G– damn it I can make nothing of my Ideas there has been such a fall of rain from the same quarter—you shall not see it for I'll cut it before you can come—tell me Dear Sir when you Purpose coming to Bath that I may be quick enough in my Motions—Shakespears Bust is a silly smiling thing,[2] and I have not sense enough to make him more sensible in the Picture and so I tell ye you shan't see it. I must <make> a plain Picture of Him standing erect,[3] and give it [*word scratched out*] <an> old look as if it had been Painted at the time he lived and there we shall fling 'em Damme

poor Mrs Pritchard[4] died here on Saturday <night> 11 o'Clock—so now her performance being no longer present to those who must see and hear, before they can believe, [*word crossed out*] Will you know my dear Sir [*word crossed out*] but I beg pardon, I forgot—Time puts all into his Fobb, as I do my Time-keeper, watch that my dear.

Who am I but the same
Think you
TG

Impudent scoundrel says Mr. G –
Black Guard

Bath 22nd Ag^st^ 1768

[*Addr.*] To / David Garrick Esqre / London—
[*Postmark*] 24 AU BATH

'an immediate Ray darting <down> upon his Eye turn'd up for the purpose'

X-ray of the portrait of Shakespeare underlying the full-length of Johann Christian Fischer
The Royal Collection © Her Majesty Queen Elizabeth II (detail)

1 This is evident in the X-ray photograph (Postle, op.cit., fig.2, repr. above).
2 Probably the tomb effigy by Gerard Johnson in Holy Trinity Church, Stratford-upon-Avon (Postle, *op.cit.*, p.378).
3 Gainsborough seems not to have proceeded with this simpler concept (Postle, *op.cit.*, p.379).
4 Hannah Pritchard (1709–68), one of the greatest actresses of the day, is described as having been 'one of the most conspicuous stars in the Garrick galaxy' (DNB).

In November 1768 Gainsborough received a letter from Reynolds inviting him to become one of the thirty-six members of the newly founded Royal Academy of Arts. In common with most of the leading artists of the day he defected from the Society of Artists, of which he had been admitted a Fellow at the time of its incorporation in 1765, but which more recently, and especially under the presidency of his old friend, Joshua Kirby, had suffered from constant internal wrangles. He was extremely proud of his diploma from the Academy, 'sign'd with the King's own hand'.

Joshua Kirby (1716–74)
Canvas, 41.9 x 29.2. Late 1750s
Victoria and Albert Museum

37

TO JOSHUA KIRBY[1] 5 DECEMBER 1768

MS. Royal Academy of Arts

Mr President & Gentlemen Directors of The Society of Artists of Great Britain, I thank ye for the honor done me in appointing me one of your Directors; but for Particular Reasons[2] I beg leave to resign, and am

Gentlemen

your most Obedient &

Obliged humble Servant

Tho Gainsborough

Bath Decem^r 5th 1768

[*Addr.*] To / Jos^a Kirby Esqr / President of The Soc. Artists of Great / Britain, to the left at the Turks- / Head in Gerrard Street. St Annes / London
[*Postmark*] 7 DE BATH

1 Joshua Kirby (1716–74), who settled in Ipswich as a house and coach painter in about 1738, was also a topographical draughtsman, a writer on perspective (he moved to Lon-

don in 1755 to teach the future king) and later an architect, George III appointing him clerk of the works at Kew Palace. Although intensely pious he and Gainsborough were lifelong friends, Gainsborough so loving him that he requested in his will to be buried beside him in Kew churchyard. Kirby was elected President of the Incorporated Society of Artists in October 1768, but faction and ill health led him to resign in 1770; he must have been aware that Gainsborough was intending to leave the Society before receiving this formal letter.

2 His invitation to join the newly established Royal Academy of Arts.

Gainsborough's friend William Jackson, of Exeter, may often have been in Bath. He was certainly there in November 1767 to conduct his setting of Milton's Lycidas, *when Giardini and the Linleys were among the performers. In corresponding with him, Gainsborough brought into play apt analogies between the arts of music and painting which reflect his own lyrical and intuitive attitude towards pictorial composition.*

38

TO WILLIAM JACKSON [DATE UNKNOWN]

MS. Royal Academy of Arts

Dear Jackson

I thought you was sick as I had not seen you for some Days, and last night when I went to the Play in hopes of meeting you there, Mr Palmer confirm'd my fears; [*word crossed out*] I fully intended putting on my thick shoes this Morning, but have been hinder'd by some Painter Plagues;[1] pray send me word whether there is any Occasion for Doctor Moysey to come to you, in Palmers opinion, damn your own, for you are too much like me to know how it is with you. The Doctor shall come in a Moment if there is the least occasion and I know he will with pleasure without your touching your breeches pocket. I'll be with you soon to feel your pulse myself

so God mend you

T Gainsborough

Tuesday Morng

I have spoilt a fine piece of drawing paper for you because I had no other at hand, and in a hurry to know how you are—

[*Addr.*] To / Mr. Jackson / at Mr. Palmer's

1 Unwelcome sitters.

In about 1767 or 1768 Gainsborough was involved in an important commission for Lord Shelburne, later first Marquess of Lansdowne. Shelburne was a staunch supporter of the great Earl of Chatham and served him as Secretary of State in these years, distinguishing himself by pursuing a deeply understanding and statesmanlike policy towards the rebellious American colonists. The scheme was for the decoration, by Barret, Deane, Gainsborough and Wilson, of the drawing-room of Bowood, his newly finished Adam house near Bath, 'with a particular injunction that each artist would exert himself to produce his chef d'oeuvre, as they were intended to lay the foundation of a school of British landscapes'. Gainsborough's contribution, indeed a masterpiece, is now in the Toledo Museum of Art. The artist remained a friend of Shelburne for the rest of his life, and once met, at Bowood, the brilliant Whig member for neighbouring Calne, John Dunning, later Lord Ashburton, who was then solicitor-general (Dunning is celebrated in history for the motion he carried in the House of Commons in 1780 that 'the influence of the crown has increased, is increasing, and ought to be diminished').

39

TO WILLIAM JACKSON 2 SEPTEMBER [YEAR UNKNOWN]

MS. Royal Academy of Arts

Bath Sepr 2d.

My dear Jackson

I should have wrote to you sooner, but have been strangely hurried since I left Exeter—In my Way home I met with Ld. Shelburne,[1] Who insisted on my making Him a short Visit, and I don't repent going ('tho I generally do to all Lord's <Houses>) as I met with Mr. Dunning[2] there—There is somthing exclusive of the Clear and deep understanding of that Gentleman most exceedingly pleasing to me—He seems the only Man who talks as Giardini plays, if you know what I mean; He puts no more motion than what goes to the real performance, which constitutes that ease & gentility peculiar to damn'd clever Fellows, each in their way—I observe his Forhead juts out, and mine runs back a good deal more than common, which accounts for some difference betwixt our Parts—no doubt, with me, but he has an uncommon share of Brains and those disposed so as to overlook all the rest of his Parts, let them be ever so pow-

'Mr Dunning . . . Sober Sense and great acuteness are mark'd very strong in his Face'.

Joshua Reynolds
John, 1st Lord Ashburton (1731–83), from the double portrait with his sister
Canvas, 129.5 x 187.7
c.1782–83
Tate Gallery (detail)

erful—He is an amazing compact Man in every respect; and as we get a sight of every thing by comparison only think of the difference betwixt Mr Dunning almost motionless, with a Mind brandishing, like Lightning, from corner to corner of the Earth, whilst a Long cross made fellow only flings his arms about like threshing-flails without half an Idea of what he would be at—And besides that neatness in outward appearance, his Store=Room seems cleared of all french Ornaments and gingerbread Work, every thing is simplicity and Elegance & in its proper place; no disorder or confusion in the furniture as if he was going to remove[3]

Sober Sense and great acuteness are mark'd very strong in his Face, but if those were all, I should only admire Him as a great Lawyer; but there is a Genius (in our Sense of the Word)[4] [*word torn*] shines in all <He> says—In short Mr Jackson of Exeter, I begin to think there is something in the Air of Devonshire that grows Clever fellows I could name 4 or 5 of you, superior to the product of any other County in England –

Pray make my Compliments to one <Lady> who is neat about the Mouth[5] if you can guess & believe me

Most faithfully yours
Tho Gainsborough

[*Addr.*] Mr Jackson / Musician at / Exeter

[*Postmark*] BATH

1 William Petty, 2nd Earl of Shelburne, later 1st Marquess of Lansdowne (1737–1805), then aged about thirty. An unpopular politician largely due to his dislike of party, Shelburne was liberal and forward-looking and Bowood a focus for radical and intellectual society. He was also one of the great collectors of his age, and clearly enjoyed a warm relationship with Gainsborough (see also Letter 103).

2 John Dunning, later 1st Baron Ashburton (1731–83), was a brilliant barrister and one of the most powerful orators of his age. He was Member of Parliament for Calne (close to Bowood), 1768–80, through the influence of Lord Shelburne, and strongly opposed the high-handed ministerial policy towards the American colonies. Reynolds portrayed him posthumously with Shelburne and Isaac Barré, 1788–89, in one of the finest of his group portraits (Earl of Northbrook, on indefinite loan to Baring's Bank, London).

3 An extended metaphor for an orderly mind. 'Gingerbread work' was a term originally applied by sailors to the carved and gilded decorations of a ship, and hence to architectural or other ornament of a gaudy and tasteless kind (OED).

4 Probably distinctive character, as in the familiar eighteenth-century expression, 'genius loci', used in respect of gardens distinctive of a particular place.

5 Mrs Jackson.

Gainsborough was not only a lover of music and friend of musicians — like his revered predecessor, Van Dyck — but a fine extempore player, possessing a natural, if untrained, ear and taste. His friend Henry Bate-Dudley said that 'His performance on the Viol de Gamba was, in some movements, equal to the touch of Abel. He always plays to the feelings.' He had a singular passion for possessing the instruments from which such friends of his were able to draw exquisite sounds, and once gave Abel two fine landscapes in exchange for a viol da gamba. His knowledge of musical instruments was considerable; he 'took great pains to buy the best, & would give large prices for them.' Increasingly, as the 1760s wore into the 1770s, Gainsborough resented the annual round of run-of-the-mill face painting, and no less the round of entertainments and aimless tittle-tattle into which he was drawn by the marriageable age of his daughters. The elder, Margaret, who never married, was seriously ill in the autumn of 1771. As John Palmer told Garrick, Dr Moysey 'paid no attention to her, declaring that it was a family complaint and he did not suppose she would ever recover her senses again; so that Gainsborough was obliged to call in Schomberg and Charlton, who called it by its right name, a delirious fever, and soon cured her'.

The Music Party
Red chalk drawing, 24.1 x 32.4. Late 1760s or early 1770s
British Museum

40

TO WILLIAM JACKSON 4 JUNE [YEAR UNKNOWN]

MS. Royal Academy of Arts

My Dear Jackson

I am much obliged to you for your last Letter, and the Lessons rec^d^ before; I think I now begin to see a little into the nature of Modulation and the introduction of flats & sharps; and when we meet you shall hear me play extempore—My Friend Abel[1] has been to visit me, but he made but a short stay, being obliged to go to Paris for a Month or six weeks, after which He has promised to come again There never was a poor Devil so fond of Harmony, with so little knowledge of it; so that what you have done is pure Charity—I dined with Mr Duntze[2] in expectation (and indeed full assurance) of hearing your scholar Miss Floud[3] play a little, but was for the second time flung;[4] she had best ['take care' *crossed out*] beware of the third time, lest I fling Her, and if I do I'll have a Kiss before

She is up again—I'm sick of Portraits and wish very much to take my Viol da Gam and walk off to some sweet Village where I can paint Landskips and enjoy the fag End of Life in quietness & ease[5]

But these fine Ladies & their ['D–mnd' *crossed out*] Tea drinkings, Dancings, Husband huntings &c &c &c will fob me out of the last ten years, & I fear miss getting Husbands too—But we can say nothing to these things you know Jackson, we must Jogg on and be content with the jingling of the Bel[ls], only d–mn it I hate a dust, the kicking up a dust; and being confined in Harn[ess] to follow the track, whilst others ride in the Waggon, under cover, stretching their Legs in the straw at Ease, and gazing at Green Trees & Blue Skies without half my Taste[6] That's d–mn'd hard

My Comfort is, I have 5 Viol's da Gamba, 3 Jayes[7] and two Barak Normans[8]—

Adieu Dear Jackson

and believe me ever & sincerely yours

Tho Gainsborough

Bath June 4th

[Addr.] To / Mr. Wm. Jackson / Fore street / Exeter

[*Postmark*] BATH

1 Carl Friedrich Abel (see Biographical Register), the last of the great virtuosi of the viola da gamba, performed regularly in Paris and had a pupil there.

2 John Duntze (died 1795), of Rockbeare House, Exeter, was a prominent woollen merchant in that city and founder partner in 1769 of the Exeter Bank. He was Member of Parliament for Tiverton, the centre of serge manufacture, 1768–95, and was created a baronet in 1774.

3 Miss Floud was probably one of the daughters of Alderman Flood, of Exeter. Elizabeth, his second daughter, was portrayed by Jackson's son-in-law, John Downman, in 1778 (Fitzwilliam Museum, Cambridge).

4 Rejected. Metaphor from riding: flung to the ground.

5 This much-quoted remark was made at the end of the season to an intimate friend. Gainsborough was clearly exasperated by the incessant demands of run-of-the-mill society portraiture, and no less by the social round inseparable from the fact that his wife had two daughters to marry off. The 'sweet Village' existed only in his imagination, but nonetheless it was an idyllic existence for which he longed.

6 As Sir Michael Levey has suggested ('The Genius of Gainsborough', *Christie's International Magazine*, October 1990, p.2), the wagon, which featured constantly in Gainsborough's later landscape imagery, seems to have constituted a symbol for the human passage through life. This connotation is clear in the present context.

7 Henry Jaye is first mentioned as living in Southwark in 1610. His descendants were viol and violin makers for nearly two hundred years.

8 Barak Norman was a maker of violins, violoncellos and bass viols active during the Restoration period.

'others ride in the Waggon . . . stretching their Legs in the straw at Ease, and gazing at Green Trees & Blue Skies'
Boy Reclining in a Cart
Pen and brown ink, with grey and brown washes, 17.6 x 22.1. Late 1760s
British Museum

In about 1767, largely under the influence of Rubens, Gainsborough lightened his palette and began to introduce a richer variety of tints into his modelling. Light reflected onto surfaces from the setting sun might be rendered in mingled hues of red, yellow, orange, blue and purple. He also used much bolder impasto. In 1772 his handling of paint was criticised in the reviews of the Academy exhibition: one reporter declared that ' his colours are too glaring', another that 'he throws a dash of purple into every colour'. Jackson sent two landscapes to the Academy of 1771, and at about this time, lacking a musical position (he was not appointed organist of Exeter Cathedral until 1777), he thought seriously of giving up music for painting, about which he was prone to theorize. Gainsborough, aware that he lacked genuine talent, gave him guarded encouragement.

41

TO WILLIAM JACKSON[1] 6 FEBRUARY [PROBABLY 1770]

MS. Royal Academy of Arts

Dear Jackson

Is it true that you broke your Neck in going home! I have not seen Palmer but only the day after your departure to learn the truth — it is a current report <here> that the Great and the amiable Mr Jackson got a Mischief in going home, that you had tied your horse by the head so fast, that his head was dragg'd off in going down a hill, and that you order'd the driver (like a near sighted Man) to go back for the horses body, and that the Chaise horses frightend at the sight of the boys riding up upon a Horse without a head, took fright and made for Exeter — and that you unwilling to leave your Horse in that condition took a flying leap out at the window, and pitch'd head foremost into a hollow Tree[2] — Miss D — l[3] has heard this Story, and says if it be true she'l never touch a Note again. I hope to hear from either Palmer or Bearing[4] when I see them, some more favourable account of you. I'm but little dispos'd to pitty you because you slip'd away so dam'd sly without giving me any more time than you had to jump into the hollow tree

Pray if your damn'd long fingers escaped lets hear from you soon, and in the mean time I'll pray that it's all a lie

believe me yours sincerely

Tho Gainsbor[ough]

Bath Feb: 6th

Will you meet me at London any time! and I'll order Business Accordingly —

[*Addr.*] To / Mr Jackson

1 This letter was endorsed by Jackson: 'This parcel of letters are Kept for my Brother T: J: if ever he returns to England but if not during my life they should be burnt'.

2 The reference to Jackson's accident links this letter with Letter 42, while the reference in the latter to the gift of a harp links both to Letter 43, dating probably from April 1770, when the harp had been returned.

3 Miss D—L, a musician, presumably a friend or pupil of Jackson, has not been identified. Susan Sloman has suggested that she may have been a member of the Delaval family (letter to the compiler, 27 April 2000).

4 Probably Jackson's patron, John Baring (1730–1816), of Mount Radford, Exeter. A wealthy cloth merchant, he was co-founder with his brother Francis of Baring's Bank, and Member of Parliament for Exeter, 1776–1802.

42

TO WILLIAM JACKSON [PROBABLY FEBRUARY 1770]

MS. Royal Academy of Arts

Dear Jackson

If your Neck is but safe, damn your Horses head[1] — I am so pleased with both your Remarks, & your Indigo, that I know not which to admire most, or which to think most of immediate use; the Indigo you leave me in doubt whether there be any more to be got, whereas I am pretty sure of some more of your thoughts now we are fairly settled into a correspondance; your Observations are like all yours, just, natural, and not common — your Indigo is cleare, like your understanding & pure as your Music, not to say exactly of the same Blue of that Heaven from whence all your Ideas are reflected — to say the truth of your Indigo, 'tis delightful, so look sharp for some more (& I'll send you a drawing —) and for your thoughts, I have often flatter'd myself I was just going to think so — the lugging in Objects whether agreeable to the whole or not is a sign of the least Genius of any thing, for a person able to collect in the Mind, will certainly groupe in the Mind also; and if he cannot master a number of Objects, so as to introduce them in friendship, let him do but a few — and that you know my Boy makes Simplicity — one part of a Picture ought to be like the first part of a Tune, [*part of word crossed out*] that you ['could' *crossed out*] can guess what follows, and that makes the second part of the Tune, and so I've done –[2]

My Respects to Mr Tremlett[3] — Bearing did not call upon me, I hear he's gone from Bath

The Harp is packed up to come to you and you shall <u>take it out</u> with Miss as I'll not <u>take</u> any thing for it[4] but give [it] to you to twang upon when you can't twang upon Mrs Jackson, to whom pray my Comp^ts^ if there is no impropriety in the Introduction [*the rest of this page, three lines, has been cut off, probably for the signature*]

[*Addr.*] To / Mr William Jackson / Musician at / Exeter

[*Postmark*] BATH

1 The references to Jackson's neck being safe relates this letter closely to Letter 41.

2 Gainsborough's advice reflected the increasing maturity and focus of his own landscape compositions: in his early work there had been a tendency, absorbed from Dutch painting, towards 'the lugging in Objects whether agreeable to the whole or not.'

3 Mr Tremlett, presumably a mutual friend in Exeter, has not been identified.

4 An example of Gainsborough's natural generosity.

'one part of a Picture ought to be like the first part of a Tune, ... that you ... can guess what follows, and that makes the second part of the Tune'

Peasants Returning from Market
Canvas, 121.3 x 170.2. c.1767–68
Toledo Museum of Art, Ohio (Edward Drummond Libbey Endowment)

43

TO WILLIAM JACKSON [PROBABLY APRIL 1770][1]

MS. Royal Academy of Arts

Dear Jackson

Methinks I hear you say, all Friendship is my [*word scratched out*] and all sincerity my [*word scratched out*] only because I have not had time, since my hurry of finishing two full lengths & a Landskip for the Exhibition,[2] to answer your last two Letters—But don't be in a hurry to determine any thing about me, if you are, ten to one you <are> wrong; [*short word crossed out*] those who can claim a longer acquaintance with me than Mr Jackson knowing at this moment but very little of my real temper. I'm heartily sorry that you don't come to reside nearer Bath, as you expected not because you are disapointed of the advantages of conversing with me & my Works, but because I am deprived of much greater advantages of sucking your sensible skull, and of the Opportunity I might possibly have of convincing you how much I shall allways esteem your various and extensive Talents, not to mention what I think still better worth mentioning, namely your honesty, & undesigning plainness & openness of soul—They say your Mind is not Worldly, no said I, because its heavenly—I think a tollerable reason Master Mathews[3] –

I fear my Lad I shall have it this Exhibition for never was such slight dabs presented to the Eyes of a Million. but I grow dauntless out of meer stupidity as I grow old, and I believe any one that plods on in any one way, especially if that one way will bring him bread & cheese as well as a better, will grow the same.

You mention'd somthing you had committed to paper upon Painting, I hope you have not committed Painting upon the same paper, because you know I am to see it—Mr Palmer was going to London the last time I saw him so I fear it may be some time before you receive this Letter, but as soon as you do shew how well you can forgive by a speedy answer.

The Harp is come back and I'm sorry you thought it worth the pains of returning as the Lady was not wo[rthy] of it—I suppose you had playd upon her til you was tired and so would not let her have it[4]—thanks for the Indigo—a little of it goes a great way, which is lucky—

Adieu Dear Jackson and believe
me most truly & sincerely yours
Tho Gainsborough

respects to Mr Tremlet

[*Addr.*] To / Mr. Jackson at / Exeter

1 See note 2.
2 The only years in which Gainsborough painted two full-lengths and a landscape for exhibition were 1769 and 1770. The self-deprecatory reference later in the letter to their being 'slight dabs' might fit the spirited handling characteristic of either year, but the reference in this passage to *this* Exhibition suggests that Gainsborough was writing of the second Royal Academy Exhibition, i.e. that of 1770.
3 Possibly a reference to 'Captain' Mathews, a plausible and extravagant young man-about-town who arrived in Bath that year (see Letter 57, note 4).
4 A teasing reference to Jackson's weakness for pretty young women.

44

TO WILLIAM JACKSON [DATE UNKNOWN]

MS. Royal Academy of Arts

Dear Jackson

I will confess to you that I think it unpardonable in me not to speak seriously upon a subject of so much consequence as that which has employd us of late; therefore you shall now have my thoughts without any humming[1] swearing or affectation of Wit[2] — Indeed my Affection for you would naturally have led me that way before now, but that I am soon lost if I pretend to reasoning; and you being all regularity & Judgment, I own provoke me the more to break loose; as he who cannot be correct, is apt to divert the Eye with a little freedom of handling but no more of it

I must own your calculations, & comparison betwixt our different professions, to be just, provided you remember that in mine a Man may do great things, and starve in a Garret, if he does not conquer his Passions and conform to the common Eye in chusing that branch which they will encourage, & pay for.[3] Now there cannot be that difference <betwixt Music & Painting> unless you suppose that the Musician Voluntarily shuns the only profitable branch, and will be a Chamber Counsel[4] when he might appear at the Bar — you see I'm out of my Subject already — But now in again — If Music will not satisfye you without a Certainty (which by the by is nonsense begging your pardon, for there is no such thing in any profession) then I say be a Painter — you have more of the Painter than half those that get money by it, that I will swear, if you desire it, upon a Church Bible — you want a little Drawing & the use of pencil & Colors which I could put into your Hand in one Month, without medling with your Head; I propose to let that alone, if you'l let min[e] off easey — There is a branch of Pai[nting] next in Profit to Portrait, and quite [in] your power without any more drawing than I'll answer for your having, which is Drapery & Landskip backgrounds.[5] perhaps you don't know that whilst a Face painter is harras'd to death the drapery painter sits and earns 5 or 6 hundred a year, and laughs all the while — ['perhaps' *crossed out*] your next will be to tell me what I know as well as yourself Viz^{t} that I'm an impertinent Coxcomb — this I know, & will speak out if you kill me for it, you are too modest too diffident too sensible & too honest ever to push in Music so now Kiss my Arse[6] [*these last five words struck out in a later hand*]

Sincerely
TG –

[*Addr.*] To. / Mr William Jackson / Exeter

1 Deception; 'hum' was short for 'humbug' (OED).
2 Amal Asfour and Paul Williamson ('Gainsborough's Wit', *Journal of the History of Ideas*, Vol.58, 1997, No.3, pp.479–501) demonstrate how 'Gainsborough's letters show his affinity with aspects of eighteenth-century wit and reveal his awareness of the long-running argument about wit and judgement' (pp.479–80).
3 Portraiture, not the recognized academic summit in the hierarchy, history painting, connoisseurs of which generally preferred to buy Old Masters.
4 Lawyer who prepares briefs for the advocate.
5 Gainsborough himself rarely employed a drapery painter, but most of the leading eighteenth-century portrait painters did. It could be a lucrative business. Joseph van Aken, for example, who worked chiefly for Thomas Hudson and Allan Ramsay, made a considerable fortune. Peter Toms was elected a Royal Academician.
6 Fielding explained the wit of this expression as 'in desiring another to kiss your a— for having just before threatened to kick his' (*Tom Jones*, 1903 ed., vol.1, p.308).

For the first exhibition of the Royal Academy in 1769 Gainsborough not unnaturally took particular pains, contributing one of the grandest female full-lengths he ever painted, and one consciously in the Van Dyck tradition, the marriage portrait of the twenty-year-old Lady Molyneux, now in the Walker Art Gallery, Liverpool, which was singled out for praise by contemporary critics. But, already by the following year, Gainsborough was showing signs of dissatisfaction with the hanging policy. The Academy's 'Monstrous large Room' in Pall Mall seems to have been less satisfactory, at least for the appreciation of smaller pictures, than the exhibition room of the Society of Artists; Newton, the Secretary, was evidently something of a snob, and small pictures he considered unimportant might well be skied.

45

TO WILLIAM JACKSON 9 JUNE 1770

MS. Gerard Mackworth Young (formerly)

My Dear Jackson Bath June 9th 1770

I have been most unaccountably hinder'd from writing to you, from time to time and I flatter myself as that is really the case you'l think me a clever fellow for not endeavouring to account for it. I saw you at the Exhibition, and as I expected, hung a mile high[1] — I wish you had been a <created> Lord before my sending the Picture, then that puppy Newton[2] would have taken care you had been in sight. I wonder if any of your Acquaintance knew you besides myself! This I'll swear, they none of them know your Rogues tricks half so well as I do and <yet> at the same time Value you for your honesty. I believe I shall come this Autumn to Exmouth to bathe in order to stand next Winter.[3] My Wife seems coming into the scheem.

let me know if I must send you your Head, or whether you can do with the half one you already are in possession of[4] none but a half-headed fool would pay you this Compliment — mark that — and make my Compliments to the Sensible & agreeable Mr Tremlet; If I come I'll plague Him enough Ill warrant you.

Well, God bless you, I can't think of any more Nonsense and you don't admit of Drawing in Letters,[5] or else I could add a triffle more for your amusement —

believe me Dear Jackson

Ever yours

Tho Gainsborough

Observe the reason I have not Answered your last sooner I have been 3 months from home, at Mr. George Pitts Country House[6]

[*Addr.*] To / Mr. Jackson / Exeter. —/ no haste

1 The portrait, in a Scottish private collection (not known to Waterhouse), was a 30 x 25 inch canvas.

2 Francis Milner Newton (see Biographical Register) was Secretary of the Royal Academy, 1768–88.

3 Gainsborough stood at his easel. Ozias Humphry noted that 'he commonly painted standing' and Philip Thicknesse, in his short biographical sketch written in 1788, remarked that 'he stood, not *sat* at his Palate, and consequently, of late years at least, five or six hours work every morning, tired him exceedingly.'

4 A complex explanation of this remark is offered in Amal Asfour and Paul Williamson, ' "Rogues Tricks" — The Problem of Gainsborough's Portrait of Jackson', *Gainsborough's House Review*, 1996/97, pp.140–41. A simpler one is that Gainsborough was merely making a joke about Jackson's actual head.

5 In fact, only two of Gainsborough's surviving letters (fragments: see Letters 3 and 8) contain drawings; but sketches of coaches, figures, dogs being scolded and other detail are supposed to have embellished the pages of a series of letters to Lady Tynte which, unfortunately, perished in a country house fire. Lady Tynte was the wife of Sir Charles Kemeys Tynte (1710–85), of Halsewell, Somerset.

6 George Pitt, later Lord Rivers (see Biographical Register), who lived at Stratfieldsaye, in Hampshire (later sold to the Duke of Wellington).

George Pitt, 1st Baron Rivers (1721–1803)
Canvas, 232.4 x 152.4. R.A. 1769
Private Collection, England

There is little evidence that in later life Gainsborough was prepared to do portraits anywhere but in his own studio. An exception was in the case of the full-lengths of the Ligoniers, which he executed at Stratfieldsaye. George Pitt, later Lord Rivers, for whom Gainsborough had a particular affection, was anxious to have portraits done of his daughter and son-in-law before he went off as ambassador to Madrid. They were shown at the Academy of 1771. It is of interest to note that Gainsborough spent so long on the job (he was three months at the house). As Thicknesse wrote in an article in 1770: 'Mr. Gainsborough not only paints the face; but finishes with his own hands every part of the drapery, this, however trifling a matter it may appear to some, is [as] of great importance to the picture as it is fatigue and labour to the Artist. The other eminent painters either cannot or will not be at that trouble.' It was at this period, sometime between 1770 and 1772, that Gainsborough raised his portrait prices once again, to thirty guineas for a head, sixty guineas for a half-length and one hundred guineas for a full-length; his fees were now well ahead of any of his rivals except Reynolds, who had been charging a hundred guineas for a full-length more than a decade earlier and had already raised his fee to a hundred and fifty in 1764.

46

TO JAMES UNWIN 10 JULY 1770

MS. Institut Néerlandais, Paris

My Dear Friend Bath July 10th 1770

Ever since the receipt of your last undeserv'd favor, I have been toss'd about like a ship in a storm; I went by appointment only to spend two or three Days at Mr George Pitt's country House, by way of taking leave of him, as a staunch Friend <of mine> before his going to Spain, and behold he had got two whole length Canvasses, & his Son & Daughter L^{d} & Lady Ligonier in readiness to take me prisoner for a months work[1] — you'l say I might have wrote to you from thence, and so I certainly should but that I left your Letter at home, & forgot your direction — It may seem very odd, and I'll lay fifty pounds you'l think 'tis a d — n'd lie, but the D — l fetch me if I have been able to direct a Letter to you these 5 years owing to your removal from Essex I have been just going to write to your Brother many times for your direction but have been always prevented by the curs'd Face Business — If you'l believe me,

Penelope, Viscountess Ligonier (1749–1827)
Canvas, 240 x 157.5. R.A. 1771
Henry E. Huntington Art Gallery, San Marino, California

my Dear Friend, there is not a man in the World who have less time to call his own, and that would so willingly spend some of it in the enjoyment of an Old Acquaintance My Regard for you was originally built upon such a foundation that you know no time can shake, nor ought not, but the nature of face painting is such, that if I was not already crack'd, the continual hurry of one fool upon the back of another, just when the magot bites,[2] could be enough to drive me Crazy.

Let us, for an experiment try what a renewal of our Acquaintance would do towards making me behave well for the future; you say if I would come and see you in Derbyshire, you w^{d}. return our Visit to Bath—By G— if you will come this Autumn and bring M^{rs}. Unwin for six weeks, and make our house your home, I'll pack up all my Drawing things, and see Derbyshire next summer, if I'm alive.

What say you? let us be at a word now

I'm so ashamed to mention M^{rs}. Unwin's Picture that D—mme I wish I was a Razor-grinder—I'll begin a new one of Her & you together if you'l come. Poor M^{rs}. Saumarez too, o Lord[3]—[*word torn: presumably* 'that'] I should behave worst to my best Friends [*word torn: presumably* 'and'] [b]est to my worst—I hate myself for this 'tho even my Enemies say I have some good qualities If there is any one Devil uglier than another 'tis the appearance of Ingratitude join'd to such a Face as mine.

let me before I get more out of patience with myself, tell you that my Wife & Daughters desire their best Respects to yourself & M^{rs}. Unwin; & hope you'l agree to my proposal.

Beleive me Dear Sir yours Affectionatly

Tho Gainsborough

[*Addr.*] To / James Unwin Esqre / at Wooton Lodge near Ashburn / Derbyshire [*Postmark*] 13 JY BATH

1 George Pitt had sought this lengthy extension of a proposed two or three days' visit so that Gainsborough could paint full lengths of his daughter, Penelope, and his son-in-law, Edward, on the latter's succession to the title of Viscount Ligonier (both Huntington Art Gallery, San Marino, California: Waterhouse, Nos.442 and 443, pls.130 and 131).

2 Just when the fancy takes me (to do something for my own enjoyment). 'I shall do it, when the magot bites' was a French proverb (OED).

3 Both Mrs Unwin's and Mrs Saumarez's portraits were first mentioned seven years before, in a letter dated 24 July 1763 (Letter 9). The three-quarter-length of Mrs Unwin is in a Canadian Private Collection (Waterhouse, No.688); the portrait of Mrs Saumarez has not so far been identified.

47

[TO AN UNKNOWN RECIPIENT] [DATE UNKNOWN]

MS. Royal Academy of Arts (Jupp Collection, vol.1., fo.60/9)

[*letter missing*]

Adieu

my Valuable Old Friend
'til I am enabled to give you
a better Letter – My best Affections
attend you all –

Tho Gainsborough

In the eighteenth century, when friends came for a visit, they usually stayed for a much longer time than is customary nowadays. To start with, travel was long and tiring if not arduous: the fastest time on the road from London to Bath was still twenty-four hours in 1763, though it was ten by the end of the century. Gainsborough's accommodation in the Circus was evidently insufficient for more than one couple, with attendant servants, staying at a time; and Thicknesse tells us that, in any case, his wife, with more than one eye upon the housekeeping, did not encourage him to entertain his friends at home.

48

TO JAMES UNWIN 15 NOVEMBER 1770

MS. British Library Add. MS.48964, fo.17r, 17v, 18r,18v

My Dear Friend

The reason and only reason I did not answer your last Obliging Letter was that just at the time I received it, a Lady, her Son & servants arrived at our house upon a long invitation from my Wife, whose acquaintance She is, to stay at our House; this you may guess was a pleasant Circumstance as I was about to appoint a time for our pleasure of seeing you & Mrs. Unwin; I have been ever since harkening to the time of her intention of going that I might answer your Letter, but behold (owing to warm intreaties from some part (not the most insignificant of my Family) She now proposes to spend her Christmas here. We never had above a Bed & a half to spare in our lives, and so I am reduced to offer my Friendship only to take Lodgings for you according to your directions if you favor me with them I am sorry to hear that Bath waters have any part in the Occasion of your coming; I hope we shall ride often together, and set you up for another seven years.

Believe me Dear Sir (with [*word crossed out, probably* 'best'] all our joint Comp^{ts}. to

M^{rs}. U. <& self>

yours most truly

Tho Gainsborough

Bath

Novr. 15th. 1770

[*Addr.*] To / James Unwin Esq$^{\underline{re}}$ / at Wooton Park near Ashbourn / Derbyshire

[*Postmark*] 17 NO BATH

In the late 1760s and early 1770s Gainsborough executed a number of portraits in pastel, a medium well suited for an intimate likeness and much favoured in the eighteenth century: his main competitor at Bath was his friend William Hoare, who was a specialist in the genre, as were Francis Cotes, the latter's pupil John Russell, and Daniel Gardner (the last two working almost exclusively as pastellists). In later years, however, perhaps because of the fragility of the chalk, so difficult to preserve, Gainsborough seems to have preferred the medium of oil on paper for smaller portraits of this sort.

49

TO THE HON. EDWARD STRATFORD, LATER 2ND EARL OF ALDBOROUGH[1] 21 MARCH 1771

MS. Houghton Library, Harvard University (Locker-Lampson-Warburg-Grimson Album, fo.128)

Sir,

I had the honor of your Obliging Letter last night, and sent the inclosed both as directed, and to one of them you have the Inclosed Answ[r] I am sorry you have had so much trouble in the affair you mention, 'tho I understood by the news papers that you had recover'd the Plate & Jewells, and that the Rascals were hang'd out of the way, as they richly deserved.

I am daubing away for the Exhibition with all my might, and have done two large Landskips which will be in two handsome frames (exclusive of 3 full length Portraits) and think whether you have recover'd your Riches or not, you ought to purchase them, because you have enough left, and the Landskips are the best I ever did, & probably will be the last I shall live to do.[2] I wish that yours and M[rs] Stratfords Portraits had been whole lengths that I might have Exhibited you, & have got Credit; but half lengths are overlook'd in such a Monstrous large Room[3] and at a Miles Distance.

I'm sorry your Chalk Drawings got Rubbed as they were muzzy enough at first, as indeed all Chalk Drawings of Portraits must be so Small and the Chalk so soft—I shall very willingly retouch them or do any thing else for you, when I come to Town well knowing that if ever I am Knighted or have any thing to do at S[t] James's it must be through your Interest and singular Friendship for me[4]—You may depend upon my utmost care to do every thing [*word torn*] your Pictures according to your direc[tions] and that you shall have them as soon as these Exhibition Pictures are pack'd up which will be in a Week.

I beg my humble Service to M[rs]. Stratford I am

Sir your most Obedient & humble

Servant

Tho Gainsborough

Bath March. 21st 1771

Pardon the Vulgar form of this Letter occasion'd by the unlucky shape of the Card Inclosed.

[*Addr.*] To / The Hon[ble] Mr Stratford

1 Edward Stratford, a wealthy patron (see Biographical Register).

2 The two landscapes Gainsborough sent to the Royal Academy have not so far been identified, nor is it clear why he should have been so apprehensive about the future at this time.

3 See illustration on p.149. The two portraits (Waterhouse, Nos.10 and 11) are untraced.

4 It is not known what connections Stratford had with the Court.

In 1770 Gainsborough painted another portrait of Garrick: a lively head and shoulders, now in the National Portrait Gallery, in which the sitter is projected almost out of the frame as though leaning forward towards an expectant audience. This was exhibited at the Academy that year. The following year he painted a copy of it as a present for James Clutterbuck, Garrick's business adviser. Gainsborough's remarkable devotion and feeling of indebtedness towards Garrick, a vain and difficult man by all accounts, is evident from Clutterbuck's letter to the great actor: 'because he owes you so much [he] thinks it is not in his power to pay you enough . . . The unbounded liberality Gainsborough possesses hath inclined him—contrary to my wishes and expectations—to add a frame (price 55s.) to my picture.' Gainsborough seems also at this time to have done a pastel of Garrick's two daughters for which likewise he refused payment.

50

TO DAVID GARRICK [DATE UNKNOWN]

Untraced (H.W. Underdown sale, Sotheby's, 28 June 1927, lot 395, bt. Tregaskis)

With this sensible scull of mine I have order'd my Business so as to have three sitters one after another to-morrow, besides having caught a d—m'd cold by riding in the rain this afternoon, so that I fear I cannot call in the formal manner I promised[1] to take my leave of you to-morrow ... I shall never think any touch of my hand capable of expressing a hundredth part of my obligation and gratitude to you and that if I ever spy but a glimmering of any acknowledgemt for the Chalk scratch[2] . . . except your speaking kindly of me I swear by Saint Luke's pencil you shall never see touch, scratch or blot more of

My dear Friend

Yours very sincerely

Tho. Gainsborough

1 A few additional words derive from the extract published in the catalogue of the Charles Fairfax Murray sale, Sotheby's, 5 February 1920.

2 Payment when it was intended as a gift.

51

TO DAVID GARRICK [1771]

MS. Victoria and Albert Museum (Forster Bequest)

My Dear Sir

I never will consent that any body makes a present of your Face to Clutterbuck[1] but myself, because I always intended a Copy (by my own hand) for Him, that he may one day tell me what to do with my Money, the only thing he understands except jeering at folks

I shall look upon it that you break in upon my Line of happiness in this World if you mention it; and for the Original, it was to be my present to Mrs. Garrick, and so it shall be in spight of your blood[2] –

Now for the Chalk scratch it's a poor affair, not much like the young Ladies,[3] but however if you don't remember what I said in my last, and caution your Brother of the same Rock[4] may you sink in the midst of your Glory –

I know your great Stomach and that you hate to be cram'd, but by G— you shall swallow this one bait, and when you speak of me don't let it be like a Goose but remember you are a fat Turkey

God bless all your endeavours to delight the World, and may you Sparkle to the last –

Tho Gainsborough

damn Underwood[5]

1 James Clutterbuck (1704?–76), a wealthy mercer, was Garrick's business adviser and, like Samuel Sharpe (see Letter 35, note 2), a member of the coterie which met at the Queen's Arms, St. Paul's Churchyard (Ian McIntyre, *Garrick*, London, 1999, pp.109 note, 372 and 555).

2 Hotheadness.

3 A pastel, no longer extant, of Arabella (1753–1819) and Catherine (born 1756), the two daughters of Garrick's youngest brother, George, and his first wife, Elizabeth Carrington.

4 Impediment: Gainsborough's repeated insistence that these portraits should be gifts.

5 Underwood was a youthful minor poet who had made Gainsborough's acquaintance a few years previously. Piqued because he imagined Gainsborough had promised to paint his portrait as a present and no invitation had been forthcoming, he lampooned him in a volume of satiric verse published in 1768 (to which Garrick was a subscriber) and continued to hound his victim with acrimony.

The letters Gainsborough wrote to Lord Dartmouth—three at five-day intervals, evidently replies by return of post—add up to the artist's most

William, 2nd Earl of Dartmouth (1731–1801)
Canvas, 124.4 x 99.1. 1769
Earl of Dartmouth

important statement about his attitude to portraiture. While Gainsborough was painting for the first Royal Academy exhibition a portrait (Lady Molyneux) in which one almost feel the rustle of the exquisitely executed satin dress, Reynolds produced four female portraits—inspired respectively by classical sculpture, Albano, Correggio and Guercino—in which the sitters are clothed in generalized drapery deliberately intended to give a timeless look to the pictures. It was perhaps not surprising that Lady Dartmouth should request from Gainsborough, to whom she was sitting at this time, a portrait in the new elevated style. It was not surprising, either, that he should have produced an indifferent result. Gainsborough thought that Reynolds's inventions only served to conceal individuality and likeness, the qualities which he sought. He was fully aware of the immense difficulties of portraying a sitter's physical presence and personality—with no voice and movement, as an actor would have, 'but only a face, confined to one View, and not a muscle to move to say here I am'—even using his own methods, which entailed working only from the life, and noting characteristic postures, movements and gestures. The measure of his success may be gauged by Thicknesse's remark that

'the ridiculous use of fancied Dresses in Portraits'

Frances, Countess of Dartmouth (c.1733–1805)
Canvas, 124.4 x 99.1. 1769
Earl of Dartmouth

it was possible to judge a Gainsborough portrait as though it were a living person and in many of his canvases we do have an uncanny sense that we are confronting someone as he or she actually looked at home, or went about their daily business, or walked the streets of Bath. Gainsborough finally compromised with Lady Dartmouth by painting her in a Van Dyck dress, a fashionable conceit of the time (it was at the Academy of 1770 that he exhibited the celebrated The Blue Boy, *now in the Huntington Art Gallery).*

52

TO WILLIAM, 2ND EARL OF DARTMOUTH[1] 8 APRIL 1771

MS. Staffordshire Record Office, Stafford (D(W) 1778/III/257)

Bath April 8th 1771

My Lord,

I recd the honour of your Lordship's Letter acquainting me that I am to expect Lady Dartmouth's Picture at Bath, but it is not yet arrived—I shall be extreemly willing to make any alterations your Lordship shall require, when Her Ladyship comes to Bath for that purpose, as I cannot (without taking away the likeness) touch it unless from the Life[2]

I would not be thought by what I am going to observe that I am at all unwilling to do any thing that your Lordship requires <to it> or even to paint an entire new picture for the Money I received for that, as I shall always take pleasure in doing any thing for Lord Dartmouth, but I should fancy myself a great blockhead if I was capable of painting such a Likeness as I did of your Lordship, and not have sense enough to see why I did not give the same satisfaction in Lady Dartmouth's Picture: & I believe your Lordship will agree with me in this point, that next to being able to paint a tollerable Picture, is having judgment enough to see what is the matter with a bad one. I don't know if your Lordship remembers a few impertinent remarks of mine upon the ridiculous use of fancied Dresses in Portraits[3] about the time that Lord North[4] made us laugh in describing a Family Piece His Lordship had seen somewhere, but whether your Lordship's memory will reach this triffling Circumstance or not, I will venture to say that had I painted Lady Dartmouths Picture, dressd as Her Ladyship goes, no fault (more than in my Painting in general) would have been found with it. believe me My Lord, 'tho I may appear conceited in saying it so confidently ['that' *crossed out*] I never was far from the mark, but I was able before I pull'd the trigger to see the cause of my missing: and nothing is so common with me as to give up my own sight in my Painting room rather than hazard giving offence to my best Customers. You See, my Lord, I can speak plainly when there is no danger of having my bones broke, and if your Lordship encourages my giving still a free Opinion upon the matter, I will do it in another Line.

I am Your Lordships most Obliged & Obedient
humble Servant
Tho Gainsborough

1 Lord Dartmouth (see Biographical Register).

2 Gainsborough refused to work on a portrait without the presence of the sitter.

3 Reynolds's classicizing costume.

4 Frederick, 8th Baron North, Prime Minister, 1770–81, was Lord Dartmouth's stepbrother, and the two had made the Grand Tour together, 1752–54.

'and dress it (contrary I know to Lady Dartmouths taste) in the modern Way'

Frances, Countess of Dartmouth (c.1733–1805)
Canvas, 76.2 x 63.5. 1771
Earl of Dartmouth

53

TO WILLIAM, 2ND EARL OF DARTMOUTH 13 APRIL 1771

MS. Staffordshire Record Office, Stafford (D(W) 1778/III/257)

My Lord,

I can see plainly your Lordships good nature in not taking amiss what I wrote in my last, 'tho 'tis not so clear to me but your Lordship has some suspicion that I meant it to spare myself the trouble of painting another Picture of Lady Dartmouth which time & opportunity may convince your Lordship was not the intention, and I here give under my hand that I will most willingly begin upon a new Canvas. But I only for the present beg your Lordship will give me leave to try an Experiment upon that Picture to prove the amazing Effect of dress—I mean to treat it as a cast off Picture and dress it (contrary I know to Lady Dartmouths taste) in the modern Way; the worst consequence that can attend it will be Her Ladyships being angry with me for a time—I am vastly out in my notion of the thing if the Face does not immediatly look like;[1] but I must know if Lady Dartmouth

Powders or not in common:[2] I only beg to know that, and to have the Picture sent down to me—I promise this my Lord, that if I boggle a Month by way of Experiment to please myself, it shall not in the least abate my desire of attempting another to please your Lordship when I can be in London for that purpose or Lady Dartmouth comes to Bath.

I am

your Lordships

most Obedient humble

Servant

Bath

Tho Gainsborough

April 13th. 1771

My Lord

I am very well aware of the Objection to modern Dresses in Pictures, that they are soon out of fashion & look awkward; but as that misfortune cannot be help'd we must set it against the unluckiness of fancied Dresses taking away Likenesses, the principal beauty & intention of a Portrait.[3]

1 Gainsborough believed that likeness depended on the use of contemporary dress, what people actually wore.

2 *Pari passu*, it was essential for likeness to know whether or not a female sitter used make-up in society.

3 A succinct statement of Gainsborough's considered view on the purpose of portraiture, which he would have assimilated from the books being discussed by the Hogarth circle with whom he had associated as a student (see Rosenthal, p.136).

54

TO WILLIAM, 2ND EARL OF DARTMOUTH 18 APRIL [1771]

MS. Gainsborough's House, Sudbury (1973.002)

Bath

April 18th.

My Lord

Here it is then—Nothing can be more absurd than the foolish custom of Painters dressing people like scaramouches, and expecting the likeness to appear;[1] had a picture Voice, Action, &c to make itself known, as Actors have upon the Stage, no disguise would be sufficient to conceal a person; but only a face, confined to one View, and not a muscle to move to say here I am, falls very hard upon the poor Painter who perhaps is not within a mile of the truth in painting the Face only[2] — Your Lordship I'm sure will be sensible of the Effect of Dress thus far, but I defy any but a Painter of some Sagacity (and such you see am I my Lord) to be well aware of the different Effects which one part of a picture has upon another, and how the Eye may be cheated, as to the appearance of Size &c by an artful management of the accompanyments — A Tune may be so confused by a false Bass, [*short word crossed out: probably* 'so'] that if it is ever so plain simple and full of meaning it shall become a jumble of nonsense, and just so shall a <handsom> Face be overset by a fictitious bundle of trumpery of the foolish Painters own inventing[3] — For my [*short word crossed out: probably* 'own'] part (however your Lordship may suspect my Genius for Lying) I have that regard for Truth, that I hold the finest invention as a meer slave <in Comparison >: I believe I shall remain an Ignorant fellow to the end of my days, because I never could have patience to read Poetical impossibilities, the very food of a Painter: <especially> if he intends to be Knighted [*word crossed out*] in this Land of Roast Beef. So well do Serious People love froth[4] —

But where am I my Lord! This my free Opinion in another Line with a Witness —

forgive me my Lord I'm but a Wild Goose at best — all I mean is this, Lady Dartmouth's Picture will look more like and not so large when dress'd properly; and if it does not, I'll begin another. it is safe arrived.

I am your Lordships most

Obedient

Tho Gainsborough

1 An attack on contemporary artists' practice of dressing people (especially female sitters) in classicizing or masquerade costume without concern for their individuality.

2 Like all good portrait painters, Gainsborough realized that the depiction of an individual human being depended upon an accurate portrayal of every aspect of their persona: physical presence, expressions, gestures, movements, in conjunction with psychological insight.

3 A statement of the view expressed at the beginning of the letter.

4 A dig at the encouragement of classical, mythological and literary subject-matter as a source for painting, especially by Reynolds, who had been knighted in 1769.

For Gainsborough, always an original and always adventurous as far as techniques were concerned, the early 1770s were years of unusually restless experimentation. His earliest aquatint dates from this period, as does his discovery that Bristol-made white lead was of better service than white chalk, a secret he kept close. In 1772 he sent to the Academy two large, and ten smaller, 'drawings in imitation of oil painting'. Such landscape drawings were in a variety of media—oil, gouache, watercolour, and more complex media he devised himself—and some of the larger ones that survive are on as many as six pieces of paper joined together (none survives on a single piece as one finds later in the work of Turner). The purpose of the technique was not only rapidity of execution but an enhancement of the natural effects he sought in his oils through the luminosity of the paper. Gainsborough was infinitely generous in instructing his friends in the art of drawing.

55

TO THE HON. CONSTANTINE PHIPPS, LATER 2ND BARON MULGRAVE[1] [1771 OR 1772?]

MS. Major P.A.V. Biddulph, Stevenage

Dear Sir

I'm allways glad when my first Letter is off to a person I would keep up a Friendly & usefull correspondence withal, as there are a few forms & Comp^{ts}. expected, which when once settled, never need be repeated. And you seem to have done me full justice in your last favor, in return for a very saucy Letter. Most people spend ten years in what you & I seem to have very dexterously hop'd over at once, so that now, like experienced officers, let us proceed to Business.

I wish to having a Draw, as much as you can possibly desire it; and what I have to say to you upon the Subject, you shall have without any flourishes or round about pieces of Art. you know, Sir, I set you to this [*lsketch of foliage*] meerly to free your hand, but you are not to understand that for Drawing—Therefore remember that there must be truth of hand, as well as freedom of hand in Drawing. If you ask me how you are to distinguish when you are exercising truth and when freedom, I answer you, that no ['real' *crossed out*] exercise in Drawing can be, but in sketching the real form of some Object, a Head; or Hand, a Tree, a House; freedom is only the manner, in which a Master would do the same thing, different from a stiff handed scholar—All I meant by scribling of Boughs was to set your hand

Gainsborough Dupont
Constantine Phipps, 2nd Baron Mulgrave (1744–92)
Canvas, 76.2 x 63.5
Whereabouts unknown

agoing; now you must stick a little Plaister-Head upon a wire, like a Traitor upon Temple Bar, and draw away in your Closet, all round, in every View: When you can sketch the Outward form, and touch in the parts so that it is not half as big again or half as small again as the head you draw from, then you may [*short word crossed out: probably* 'be-'] begin to express a little light & shade, with common black & white Chalks <upon blue paper> but very faintly, and not before you can sketch freely. Thus I freely tell you the Road, if you are disposed to set off in Earnest and by G — nothing can be done in the trifling way out of a Boarding school

Dear Sir

Yours most sincerely

Tho Gainsborough

Bath
Sunday Morning
before breakfast — Boots on. fine Morning –

1 Constantine Phipps, a close friend from this time on (see Biographical Register).

56

TO THE HON. CONSTANTINE PHIPPS, LATER 2ND BARON MULGRAVE 13 FEBRUARY 1772

MS. The Marquess of Normanby, Mulgrave Castle

Honble Constantine & Dear Uniform Lappell[1]

I snatch a moment betwixt the sittings of such another stiff three quarter Portrait as your Own, to acknowledge your Obliging & Friendly Letter

By G — You are the only Great Man, except George Pitt, that I care a farthing for, or would wear out a pair of Shoes in seeking after; long-headed[2] cunning people, and rich fools are so plentiful in our country that I don't fear getting now & then a Face to paint for Bread; but a Man of Genius, with truth & simplicity, sense & Good-nature, I think worth his weight in Gold — so Sir, tell me no more of that vile sketch of you, but frame this, with naval Ornaments[3] & hang it up in its stead. Methinks I would fain have you join <a little> Drawing to your valuable accomplishments, which I'm sure you'l conquer as far as your wishes can reach, if you will but think it worth your while; & I'm sure I shall be proud of being your Master — your greater & more useful acquirements can never suffer by joining this innocent amusement to them. But I'm telling you what you know, for which I ask your pardon —

I have been trying a large Cartoon Landskip in the Way of the Drawings I sent by Zaffani[4] as they run off so quick, & intend two spanking ones for the Exhibition, if I succeed in getting large Paper made on purpose, as I have wrote for to the Paper Mills for the joinings I dont admire being seen through all the Work.[5] Remember you are in my Secret about the White[6] ['and' *crossed out*] I intend you shall have a Couple of Drawings in that way as soon as I can please myself half so well as I did in keeping you up with little Sensible George[7] 'til four o'Clock.

Heavens preserve you from the Vices & Corruptions of the Age, in Manly Sincerity of Heart & great pursuits, the Wish of

your Likeness Man

Tho Gainsborough

Bath Feb: 13th 1772

God knows when I shall come to Town, Stratford is damnably out of humour about his Pictures not being finished because the Frames hang up in his best Visiting Room in readiness. He Writes every post, partly to shew me how Angry he is, & partly how well he can Write.

'I have been trying a large Cartoon Landskip'

Rocky Wooded Landscape with Drovers and Cattl. Paper mounted on board. 100.3 x 124.5. c.1771-72. Buscot Park (Faringdon Collection)

1 This waggish form of address, with its naval reference, was a play on words: Lepell was the Christian name of Phipps's mother.

2 Artful (1735). Dickens described long-headed people as men of the world, knowing dogs (OED).

3 Presumably symbolic references to Phipps's career in the Navy to embellish the frame, as was often the case with paintings of battle scenes. The 'this' Gainsborough asked him to frame would appear to be the present letter, or a drawing enclosed with it. The 'vile sketch' was the head-and-shoulders portrait exhibited at the coming Academy, 1772 (97) (Marquess of Normanby, Mulgrave Castle: Waterhouse, No.508).

4 Johan Zoffany (1733–1810), the master of the conversation piece, whom Gainsborough would have known through his patron, David Garrick.

5 Gainsborough sent two large drawings in imitation of oil paintings to the Royal Academy Exhibition of 1772; Susan Sloman has pointed out (in a letter to the compiler, 25 November 1999) that the first really large (53 x 31 in.) sheets of paper were not produced by Whatman until 1773, and all Gainsborough's drawings of this description which survive today were done on several sheets of paper joined together.

6 See Gainsborough's letter to Jackson, 29 January 1773 (Letter 64).

7 George Pitt, later Lord Rivers (see Biographical Register).

57

TO THE HON. CONSTANTINE PHIPPS, LATER 2ND BARON MULGRAVE 31 MARCH 1772

MS. Major P.A.V. Biddulph, Stevenage

Dr Sir

I thought you was burning your fingers in some Marriage Bill or Act[1] that I had not heard from you—I like your sketches and see no reason why you should not draw away as much and as long as you find any Pleasure in it—I have thought of a s[c]:heem for you, by which I can correct & examine or rather examine & correct, your Drawings, as you send them to me by Letter; and this is by sending you some little Plaister Heads,[2] of which I have duplicate Casts; so that you have nothing to do but stick them up upon a wire & Draw for Life

I shall still stick mine of the same upon a wire to examine your Outlines (which is all I would have you trouble yourself with at first) and by return of post, after receiving your sketch, send you it corrected, with hints to go on—Is not this a bright thought, to teach you to draw by Letter? I challenge you to take any View of the heads, or any Effect of light & shade that I cannot immediatly place mine in the same, just as well as if I was present at your Drawing from your own—

Observe to place your Heads exactly upon a level with your Eye, so as to look neither upwards nor downwards to View it. I shall send them in a little Box by the next Machine—

I am D^r^. Sir

your most Obed St

Tho Gainsborough

Bath March 31st. 1772

P.S.

Miss Linley is walkd off sure enough [*word crossed out*] with young Sheridan;[3] but He is not at the bottom of the mischief, he is supposed to be only half way [*word scratched out*]—M—ews is the scoundrel supposed (and with much reason) to have undone the poor Girl[4]—it vexes me much; I could fight about it, because I was just finishing her Picture for the Exhibition.[5] I feel for Poor Linley[6] much. though in my private Opinion he did not take quite care enough; but [*word illegible*].

Elizabeth Linley (1754–92)
Canvas, 76.2 x 63.5. c.1775
Philadelphia Museum of Art:
The George W. Elkins
Collection

Captain Thomas Mathews (1741–1820)
Canvas, 77.5 x 64.5. 1772
Museum of Fine Arts,
Boston: Julia Cheney
Edwards Collection, 1925

Thomas Linley, Sr. (1733–95)
Canvas, 74.9 x 62.2
Late 1760s
Dulwich Picture Gallery

1 The Royal Marriage Act, which was passed in the House of Commons on its third reading on 24 March 1772,was bitterly contested as an extension of royal prerogative and as an oppressive restraint contrary to all religious principle. Arising from scandals surrounding the throne, notably the secret marriages of the Dukes of Cumberland and Gloucester and the flagrant adultery of the King's sister, the Queen of Denmark, it provided that no descendant of George II could marry without the consent of the King, if under twenty-five, or, if over that age, Parliament were to disapprove.

2 Similar plaster heads are seen in Gainsborough's portrait of Martha Harley (later Mrs George Drummond) with her porte-crayon, c.1778 (last recorded in the Palace Foundation sale, Sotheby's, 16 November 1988, lot 57 (repr. col.), bt. Lady Abdy: Waterhouse, No.212), who seems to have been following the same system of instruction (see Hugh Belsey, 'Two Works by Gainsborough: The master in two guises: a drawing and a portrait', *National Art Collections Fund Annual Review*, year ended 1992, p.11).

3 Elizabeth Linley (1754–92) (see Letter 30, note 1) eloped with Richard Brinsley Sheridan (1751– 1816), when she was eighteen.

4 'Captain' Mathews, a young married man whom Elizabeth's father (see note 6 below) had allowed to become a family friend and to be his daughter's escort, but who subjected her to increasingly intolerable sexual harassment. She was finally rescued by Sheridan, who humiliated Mathews by forcing him to beg for his life and breaking his sword to pieces after defeating him in a duel. It was presumably Gainsborough's anger which led him not to finish his portrait of Mathews, seen in his studio in Bath in December 1772 (Museum of Fine Arts, Boston: Waterhouse, No.473, pl.151).

Sir William Pulteney (1729–1805)
Canvas, 237.5 x 149.9
R.A. 1772
Yale Center for British Art, New Haven (Paul Mellon Collection)

5 The double portrait of her and her sister Mary (1758–87) at full-length (Dulwich Picture Gallery, London: Waterhouse, No.450, pl.145).

6 Thomas Linley, Sr (1733–95), their father. Linley later (1776) became a patentee of Drury Lane Theatre with Sheridan, and was responsible for the music there.

58

TO WILLIAM JOHNSTONE PULTENEY[1] 1772 [PROBABLY APRIL]

MS. Pierpont Morgan Library, New York (MA 1263 (329))

Sir,

I generally view my Works of a Sunday, 'tho: I never touch;[2] and I think we could still finish a little higher, to great advantage, if it would not be intruding too much upon your good nature, to bestow one more little <sittting> of about half an hour, either to morrow morning, or any other, most agreeable to yourself. I am fired with the thoughts of Mrs. Pulteney's giving me leave to send you to the Royal Exhibition, and of making a good Portrait of you,[3] therefore hope Sir you will be so good to pardon my giving you all this trouble.

I am

Sir your most Obliged &

most Obedient humble Servant

Tho Gainsborough

Circus

Sunday Evening

[*Addr.*] To / —Pulteney Esq—

1 Sir Willliam Johnstone Pulteney (1729–1805), of Westerhall, Dumfriesshire, who succeeded as the 5th baronet in 1794. He made a fortune acquiring land in America.
2 Unlike Reynolds, Gainsborough was a strict observer of the Sabbath.
3 Pulteney must have obliged, as the portrait of him (at full length: Yale Center for British Art, New Haven: Waterhouse, No.565, pl.144) is unusually highly finished, and was duly exhibited at the Royal Academy exhibition of 1772 (96), which opened on 24 April.

Gainsborough's work on the full-length of William Pulteney, as well as his group of experimental landscapes, for the Academy of 1772, effectively prevented him from completing his commission for Edward Stratford, who, as he had told his friend Constantine Phipps in February, had been writing to him every post complaining of the delay. Gainsborough took refuge in his duty to the Academy—there is for the second time a hint that a knighthood was more than a faint possibility—and in a bohemianism which, in spite of temptations, prostration and some lack of order in his studio routine, he was probably far from accepting as an artistic norm.

59

TO THE HON. EDWARD STRATFORD, LATER 2ND EARL OF ALDBOROUGH 1 MAY 1772

MS. Henry E. Huntington Library, San Marino, California

Dear Sir

When you mention Exhibition Pictures, you touch upon a String, which once broke, all is at an End with me; but I do assure you, nay I swear by Saint Luke's Pencil,[1] I have not dress'd[2] nor sent a finished half length out of my doors since yours have been in hand;[3] so that I beg you to have patience to hear me, and I beg Mrs Stratford to keep you in good

After James Tassie (1735–99)
Edward, 2nd Earl of Aldborough (d. 1801)
Replica of a paste medallion
Scottish National Portrait Gallery

nature for a moment, I do solemnly promise you to finish your Pictures in my best manner before any other from this time. I was obliged to cobble up somthing for the Exhibition or else (so far from being knighted) I should have been expel'd the Society, and have been look'd upon as a deserter, unworthy my Diploma sign'd with the Kings own hand,[4] which I believe you have seen most beautifully framed & hung up in my Painting-Room, behind the Door—

Do good Sir let me know for certain when you think of returning home from abroad, and if I disapoint you of seeing your Pictures hung in their Places with my own Eyes, I'll give you leave to boil me down for Painters Drying oil, and shiver my Bones into Pencil = Sticks—could Shakespeare with his Mother Madam fancy[5] say more—I wish you would recollect that Painting & Punctuality mix like Oil & Vinegar,[5] & that Genius <&> regularity are utter Enemies, & must be to the end of Time—

I would not insinuate that I am a Genius any further than as I resemble one in your Opinion, who think I have no such thing as punctuality about me—In short Sir, I throw myself at your Feet, & thank God most sincerely that I am not any nearer to them, for surely you could not help kicking me—However Sir [de]pend upon this, that I am most sincerely

Your ever Obedient & humble

Servant

Tho Gainsborough

Bath

May 1st. 1772 –

[*Addr.*] To / The Honble Edwd. Stratford / Dean Street

1 Saint Luke is the patron saint of painters.

2 Completed the costume.

3 They had been in hand since at least March 1771 (see Letter 49). Rosenthal (p.53) attributes Gainsborough's procrastination to annoyance that so wealthy a man had not commissioned full-lengths.

4 Every Royal Academician received a Diploma, and in turn was expected to present a Diploma picture to the Academy. Gainsborough never submitted the required picture, and it was not until 1799, eleven years after his death, that his daughter, Margaret, presented a large landscape (Waterhouse, No.1007) 'in compliance with the intention of her late father'.

5 The reference is puzzling, but Gainsborough may have had in mind Hamlet's frequently addressing his mother as Madam and his desire to please her, as in 'I shall in all my best obey you, Madam' (Act I, sc. ii, l.120). (I am very grateful to Roger Pringle and Dr. Robert Smallwood, of the Shakespeare Birthplace Trust, for so kindly pointing me in this direction). *Hamlet* was certainly in the repertory of the Theatre Royal, Bath during Gainsborough's time there, and he is likely to have seen it performed.

60

TO THE HON. EDWARD STRATFORD, LATER 2ND EARL OF ALDBOROUGH [1772]

MS. [Card] Henry E. Huntington Library, San Marino, California

Mr Gainsborough presents his Compts. to Mr Stratford; He does not understand whether Mr Stratford means to have the Dog painted seperate by Monsieur Dupont,[1] or again put into Mrs. Stratford's Picture to spoil it; so cannot say any thing about it to Day.

But with regard to Mrs. Stratford's Drawing,[2] Mr G— will expect the honor of seeing Mrs. Stratford to morrow Evening (Dressd) at any hour agreable to Mrs. Stratford.

1 Gainsborough Dupont (see Biographical Register), who became Gainsborough's studio assistant that very year. It is curious that Gainsborough, who excelled with dogs, should have deputed this task to his new young assistant.

Gainsborough Dupont (1754–97)
Black chalk and stump, coloured chalks and watercolour, varnished, 16.5 x 14.1
Early 1770s
Victoria and Albert Museum

2 This was probably a pastel, a medium which Gainsborough was using at this time. If the drawing was completed, it has not survived.

As always, his impulsive temperament to blame, Gainsborough never made a trip to London when he ever did entirely what he intended; and, in spite of his scare in 1763, found it difficult to resist a pretty girl who put temptation in his way. It was their female acquaintances he meant when he wrote to his fellow-painter, Cipriani, in 1774: 'I hope that all our Friends are well towards the City?'

61

TO THE HON. CONSTANTINE PHIPPS, LATER 2ND BARON MULGRAVE 28 MAY [1772][1]

MS. The Marquess of Normanby, Mulgrave Castle

Dear Sir

My Flight to Town was so sudden & transient, that did not your Obliging Letter convince me that I really call'd at your House I should think it rather

Johann Christian Bach (1735–82)
Canvas, 74.3 x 61.6. 1776
Civico Museo, Bologna
(Bibliografico Musicale)

an agreeable Dream — I was sorry I did not hit the moment just to shake you by the hand — who knows but a hearty Shake from me might have proved like a Magnet and have shaken a freedom of hand into your Drawing for ever — I was hugging myself as I pass'd through Harley street, that as I had not met one Fidler or Hautboy Man, I should doubtless have leisure to wait upon you again, but behold, not three doors from yours, I ran my head plump in Abel's fat Guts.[2] He promised I should hear a Man blow half notes upon the French[3] if I would dine with Him; I found Fisher, Bach & Duport,[4] all ready to make a finish of me for the Day I had to stay in Town, so that not a Friend, a Picture, or any thing I liked could I enjoy — except only a little Venus rising from the Sea[5] in my way to my Lodgings, the same that is puff'd off at our Exhibition I believe for her hair was d — md red.[6]

Adieu

Dear Sir & believe me

Your most Obedient &c

Tho Gainsborough

Bath May 28th.

1 The year is established by the reference at the end of the letter to Barry's exhibited picture (see note 6 below).
2 Abel was extremely portly. See also Biographical Register.
3 The French horn.
4 Johann Christian Fischer (see Biographical Register) was a distinguished oboeist. Johann Christian Bach (1735–82), the eldest son of Johann Sebastian Bach, was an opera composer who settled in London in 1762 and became music master to Queen Charlotte; until his marriage in 1773 he shared a house with Abel, with whom he organized a series of subscription concerts. Jean-Pierre Duport (1741–1818), the celebrated 'cellist, came to England in 1769. In 1773 he accepted the invitation of Frederick the Great to become the first 'cellist of the royal chapel in Berlin.
5 A prostitute. According to Hesiod, Venus, the goddess of love and fertility, was born out of the sea, from the foam produced by the genitals of the castrated Uranus when they were cast upon the waters.
6 James Barry exhibited his *Venus rising from the sea* in 1772. Horace Walpole described her as 'dragging herself up to Heaven by a pyramid of her own red hair'.

Gainsborough's difficulty in satisfying himself with a portrait not done from the life is illustrated by a letter to Garrick in which he announces the belated dispatch of a portrait of the great actor, a present to Mrs Garrick, of which he had been trying to make a copy for himself.

62

TO DAVID GARRICK 22 JUNE 1772

MS. Victoria and Albert Museum (Forster Bequest)

Dear Sir

I ask pardon for having Kept your Picture so long from Mrs Garrick— It has indeed been of great service in keeping me going, but my chief reason for detaining it so long, was the hopes of getting one copy <u>like</u>, to hang in my own Parlour, not as a show Picture, but for my own enjoyment,[1] to look when I please at a Great Man, who has thought me worthy of some little notice; but not one copy can I make which does not as much resemble Mr Garrick's Brother as Himself—so I have bestow'd a drop of excellent Varnish to keep you out, instead of a falling tear at parting and have only to beg of Dear Mrs Garrick to hang it in the best light she can find out, and to continue puffing for me in the manner Mr Keate[2] informs me She does—That you may long Continue to delight &

surprise the World with <your Original> Face whilst I hobble after with my Copy is the sincere wish

of Dear Sir

your most unaccountable

& Obedient Servt

Tho Gainsborough

Bath June 22d. 1772

P.S. The Picture is to go to London by Wiltshire's Flying Waggon[3] on Wednesday next, and I believe will arrive [*two or three words scratched out*] by Saturday Morning—

[*Addr.*] To / David Garrick Esqr / London –

[*Postmark*] 24 JU BATH

1 Susan Sloman has shown how portraitists working in Bath liked to be able to include portraits of performers in their show rooms, so that visitors, who would have seen them at the theatre or assembly rooms, 'could judge for themselves how good a likeness the artist achieved' ('Artists' Picture Rooms in Eighteenth-Century Bath', *Bath History*, vol.VI, 1996, p.137). Gainsborough is stressing that this was not his purpose.

2 Probably George Keate (1729–97), an amateur poet and artist who had been given the freedom of Stratford-upon-Avon at the time of the Shakespeare Jubilee celebrations, 1769.

3 See Biographical Register.

In 1771 Philippe Jacques de Loutherbourg, the French landscape painter, settled in London with an introduction to Garrick, and achieved a rapid success as the most accomplished and inventive, not to say sensational, scene painter of his day. He and Gainsborough became friends, and may have worked together for the stage: certainly Gainsborough was involved with decor, for he is known to have executed on glass an over-life-size Comic Muse, one of a number of such transparent paintings lit from behind by candles, for Bach and Abel's new concert room in Hanover Square, opened in February 1775. However, he was not wholly sympathetic to the revolutionary ideas of de Loutherbourg, although he was entranced by the latter's Eidophusikon, *sequences of moving scenery on a model stage accompanied by dramatic sound effects and music by Dr Arne, an entertainment which took London by storm in 1781. In the early 1770s he may have been criticized himself for the 'glaring' colour of his painting, but Sir Francis Bourgeois remembered that Gainsborough used to tell him that 'chaste colouring was as necessary to a picture as*

Philippe Jacques de Loutherbourg (1740–1812)
Canvas, 76.5 x 63.2
R.A. 1778
Dulwich Picture Gallery

modesty to an artist'. Gainsborough disliked excess in any art form and detested the stridency of the percussion bands and overlit stage which, in the interests of illusion, had become fashionable in the London theatre under the aegis of Domenico Angelo and de Loutherbourg.

63

TO DAVID GARRICK [1772]

MS. Yale University Library, New Haven

My Dear Sir

When the streets are paved with Brilliants, and the Skies made of Rainbows I suppose you'l be contented, and satisfied with Red blue & yellow[1] – It appears to me that Fashion, let it consist of false or true taste will have its run, like a run away Horse; for when Eyes & Ears are thoroughly debauch'd by Glare & noise, the returning to modest truth will seem very gloomy for a time; and I know you are cursedly puzzled how to make this retreat without putting out your lights, and losing the advantage of all our new discoveries of transparent Painting &c &c How to satisfye your tawdry friends, whilst you steal back into the mild Evening gleam and quiet middle term.[2]

Now I'll tell you my sprightly Genius how this is to be done. Maintain all your Light, but spare the poor abused Colors, til the Eye rests & recovers— Keep up your Music by Supplying the place of Noise, by more Sound, more Harmony & more Tune; and split that curs'd Fife & Drum—[3]

Whatever so great a Genius as Mr Garrick may say or do to support our false Taste, He must feel the truth of what I am now saying, that neither our Plays, Painting, or Music are any longer real Works of Invention but the abuse of Nature's lights, and [wha]t has already been invented i[n] [form]er Times—

Adieu my dear Friend

any Comm^ds to Bath

Sunday Morng—

a Word to the Wise;[4] if you let your Portrait hang up so high, only to consult your Room, and to insinnuate somthing over the other Door, it never can look without a hardness of Countenance and the Painting flat: it was calculated for breast high & will never have its Effect or likeness otherwise.[5]

[*Addr.*] David Garrick Esqr

1 Gainsborough expressed his irritation at the excesses then prevalent on the London stage, the fashion for which he recognized had to run its course, in this letter to Garrick, who had engaged the brilliant French stage designer, Philippe Jacques de Loutherbourg, for the 1771–72 season. But, far from acceding to Gainsborough's strictures, 'Garrick responded, not by putting on the brakes, but by releasing the inventiveness of de Loutherbourg' (George Winchester Stone, Jr., and George M. Kahrl, *David Garrick, A Critical Biography*, Southern Illinois University Press, Carbondale and Edwardsville, 1979, p.329). After Christmas 1773 Garrick and de Loutherbourg mounted their most spectacular collaboration, a pantomime entitled *A Christmas Tale*, which, according to a contemporary account, included 'a forest scene, where the foliage varies from green to blood color. The contrivance was entirely new and the effect was produced by placing different coloured slides in the flies and side scenes, which turned on a pivot and with lights behind which so illuminated the stage as to give the effect of enchantment' (I am indebted to Iain Mackintosh for this quotation and the contents of note 2 below: letter to the compiler, 8 August 1999). *A Christmas Tale*, enthusiastically acclaimed by the public, continued in performance until April 1780.

2 The 'mild Evening gleam' refers to Garrick's standard, unchanging lighting, with the lights in the auditorium—oil and candle—remaining on during the performance. The 'quiet middle term' meant the centre of the stage, away from the footlights. See also Ian McIntyre, *Garrick*, London, 1999, who describes the innovations Garrick introduced from French stage and lighting techniques in the 1765–66 season at Drury Lane (pp.371–72).

'a Word to the Wise; if you let your Portrait hang up so high, only to consult your Room, and to insinnuate somthing over the other Door, it never can look without a hardness of Countenance and the Painting flat: it was calculated for breast high & will never have its Effect or likeness otherwise'

David Garrick (1717–79)
Canvas, 76.2 x 63.5
R.A. 1770
National Portrait Gallery

3 Combination of shrill and loud sound characteristic of a military band.
4 A witty allusion to the new play, *A Word to the Wise*, performed at the Theatre Royal, Bath, between 30 April and 26 May 1772 (Arnold Hare (ed.), *Theatre Royal, Bath: A Calendar of Performances at the Orchard Street Theatre 1750–1805*, Bath, 1977, p.38). The letter probably dates from close to this time.
5 Probably in more cases than one realizes, Gainsborough adjusted his handling to suit a position in which a client intended a picture to be hung. In this case either Gainsborough assumed it was to be hung 'breast high' or else Garrick changed his mind about the positioning.

Gainsborough's fascination with techniques, his determination to have exactly the right materials — Bristol white lead, for example, he found more the temper of white chalk for use in his drawings than the London variety — and his enthusiastic spirit of experimentation, like a chemist in his laboratory, are well attested, but they are nowhere more tellingly revealed than in the long description of a process for making varnished drawings he sent to Jackson in 1773.

64

TO WILLIAM JACKSON 29 JANUARY 1773

MS. Yale Center for British Art, New Haven

Dear Jackson of Exeter

There is not a Man living that you can mention (besides your self and one more, living) that shall ever know my secret of making those studies you mention—I have a real regard for you, and would tell you any thing except One [*space*] in the World & that shall die with me.

You may acquaint your Friend that you tried your strength with me for the secret, but the fixing the White Chalk ['you find' *crossed out*] previous to tinging the Drawing with water-Colors, you find I am determin'd never to tell to any body; and here you'l get off, for no Chalk is used. and so keep it close for your own use; and when you can make a Drawing to please your self by my directions Send it to me & I'll tell you if they are right[1]

Mind now—take half a sheet of blotting paper such as the Clerks and those that keep books put upon writing instead of sand; 'tis a spongy purple paper. paste that and half a sheet of white paper, of the same size, together, let them dry, and in that state keep them for use—take a Frame of deal about two Inches larger every way, and paste, or glue, a few sheets of very large substantial paper, no matter what sort, thick brown, blue, or any; then cut out a square half an Inch less than the size of your papers for Drawing; so that it may serve for a perpetual stretcing Frame for your Drawings; that is to say after you have dip't your drawing as I shall by & by direct in a liquid, in that wet state you are to take, and run some hot glue and with a brush run round the border of your stretcher, gluing about half an Inch broard which is to receive your half an Inch extraordinary allow'd for that purpose in your drawing paper, so that when that dries, it may be like a drum. Now before you do any thing by way of stretching, make the black & white of your drawing, the Effect I mean, & disposition in rough, Indian Ink shaddows & your lights of Bristol ['London' *crossed out*] made white lead which you buy in [*word crossed out*] lumps at any house painters; saw it the size you want for your white chalk, the Bristol is harder and more the temper of chalk than the London. When you see your Effect, dip it all over in skim'd milk; put it wet on [your] Frame <just glued as before observed to> let it dry, and then you correct your [*word illegible*] with Indian Ink <which dry> & if you want to add more

Wooded Landscape with Herdsman Driving Cattle Downhill
Varnished drawing in mixed media, 21.9 x 31.6
Early 1770s
Birmingham Museums and Art Gallery

lights, or other, do it and dip again, til all your Effect is to your mind; then tinge in your greens your browns with sap green & Bistre, your yellows with Gall stone & blues with fine Indigo &c &c—When this is done, float it all over with Gum water, 3 ounces of Gum Arabic to a pint of water <with Camels pencil> let that dry & varnish it 3 times with Spirit Varnish such as I sent you; tho only Mastic & Venice Turpinetine is sufficient, then cut out your drawing but observe it must be Varnishd both sides to keep it flat trim it round with a Pen Knife & Ruler, and let any body produce the like if they can, stick them upon a white paper leaving a Margin of an Inch & half round.

Swear now never to impart my secret to any one living—

Yours Sincerely

Tho Gainsborough

Bath Jan: 29th 1773

[*Addr.*] To / Mr Willm Jackson / Musician at / Exeter
[*Postmark*] BATH

1 The process described in this letter was first studied in detail in an unpublished thesis by Sophie Crombie, 'A Discussion of a Technique for Varnished Drawings Described by Thomas Gainsborough in a Letter of 1773', Courtauld Institute of Art, Department of Technology, 1971. More recently, Jonathan Derow has identified fifty-nine examples of the process Gainsborough described: see his unpublished thesis, 'Thomas Gainsborough's Varnished Watercolor Technique and its Place in the History of English Landscape Watercolor Painting', A.B., Harvard University, 1988. Derow published an abridged account of his research in his article, 'Gainsborough's Varnished Watercolor Technique', *Master Drawings*, vol.26, no.3, Autumn 1988, pp.259–71.

Jackson said that Gainsborough 'scarcely ever read a book', but he was certainly acquainted with some of Reynolds's annual (later biennial) discourses to the students of the Royal Academy. He was sent a copy of the fifth one (delivered in December 1772) by his friend William Hoare, and his comments on it show that he was also familiar with the third and the fourth. He was quite prepared to accept Reynolds's concept of the 'Great Style'—the idealized expression, leaving out all particularities, of heroic actions or of subjects with universal application—but thought it unhelpful. In the first place, patrons preferred to buy Old Masters when they wanted history pictures (subjects from Greek or Roman history or mythology, or from the events of the Bible): secondly, it was of no use for portraits, which patrons did commission. The 'Ornamental Style', which, Reynolds argued, characterized the Venetian painters—whose pictures, especially those of Veronese, were full of incident and colourful groups of figures—was a different matter. So was the 'characteristical style', or style 'supported by the painter's consistency in the principles which he has assumed', and Gainsborough seized upon Reynolds's approval of Watteau as, like Rubens, an example of a painter with a complete consistency of pictorial ideas, not seeking, mistakenly, to elevate his work and impose upon the spectator with features drawn from the great style. Watteau, the greatest artist of the French rococo, was, of course, the most admired contemporary painter of Gainsborough's youth in London.

65

TO WILLIAM HOARE[1] [1773]

MS. Pierpont Morgan Library, New York (MA 1263 (329))

Mr Gainsborough's Respects to Mr Hoare, and is much obliged for the sight of Sir Joshua's Discourse[2] which he thinks amazingly clever, and cannot be too much admired (together with its Ingenious Author) by every candid lover of the Art. The truth of what He observes concerning Fresco, and the Great Style, Mr G. is convinced of by what he has often heard Mr Hoare say of the works of Rafaelle & Michel Angelo—But betwixt Friends Sir Joshua either forgets, or does not chuse see that his Instruction is all adapted to form the History Painter, which he must know there is no call for in this country. The Ornamental Style (as he calls it) seems form'd for Portraits. Therefore he had better come down to Watteau[3] at once (who was a very fine Painter tak-

William Hoare (1707–92)
Self-Portrait
Pastel, 49.5 x 38.1.
c.1742
Royal Academy of Arts, London

ing away the french conceit) and let us have a few Tints: or Else why does Sir Joshua put tints equal to Painted Glass, only to make the People talk of Colors flying, when the great style would do — Every one knows that the grand Style must consist in plainness & simplicity, and that silks & sattins Pearls & triffling ornaments would be as hurtfull to simplicity, as flourishes in a Psalm Tune; but Fresco would no more do for Portraits, than an Organ would please Ladies in the hands of Fischer;[4] there must be Variety of lively touches and surprizing Effects to make the Heart dance, or else they had better be in a Church — so in Portrait Painting there must be a Lustre and finishing to bring it up to individual Life.

As M[r] G. hates of all things the least tendency to the Sour Critic, hopes to talk over the Affair some Evening over a Glass, as there is no other Friendly or Sensible way of settling these matters except upon Canvass.

1 William Hoare (1707–92), a portrait painter in oils and pastel who by 1739 had settled in Bath, the first fashionable portrait painter to do so. The most successful practitioner in the city before the arrival of Gainsborough, he became the latter's friend, as he did of other artists, and continued to flourish himself, dying a wealthy man.

2 The *Fifth Discourse*, delivered to the students of the Royal Academy on 10 December 1772.
3 In his *Third Discourse*, Reynolds had specifically included 'the French Gallantries of Watteau' among the many classes of painting which did not presume to the Grand Style. Michael Cole elaborates on Gainsborough's reaction in 'Gainsborough's Diversions', *Word & Image*, Vol.13, No.4, October–December 1997, p.370.
4 See Biographical Register.

In 1772 a brilliant young actor named Henderson, who was the very ape of Garrick and of whom Garrick was soon to be jealous, appeared on the stage. His debut, as Hamlet, took place in Bath and, possibly through John Ireland, the future biographer of Hogarth, Gainsborough soon became acquainted with him. Henderson was, incidentally, a great admirer of Sterne and was nicknamed 'Shandy'. Gainsborough's advice to his friends was usually sound, and his letters to Henderson are no exception. His emphasis on the paramount importance of technique is characteristic. Gainsborough was always sensitive about the placing of his pictures. He had told Garrick not to hang his portrait as high as he had just to suit the decorative scheme in a particular room, as 'it was calulated for breast high & will never have its Effect or likeness otherwise'. Now his annoyance with the Academy hanging committee, already apparent, as we have seen, in 1770, had come to a head. Horace Walpole noted in his 1773 Academy catalogue, 'Gainsborough and Dance having disagreed with Sir Joshua Reynolds, did not send any pictures to this exhibition'. It seems unlikely that, at such a time, Gainsborough's intention of leaving his house in Abbey Street was connected with any thought of moving to London. He did not exhibit at the Academy again until 1777.

66

TO DAVID GARRICK 1 APRIL [1773]

Untraced (Lt. Col. R. Solly sale, Sotheby's, 23 July 1962, lot 284, bt. Ifan Kyrle Fletcher). The first and the last three phrases in the first paragraph derive from the excerpts published in Catalogue 205, C. & I.K. Fletcher Ltd., Spring 1963 (85).

. . . an amazing copy of you has appear'd on our stage[1] . . . for my own part, I think he must be your Bastard. He is absolutely a Garrick through a Glass not quite drawn to its focus, a little mist hangs about his outlines, and

John Henderson (1746–85)
Canvas, 74.3 x 61.6
1777
National Portrait Gallery
(on long-term loan to
Gainsborough's House,
Sudbury)

a little fuzziness in the tone of his voice, otherwise the very ape of all your tricks, and by G — exceedingly sensible, humble & diffident — how like you then must he be . . . Ear for modulation . . . a knack for slipping down boild Tripe . . . come out brilliant enough to split ones Ears . . .

. . . O that I could but touch his features, clean his Person, & sharpen him out into a real Garrick. Face, Person & Voice, have fallen to the share of no <u>one</u> Genius but yourself my Friend. Many as great a Genius has been hang'd, but only yourself bless'd with every requisite to the last minute touch, so as to show us <u>Perfection</u>. I'm sure it must please you to see the same thing short of you, whenever you choose to turn your head back, as the Jockeys do when they are near the Post . . .

. . . I don't send to the Exhibition this year; they hang my likenesses too high to be seen, & have refused to lower one sail to oblige me

[*Postmark*] OI AP BATH

1 John Henderson (see Biographical Register).

67

TO RICHARD WHATLEY 22 JUNE 1773

MS. British Library Egerton MS.3516, fo.168

Sir,

I hereby give you notice that I intend to quit the Duke of Kingston's House in the Abby Church yard Bath,[1] at Christmas next,

and am

Sir your most humble

Servant

Tho Gainsborough

Bath

June 22d. 1773

To Mr. Whatley, Steward to His Grace the Duke of Kingston.[2]

[*Addr.*] To Mr. Whatley / at / Bradford[3]

1 Evelyn, 2nd Duke of Kingston (1711–73), whose seat was at Thoresby, close to Clumber and Welbeck, in Nottinghamshire, owned a large area of Bath, south of the Abbey. The lease agreement with Gainsborough (dated 30 May 1760), for the most expensive house on the Kingston estate then newly built (see illustration on p. 13), is published in Susan Legouix Sloman, 'Gainsborough and "the lodging-house way",' *Gainsborough's House Annual Report*, 1991/92, p.38, note 5. I am greatly indebted to this article generally.

2 Gainsborough made five payments to Richard Whatley between 1764 and 1769, of varying amounts from £60 to £150, through his account at Hoare's Bank.

3 The Duke of Kingston also had extensive property in Bradford-on-Avon, very near Bath.

68

TO JOHN HENDERSON 27 JUNE 1773

Untraced (John Ireland, *Letters and Poems, by the late Mr. John Henderson*, London, 1786, pp.108–10)

Bath, 27th June, 1773

Dear Henderson

If you had not wrote to me as you did, I should have concluded you had been laid down; pray, my boy, take care of yourself this hot weather, and don't run about London streets, fancying you are catching strokes of <u>nature</u>, at the hazard of your constitution—It was my first school, and deeply read in petticoats I am, therefore you may allow me to caution you.

Stick to Garrick as close as you can for your life: you should follow his heels like his shadow in sunshine.

No one can be so near him as yourself when you please, and I'm sure when he sees it strongly as other people do, he must be fond of such an ape. You have nothing to do now but to stick to the few great ones of the earth, who seem to have offered you their assistance in bringing you to light, and to brush off all the low ones as fast as they light upon you.—You see I hazard the appearing a puppy in your eyes, by pretending to advise you, from the real regard, and sincere desire I have of seeing you a great and happy man.—Garrick is the greatest creature living in every respect, he is worth studying in every action—Every view and every idea of him is worthy of being stored up for imitation, and I have ever found him a generous and sincere friend. Look upon him, Henderson, with your imitative eyes, for when he drops you'll have nothing but poor old nature's book to look in.—You'll be left to grope it out alone, scratching your pate in the dark, or by a farthing candle.—Now is your time, my lively fellow—And do ye hear, don't eat so devilishly; you'll get too fat when you rest from playing, or get a sudden jogg by illness to bring you you down again.

Adieu, my dear H,
believe me your's, &c
T.G.

69

TO JOHN HENDERSON 18 JULY 1773

Untraced (John Ireland, *Letters and Poems, by the late Mr. John Henderson*, London, 1786, pp.111–13)

Bath, July 18, 1773

Dear Henderson,

If one may judge by your last spirited epistle you are in good keeping, no one eats with a more grateful countenance, or swallows with more good nature than yourself.

If this does not seem sense, do but recollect how many hard featured fellows there are in the world that frown in the midst of enjoyment, chew with unthankfulness, and seem to swallow with pain instead of pleasure;

now any one who sees you eat pig and plumb sauce, immediately feels that pleasure which a plump morsel, smoothly gliding through a narrow glib passage into the regions of bliss, and moistened with the dews of imagination, naturally creates.

Some iron-faced dogs you know seem to chew dry ingratitude, and swallow discontent. Let such be kept to under parts, and never trusted to support a character.—In all but eating stick to Garrick;—In that let him stick to you, for I'll be curst if you are not his master.—Never mind the fools who talk of imitation and copying—All is imitation, and if you quit that natural likeness to Garrick which your mother bestowed upon you, you'll be flung[1]—Ask Garrick else.

Why, sir, what makes the difference between man and man, is real performance, and not genius or conception.—There are a thousand Garrick's, a thousand Giardini's, and Fisher's, and Abels. Why only one Garrick, with Garrick's eyes, voice, &c. &c. &c? One Giardini with Giardini's fingers, &c. &c. But one Fisher with Fisher's dexterity, quickness, &c? Or more than one Abel with Abel's feeling upon the instrument? All the rest of the world are mere hearers and see'ers.

Now, as I said in my last, as nature seems to have intended the same thing in you as in Garrick, no matter how short or how long, her kind intention must not be crossed.—If it is, she will tip the wink to madam fortune, and you'll be kicked down stairs.—

'Think on that Master Ford'.[2]

God bless you,

T.G.

1 Rejected (see also Letter 40).
2 Character in Shakespeare's *The Merry Wives of Windsor* whom the amorous Sir John Falstaff attempts to cuckold.

Gainsborough's instinctive generosity and warmth of heart were demonstrated by an episode which took place towards the end of his residence in Bath. A gentleman known to his friend, Philip Thicknesse, had shot himself, leaving a woman and child in want. Thicknesse started a fund to help them but secured only twelve subscriptions. One, typically, was from Gainsborough, who was on his way to the theatre when Thicknesse encountered him and showed him a pathetic letter from the woman.

James Gillray (1756–1815)
Philip Thicknesse (1719–92)
Engraving. 1790
National Portrait Gallery (Archive Engravings Collection)

70

TO PHILIP THICKNESSE[1] [DATE UNKNOWN]

Untraced (*St. James's Chronicle*, 16/19 August 1788: published in a letter to the editor from Philip Thicknesse).

My dear Sir,

I could not go to the Play till I had relieved my Mind, by sending you the enclosed Note, and beg you will transmit it to the afflicted Woman by To-morrow's Post.

Yours sincerely

T.G.

1 Philip Thicknesse (see Biographical Register). Thicknesse refers in his memoir of Gainsborough to two other notes he had received from the artist, one when the latter dispatched his full-length portrait of the future Mrs Thicknesse to London in 1760, rolled up in a landscape of the same size: 'Lest Mrs. Thicknesses picture should have been damaged in the carriage to town, this landscape is put as a case to protect it, and I now return you many thanks for having procured me the favor of her sitting to me for it, it has done me service, and I know it will give you pleasure' (pp.19–20), the other at the time of Gainsborough's departure for London in 1774: 'God bless you and yours, I am going to London in three days' (p.31).

Though in many ways intemperate and swayed by feeling, Gainsborough was au fond *a deeply moral and religious man. Ready enough to joke about his sister, Mary, whose piety was something of an addiction, he was a believing Christian who trusted in Divine providence and mercy and, at any rate in the latter part of his residence in Bath, was a regular patron of the Church of England proprietary chapels built for, and fashionable among, the many visitors who thronged the city. Dr William Dodd, one of the most popular preachers of the day and a great favourite with the ladies, had a chapel in Bath for some years; he was a friend of Gainsborough's and sat to him for his portrait in 1773.*

71

TO THE REVD DR WILLIAM DODD[1] 24 NOVEMBER 1773

Untraced. Whitley examined this letter when it was exhibited at the New Gallery, and the first, third and fourth paragraphs of the present text follow his transcription (Whitley Papers, Dept. of Prints and Drawings, British Museum: Gainsborough box, Guard Book for 1745–1780, slip on fo.37). The second paragraph beginning with the phrase 'Be assured, dear sir', is published in the Manuscripts of Alfred Morrison, Esq., Ninth Report of the Royal Commission on Historical Manuscripts, Part II, Appendix, London, 1884, p.481, where the address is also given.

Dear Sir

My wife not being well enough to answer Mrs Dodd's obliging letter just now, & to acknowledge the receipt & return her most grateful thanks for the kind present, has employed me to do my best, though I confess myself very unequal to the task. If grateful feelings could but make their appearance upon paper with a little drawing instead of writing I should be more likely to express myself clearly upon this subject, for Sir I can't say my tints in this way are quite so regularly laid upon my pallet as I could wish for Mr Dodd's inspection. However it is some comfort to recollect that my worthy friend had heard me talk wild enough in a warm fit not to be frightened at any flight that may dash upon paper. Mrs Dodd, who has beauty & charms to do justice to any painted silk that ever was touched by the finest pencil, forgets that there is no one here worthy of such an elegant dress, but yet her seeming to think them so is a compliment equal to the charm of her generous present.

Be assured, dear sir, such politeness cannot be soon or easily forgotten, & if I was not afraid of taking from the partiality Mrs Dodd has for your

The Revd Dr William Dodd (1729–77)
Canvas, 76.2 x 63.5
1773
Prince of Wales Museum, Bombay

picture as it is now, & I thought it possible to make it ten times handsomer, I would give it a few touches in the warmth of my gratitude, though the ladies say that it is very handsome as it is; for I peep & listen though the keyhole of the door of the painting room on purpose to see how you touch them out of the pulpit as well as in it. Lord! says one, what a lively eye that gentleman has![2]

We are going this evening to the benefit of a certain musical gentleman who talks of talking by notes ere long, & then I suppose some extempore gentleman will preach by notes. We had a stranger that gave us a strange sermon last Sunday at our chapel,[3] by which I fear our good friend is not well at Weston,[4] but I shall take a walk to see him tomorrow. I have not neglected the chapel one day, since I took a liking to it, nor don't mean ever to quit it.

My wife & daughters beg to join in best compliments to Mrs Dodd & yourself, & I am most truly, Dear Sir,

Your most obliged & humble servant
Tho. Gainsborough
Bath, November 24th 1773

[*Addr.*] The Rev. Dr Dodd / Queen Street / Westminster

1 Dr William Dodd (1729–77) was a popular preacher who had a fashionable congregation at his Charlotte Chapel in Pimlico, London. Increasingly burdened by debt, in 1777 he forged the signature of his former pupil and friend, Philip, 5th Earl of Chesterfield, in order to raise money, was found out, tried and, in spite of a public outcry, hanged.

2 Gainsborough painted a half-length portrait of Dodd (Prince of Wales Museum, Bombay (Sir Ratan Tata bequest): Waterhouse, No.198) in 1773. Susan Sloman has pointed out that 'Gainsborough's principal picture room [at his house in the Circus] was probably the main south-facing room on the first floor, adjoining the painting room ('Artists' Picture Rooms in Eighteenth-Century Bath', *Bath History*, vol.VI, 1996, p.145).

3 Almost certainly the Margaret Chapel, between the Circus and the Royal Crescent. This Church of England proprietary chapel, of which Thomas Linley was one of the proprietors, and in which a fine organ by the Swiss organ-builder, John Snetzler, had been installed, was opened on 3 October 1773, when Dodd presided. (Information kindly supplied by Susan Sloman: letter to the compiler, 22 October 1998).

4 Weston was a short distance north-west of Bath, on the other side of the hill from Lansdown Road, and about a mile's walk from the Circus; Gainsborough's 'good friend' was presumably the Revd John Chapman (b.1711 or 1712), vicar of All Saints, Upper Weston, 1767–1808.

In 1774 Mary Hamilton visited Gainsborough's studio in Bath and noted in her diary: 'All portraits with the exception of two or three Landscapes. If I might presume to give my opinion I should prefer him as Landscape to Portrait Painter, yet they say he pays but little attention to the former.' It is true that Gainsborough still found it difficult to sell his landscapes, but this did not mean he was neglecting what he loved to paint most and it was at this period that he developed a new expression of his nostalgia for the old ways of life of the English countryside in his 'cottage door' subjects. The first of these was bought by the future Duke of Rutland in about 1773, and it was a version of this picture that Gainsborough painted for his old friend, Giardini, later teasing him that it was merely a copy. In March 1774 he had a harpsichord delivered to him at the Circus which Giardini had selected for him at Broadwood's. Later that year, however, and apparently unexpectedly, he made the decision to leave Bath. At this time he gave his unsold canvas of 'The Harvest Waggon', the masterpiece now in the Barber Institute, Birmingham, to his friend Walter Wiltshire of Shockerwick Park, the properous carrier whose 'flying waggons' had taken so many of his pictures up to London for him. Gainsborough's tenancy of the west wing of Schomberg House, Pall Mall, commenced towards the end of 1774, and Thicknesse refers to his departure in a letter of 23 November: 'Gainsbro is gone & settled in London'.

Schomberg House, Pall Mall. The right-hand part was Gainsborough's home in London.
Pen and watercolour drawing by an unknown artist, 13.9 x 19.4. c.1850
Museum of London

72

TO GIOVANNI BATTISTA CIPRIANI[1] 14 FEBRUARY 1774

MS. Princeton University Library, New Jersey (John Wild Collection)

Dear Sir

I should have done myself the pleasure of writing to you sooner but that I could not 'til yesterday get a sight of Mr Hamilton and his Pictures;[2] I find that he reserved the two Churches you mention'd for his House in The Crescent, and that no Price would tempt him to part with them: They are really very fine Pictures—I have done nothing but fiddle since I came from London, so much was I unsettled by the continual run of Pleasure which my Friend Giardini and the rest of you engaged me in, and if< it> were not for my Family, which one cannot conveniently carry in ones Pocket, I should be often with you, enjoying what I like <u>up to the Hilt</u>—I hope all our Friends are well towards the City?[3]

I have wrote two Letters in the little time I have been at Home to Giardini, and the D—l a word can I draw from him, 'tho in my last I fudged up a pretence of wanting a Tune that I left in his Parlour that Abel wrote for me, only to extract a word or two against his Will—I'm cursedly afraid I have affronted him with an old trick of mine, commonly call'd a hum,[4] for you must know I took it into my Head one Day as I was going in his Chariot with him to insinuate (meerly to try his temper, and a damn'd trick it was) that the Picture he has of mine of the Cottage & ragged Family, was only a Copy[5] I believe you can set him right about that, and he was cunning enough not to seem the least hurt—I repented as I generally do very soon after my folly, and the more so as he has always been the politest creature to me I ever was acquainted with—I wish my Dear Cip you would pump him a little and give me a line

I have a tollerable Picture of another rural subject which I entend for Him but I would not have him know it—

I beg my compliments [to] your [gen]teal and amiable Pupil a[nd] his fair Lady, and to Mr Bartolozzi[6] when you see Him—I should heartily rejoyce to see you all at Bath and will do my utmost to make the Place agreeable to you—

Believe me

Dear Sir

yours must truly

Tho Gainsborough

Bath Feb: 14th 1774

[*Addr.*] To / Mr Cipriani / near the Mewse: Gate Hedge Lane / Charing Cross / London

[*Postmark*] [16] FE

1 Giovanni Battista Cipriani (1727–85) was a Florentine historical painter and draughtsman who met Sir William Chambers and Joseph Wilton when living in Rome, and accompanied them back to London in 1755. He was a founder-member of the Royal Academy, and many of his drawings were engraved by his friend Bartolozzi (see note 6 below).

2 The Hon. Charles Hamilton (1704–86), the creator of the much admired rococo landscape garden of Painshill, near Cobham in Surrey. Obliged to sell his estate in 1773 owing to financial difficulties, he settled in Bath and lived first at 14 Royal Crescent and then up Lansdown Road, where he could resume gardening. His picture collection was well known to residents and visitors to Bath, and several of his paintings were copied by the young Thomas Lawrence. (Information kindly supplied by Susan Sloman: letter to the compiler, 6 November 1998).

3 In spite of his serious illness of 1763, and his determination to take greater care, Gainsborough was unable to give up his life of pleasure when he was in London, especially when he was in the company of like-minded friends.

4 A hoax ('hum' was short for humbug).

5 A replica (Hayes *Landscape Paintings*, No.106) of the first of Gainsborough's 'Cottage Door' subjects, painted about 1772–73, which had been bought by that voracious collector, Charles, 4th Duke of Rutland (1754–87).

6 Francesco Bartolozzi (1727–1815) was a distinguished etcher, notably in soft-ground (his 'red chalk' manner), who came to London in 1764 and became a founder-member of the Royal Academy. He had met Cipriani as a student in Florence, and the two became lifelong friends.

73

TO DAVID GARRICK [24 OR 25 MARCH 1774][1]

Untraced (Lt. Col. R. Solly sale,Sotheby's, 23 July 1962, lot 285, bt. Ifan Kyrle Fletcher). The last five phrases in the first paragraph derive from the excerpts published in Catalogue 205, C. & I.K. Fletcher Ltd., Spring 1963 (82)

... Had I dreamt that it w$^{d:}$ have afforded the least satisfaction to my good Friend that I should have poked my long neck & hatchet Face into his doors, in the common how d'e do way, not all the Giardini's on Earth should have prevented me; but I did not know that a first Man, assured of the affection as well as admiration of all sorts and sizes, expected every common hack to interrupt Him in his precious Moments ... that I spent an Evening with young Ranger[2] and saw him dance ... to the delight ... of pretty Ladies ... was shut up in a Viol da Gambo-case ... to be lost in the harmony of Abel's sweet sounding Instrument ...

Well, we did not make ourselves, if we had by G— you with all your Genius, could not have made anything half so clever as a Garrick, tho he is not music-mad—you pretend in your clever mixture of Love & Abuse in Palmer's Letter, to flatter me with the notion that if I had call'd Mrs. Garrick should have sat to me for a Picture, that's all a D—md L— for you'd let Dance[3] or anybody cleverer than I, sooner than put such a Feather in my cap ... May God preserve you ... long amongst your Admirers; for no man will be left behind with even Genius enough to imagine what sort of a Creature that little diamond of a Man was ...

1 The first date is given in the Sotheby catalogue, the second in the Kyrle Fletcher.

2 The part of Ranger, the young man-about-town, in Benjamin Hoadly's *The Suspicious*

Husband, was created by Garrick in 1747; he last performed the rôle on 23 May 1773. Gainsborough is presumably referring to a young actor who had taken on this part.

3 Nathaniel Dance (1735–1811), a history painter and painter of conversation pieces, who exhibited at the Royal Academy, 1769–76, chiefly portraits; he later married a rich widow and became a Member of Parliament.

Joseph Wright of Derby wrote later that he had heard 'that the want of business was the reason of Gainsborough leaving Bath', but it is unlikely that Gainsborough would have raised his prices or taken on an apprentice if work was falling off, and the number of canvasses dating from the years up to 1774 does not suggest any slackening of activity. Moreover, as Wright went on, 'the want of encouragement of the Arts, I fear, is not only felt here [in Bath] but in Town also, and artists are become so numerous that the share which falls to each is small'. Bate-Dudley tells us that, after leaving Bath, Gainsborough passed 'a short time in town not very profitably', and he was certainly careful, in those first years back in London, to take on work, however pedestrian or disagreeable; he was, however, neglectful of official duties, and in December 1775 was nearly removed from the Council of the Royal Academy to which he had been elected twelve months previously, 'having declined any office in the Academy and having never attended'.

Before long, however, Gainsborough had established himself firmly in the metropolis. In 1777 he not only obtained commissions from the royal family, but returned triumphantly to the Academy with such masterpieces as 'The Watering Place' (National Gallery, London) and 'The Hon. Mrs. Graham' (National Gallery of Scotland). In that year and again in 1778 he had sufficient money to spare to invest in Government stock; he bought a coach; and he enlarged the premises at Schomberg House with two fine studios, one above the other, each fifteen feet high and with a south easterly aspect, the windows overlooking the gardens of Marlborough House (as he worked largely by candlelight, or at least by lighting he controlled with some care, a north light was of little consequence to him). At the same time, family life was becoming more of a trial; his brother, Humphry, an inventor and Independent minister at Henley, lost his wife and then himself died; and he was angered by the relationship developing between J.C. Fischer, the oboeist, who was reputed to have 'no more intellect than his hautboy', and his elder daughter, Mary. All but one of his surviving letters to his sister, Mary Gibbon, which are particularly frank, date from the years between 1775 and 1780.

The Revd Humphry Gainsborough (1718–76)
Canvas, 59.5 x 49.5
c.1770-74
Yale Center for British Art, New Haven (Paul Mellon Collection)

74

TO MARY GIBBON 13 NOVEMBER 1775

Untraced (Fulcher 1856, pp.105–06)

London, Nov. 13th, 1775

Dear Sister

We return you our best thanks for the excellent present of fish, which turned out as good as ever was eaten, and came very timely for brother Humphry[1] to take part with us. He went home to Henley to-day, having been with us ten days, which was as long as he could well be absent from his business of collecting the tolls upon the river. He was as well as could be expected, considering his affliction for the loss of his poor wife. We did all we could to comfort him, and wish him every possible happiness, as he is a good creature. My wife has been but very indifferent with the disorder that goes about in all parts of London; it seems to be a sort of cold attended with a bad cough, and it has gone through our family, servants and all; but, thank God, we are upon the mending hand: we don't hear of many people dying of it, though 'tis universal. I am glad to hear business in the lodging-house way goes on so well. I know you would willingly keep the cart upon the wheels,[2] till you go to heaven, though you deserve to ride there in something better. I told Humphry you were a rank Methodist, who says you had better be a Presbyterian, but I say Church of England.[3] It does not signify what, if you are but free from hypocrisy, and don't set your heart upon worldly honors and wealth. I wish you long life and happiness, and remain,

Your affectionate brother,

Tho. Gainsborough

1 One of Gainsborough's elder brothers (1718–76) (see Biographical Register), who was minister of the Independent chapel in South Street, Henley.

2 See Letter 40, note 6.

3 No doubt remembering the comfort and pleasures of the Margaret Chapel he had attended in Bath (see Letter 71, note 3).

75

TO THE SECRETARY OF THE ROYAL SOCIETY OF ARTS 11 DECEMBER 1775

Untraced (Minute Books of the Royal Society of Arts, vol.21, fo.49, 13 December 1775)

Sir

Agreable to the most Obliging Order of the Society for a full Length Portrait of the late Lord Folkestone[1] I will take particular Care to Execute it in my best manner and to get it done by the beginning of October next

I am Sir

your much Obliged

and Obedient Servt

Thos Gainsborough

Pall Mall

Decr 11. 1775

1 Jacob Bouverie, 1st Viscount Folkestone (1694–1761), first President of the Royal Society of Arts, of whom Gainsborough painted a posthumous portrait after the Thomas Hudson painted in 1749 in the possession of his son, William, 1st Earl of Radnor.

'my wife is weak but good, and never much formed to humour my Happiness'

Mrs Thomas Gainsborough (1728–98)
Canvas, 76.8 x 64.1. c.1778
Courtauld Institute Galleries, London

76

TO MARY GIBBON 26 DECEMBER 1775

Untraced (Whitley 1915, pp.121–22)

Dear Sister,

I received yours and am glad your Houses and every thing go on so much to your satisfaction. I have always wish'd you happy, though sometimes we have differ'd a little in our opinions. I did all in my power to comfort poor Humphry, and should have been glad of his company a little longer, had not his business called him hence.

What will become of me time must show; I can only say that my present situation with regard to encouragement is all that heart can wish, but as all worldly success is precarious I don't build happiness, or the expectation of it, upon present appearances. I have built upon sandy foundations all my life long. All I know is that I live at a full thousand pounds a year expense, and will work hard and do my best to go through withal; and if that will not do let those take their lot of blame and sufferings that fall short of their duty, both towards me and themselves. Had I been blessed with your penetration and blind eye towards fool's pleasures, I had steer'd my course better, but we are born with different Passions and gifts, and I have only to hope that the Great Giver of All will make better allowance for us than we can make for one another.

I could now enter into particulars as my heart finds itself affected, but what would it all signify? If I tell you my wife is weak but good, and never much formed to humour my Happiness, what can you do to alter her? If I complain that Peggy is a sensible good Girl, but Insolent and proud in her behaviour to me at times, can you make your arm long enough to box her ears for me whilst you live at Bath? And (what has hurt me most of late) were I to unfold a secret and tell you that I have detected a sly trick in Molly by a sight I got of one of her Letters, forsooth, to Mr. Fischer, what could all your cleverness do for me there? and yet I wish for your Head-piece to catch a little more of the secret, for I don't choose to be flung under the pretence of Friendship. I have never suffered that worthy Gentleman ever to be in their Company since I came to London; and behold while I had my eye upon Peggy, the other Slyboots, I suppose, has all along been the Object. Oh, d—n him, he must take care how he trips me off the foot of all happiness.[1]

I desire, my Dear Sister, you will not impart a syllable of what you have here, and believe me ever yours most affectionately,

Thos. Gainsborough

December 26, 1775

Compliments of this happy season to you and love to Sally.[2]

P.S. She does not suspect I saw the letter.

1 Mary eventually married Fischer (see Gainsborough's letter to Mary Gibbon of 23 February 1780 and Biographical Register), but the marriage proved unhappy and short-lived.

2 Gainsborough's second sister, Sarah, who was presumably staying with the Gibbons for Christmas.

77

TO MARY GIBBON 10 JUNE [1776]

MS. Yale University Library, New Haven

Dear Sister

I rec[d]. your Letter and am glad to learn every thing go to your satisfaction, and Rejoyce in my Heart that you are in that way which is sure to end in peace and eternal happiness — I would have every body enjoy, unmolested, their own opinions tho I have sometimes said things to try the Temper, but I doubt not your good sense could see, and pardon —

For my Part I despair not, as I am conscious of having done my utmost, tho against all rebuffs and discouragments possible from Ignorance and evil Spirits, and at the last hazard and tryal of my own Constitution, with this reward, that I stand now just where I did; whereas if I had had my own way (with all my mighty Vices) I should have wasted many thousands — My present Situation is that of being as much encouraged as the World ['could' *crossed out*] can bestow, with every success in my business, but in the other scale, counteracted with disobedience Pride and insolence, and eternal Obraidings & reflections[1] — I was induced to try how far Jealousy might be cured by giving into her Hands every Farthing of the Money as I earn'd it, but very soon found th[at] (as a punishment for so unmanly a condesention) instead of convincing, it was a further incouragment to Govern me, and invert the order of Nature in making the Head the foot and the foot the Head; so that now I have taken the Staff into my own hands again, and purpose (God willing) to try my own Virtue and strength to walk straight and do the best for my Children let them follow the Vanity of the Age, or weakness of their Leader as they will — I am at an Age now to see right from wrong; and have a pretty good knowledge of Mankind, and I trust if I do my best, all will be well through the merits of Him who hath promised to make good our failings if we trust sincerely —

I thank God we are all pretty well except my own Health which has been but indifferent of late Bro: Humphry was here lately, and is as happy as could be expected — I leave you to act as you see proper in the affair of Penny's Money,[2] it may be of use to me when you can get it, and you'l be so good as to remit it

Believe me ever yours most
affectionatly
Tho Gainsborough

[*Addr.*] M<u>rs</u>: Mary Gibbon / Milliner / Abby Church Yard / Bath.
[*Postmark*] 10 JU
[*Inscribed*] Circus

1 References to his daughters and his wife.
2 Mr Penny was the landlord of Gainsborough's house in the Circus at Bath (information Susan Sloman).

78

TO MARY GIBBON 5 NOVEMBER 1776

Untraced (Fulcher 1856, p.107)

Nov. 5th, 1776

Dear Sister,

I have been going to write to you every post for this month past, but was desirous of acquainting you with what I done towards settling my brother Humphry's affairs, and therefore postponed writing till I had sold the stock . . . Mr. Cooper advises me to keep on the house till we can make the most of the steam-engine, (as the work, if taken to pieces, perhaps may never be put together again,) and also the maid in the house, lest any discovery should be made of it.[1] The goods are sold, but none of the books, nor have I had any account yet from Henley, so as to be able to settle anything. We hope you and Sally continue in good health and good bustling spirits, and join in best affections to you both,

T.G.

1 Mr Cooper, who became Town Clerk of Henley in 1777, was presumably the attorney acting as an estate agent. The steam engine was one of Humphry Gainsborough's most significant inventions and James Watt, who had secured a patent for a steam engine in 1769, was so apprehensive that in 1775 he filed a caveat against his fellow inventor's patent; it was this chicanery that prompted Gainsborough's concern (George H. Peters, *The Life and Work of Humphry Gainsborough*, 1948, p.21 and Hugh Belsey, *Gainsborough's Family*, exhibition catalogue, Gainsborough's House, 1988, pp.22–23).

79

TO WILLIAM JACKSON 25 JANUARY 1777

MS. Royal Academy of Arts

Jan: 25th 1777

Dear Jackson

I suppose I never drew a Portrait half so like the sitter, as my silence, since the receipt of your last, resembles Neglect and Ingratitude; owing to two of the crossest accidents that ever attended a poor fiddler—first and most unfortunately, I have been 4 times after Bach, and have never laid Eyes on Him; and secondly, and most provokingly, I have had <a> Parcell made up of two Drawings and a Box of Pencils such as you wrote for, ever since the Day after I recd. your favor inclosing the Tenths,[1] and directed for you to go by the Exeter Coach, which has laid in my Room by the neglect of two blockheads one My Nephew,[2] who is too proud to carry a bundle under his Arm, though his betters the Journeymen Taylors always carry their foul shirts so; and my d—mnd cowardly footman who forsooth is afraid to peep into the street for fear of being press'd for Sea service,[3] the only service God almighty made him for—so that my Dear Jack[son] if it was not for your being endow'd with Jobes Patience I should think my<self> deservedly for ever shut out of your favor; but surely I shall catch Bach soon to get you an Answer to your Letter; and for the Drawings ['damn me': *these two words crossed out by another hand*] if I don't carry them myself to the Inn tomorrow

There is a Letter of nonsense <inclosed with the Drawings> to plague you once more about 6ths. and 10ths.—which you may read or ['wipe your Arse with' *scratched out and* 'not' *substituted above, both by another hand*] as you hap to be in humour when you see the Drawings—til then I'm sure you can't bear the sight of my odious Hand so

no more at present as the saying is
but yours Sincerely
TG.

Pall Mall

You hear I suppose that all Lords and Members have given up their priviledge of franking to ease the Taxes, I'm sorry for it[4]—

[*Addr.*] Mr Wm Jackson / Fore Street / Exeter
[*Postmark*] 25 JA BATH

1 See also below. Sixths and tenths are musical intervals. Jackson was probably giving Gainsborough lessons in counterpoint (I owe this suggestion to Dr Oliver Davies).

2 Gainsborough's apprenticed studio assistant, Gainsborough Dupont (see Biographical Register).

3 The press gangs were unusually active at this time owing to the demands on the Navy during the War of American Independence.

4 Members of both Houses of Parliament had enjoyed the privilege of not having to pay postage on their letters—whether sent by or addressed to them—originally as a concession granted by the Crown, confirmed from 1764 by statute. It was a privilege much abused but, typically, Gainsborough disapproved of changes to existing usage.

80

TO MARY GIBBON 12 SEPTEMBER 1777

MS. Yale Center for British Art, New Haven (Paul Mellon Collection)

My Dear Sister

I have defer'd writing to acknowledge the Receipt of your Kind present of the Cheeses for some time in hopes of being able to inclose you know what; but I have been disapointed of receiving any thing privately, so must beg you to trust me a little longer—The Cheeses were disposed of exactly as you desired, and proved extreemly acceptable to all parties—

My Family had a great desire to make a Journey to Ipswich to M^{r} & Mrs Kilderbee's[1] for a fortnight, and last sunday morning I pack'd them off in their own Coach with David[2] on horse back; and Molly wrote me to let me know that they arrived very safe; but some how or other they seem desirous of returning rather sooner than the propos'd time, as they desire me to go for them by next tuesday, the bargain was that I should fetch them home—I don't know what's the matter, either people don't pay them hon[or] enough for ['people' *crossed out*] Ladies that keep a Coach, or e[lse] Madam is afraid to trust me alone at home in this great Town—However I shall find in Molly's next Letter how their inclinations stand, and will act accordingly—

Thank God I am pretty well and have got a full length in hand to employ myself in doing the Ladies Face whilst they are gone—I like to bragg when I let an Appartment as well as some Circus friends do, but I'm afraid I shall never be out of Business.

I hope every thing goes on to your Mind in the Alley,[3] and glad Sal is recover'd of her sore throat—

That every blessing may attend you as long as you live, and no doubt of perfect happiness in Eternity ever enter your mind, is the sincere wish of

your Affectionate loving Bro:

Tho Gainsborough

My love to the People in the Alley as also to Sally

Sepr 12th 1777—

[*Addr.*] Mrs Gibbon / in the Circus / Bath

[*Postmark*] 12 SE

1 One of Gainsborough's oldest friends, later his executor (see Biographical Register).

2 Gainsborough now owned a coach, and employed a coachman.

3 Possibly a reference to Lilliput Alley, between Abbey Green and Grand Parade, Bath; but Mrs Gibbon is not known to have had any business interest there (information Susan Sloman).

81

TO MARY GIBBON 22 SEPTEMBER 1777

MS. Yale Center for British Art, New Haven (Paul Mellon Collection)

Monday Sep: 22d. 1777–

Dear Sister

I hope you received mine about a week since My People are still at Ipswich and seem very well entertaind there. I was to have fetch'd them home, but Miss Read, Sir Benjamin Truman's Grand daughter is sitting for a full length and came out of Wiltshire on purpose to Sit,[1] so that I cannot go for them but I had a Letter to acquaint me that they are set out for home next Saturday Morning and will be at home on Sunday Evening—

My Dear I fear you will think me very troublesom, and bad pay into the bargain, but knowing your Nature as well as my own, I am easier to intrude on you than I should be to one less generous; and as my private necessity may in some measure alarm one so deep in religion, I shall without scruple open the truth to you, well knowing that when you are made acquainted with my motives of Action, you will sooner applaud than blame—

I have this moment 50 Guineas in my pocket that I received for the half pay from Sir Benj:[2] but you know it would be certain death to make use of a farthing of it for private as I am under everlasting engagements to deliver up to my Wife, all but Landskip deductions where she cannot come at the Knowledge of my Price[3]—The Duke of Dorset is [to] buy two Landskips as soon as his [House is] ready,[4] and there I cribb a few guineas in spite of the D—l —

Now my Dear don't think I make the worst of uses of what I squander, for as God is my Judge I do what I do more from Charity and humane feelings than any other Gratifycations; and only desire that mine may prosper and meet with friends as I have ever done fairly and generously to all with whom I have dealt—you must know that a poor wench whom I used to speak to at Bath, came to London with some worthless ungrateful Villain, and who left her to go abroad, in a poor state indeed, and is a

'The Duke of Dorset is [to] buy two Landskips as soon as his [House is] ready'

John, 3rd Duke of Dorset (1745–99)
Canvas, 76.2 x 63.5.
Intended for the R.A. 1782 but not exhibited.
Private Collection

person of that merit that if her heart was bad enough, would have no occasion for my help—But mind my Dear Sister the misfortunes of this poor Creature, whether by fretting or what, I know not, she went into a bad state of Health and a sore broke out in her Leg, which now is as wide round as the top of a Tea Cup, and down to the bone; in the greatest agony this poor Creature lay lamenting her situation without a friend—Do you think my Dear I am proof against such a sight, and would let her perish and <be> lost for want of assistance; no let me have what faults I may, that shall never lay on my conscience—The Creature would have died rather than hazard my domestic happiness, by sending any request to my House, and it was chance that I went to afford timely relief. Now my Dear if you would lend me 20 pounds I will honestly pay you soon. inclose it if you can so as to come before Sunday

T.G.

[*Addr.*] M^{rs}. Mary Gibbon / Circus / Bath—
[*Postmark*] 23 SE

The Revd Sir William Lowther, 1st Bt. (1707–88)
Canvas, 76.2 x 63.5. 1778
Private Collection, England

1 Frances Read, later Mrs William Villebois (1757–before 1801) (Viscount Cowdray, Cowdray Park, Sussex: Waterhouse, No.696, pl.164). Gainsborough had already painted Sir Benjamin Truman at full length (Tate Gallery, London: Waterhouse, No. 674, pl.117).
2 From between 1770 and 1772 and 1787 Gainsborough charged one hundred guineas for a full-length; it was customary to receive half payment in advance and half on completion.
3 It seems that his attempt the previous year to take 'the Staff into my own hands again' (see Letter 77 to Mary Gibbon of 10 June 1776) had failed.
4 In the event John, 3rd Duke of Dorset bought three landscapes in 1778, for which he paid eighty guineas each. None of them survives. The house was 38 Grosvenor Square, redecorated by John Johnson in 1776–77.

82

TO THE REVD SIR WILLIAM LOWTHER[1] 4 OCTOBER 1778

MS. Private Collection, England

Sir William

I rec^{d}. the favor of your Letter, inclosing your draft for the last payment of your Picture, which (with thanks) I acknowledge to be in full of all

Demands — I am sorry I have not succeeded in the likeness to the satisfaction of your sons;[2] every body who knows you, that saw the Picture at my House, seem'd struck with the likeness; and as to the Eyes, I should think are better with that tenderness and humanity, expressive of goodness, (and I need not add, peculiar to Sir William Lowther's Countenance) than any degree of hard brilliancy, in my opinion allways less desirable in a Mans Face — However 'though I have very seldom done good to a Likeness (struck off, as that was), by pottering at second hand upon it, I shall obey your commands in any alteration, when ever you or your Sons shall think proper to return the Picture — this I shall think my duty; but at the same time very freely confess that was it a Portrait of my own Father, I woud attempt two new ones,[3] rather than hazard a touch [*short word scratched out*] to that Face — Now you have m[y] thoughts honestly (which I declare sinc[erely] I have not advanced to spare myself half an hours work) You will do as you please; and believe me

Sir William,

Your Obedient humble

Servant

Tho Gainsborough

Pall Mall
Octo.[r] 4.th 1778

1 The Revd Sir William Lowther (1707–88), 1st Bt., father of the 1st Earl of Lonsdale, was Rector of Swillington near Leeds and a Prebend of York Minster.

2 Gainsborough painted two versions of the portrait (Private Collection, England: unknown to Waterhouse), which seem to have been intended for Lowther's two sons (see Alex Kidson, 'Thomas Gainsborough and the Revd William Lowther: an unpublished letter', *Gainsborough's House Review*, 1995/6, pp.59-60).

3 See note 2 above.

83

TO DR RICE CHARLTON 24 JUNE 1779

MS. Holburne Museum of Art, Bath

Dear Sir

I must beg pardon for not answering your Letter sooner, I have had some plaguesome sitters, and a sick House besides, but thank God all is right again. Molly had a smart Fever at the time I rec^{d} your Letter, but my next door Neighbour Doctor Heberden[1] sent Her to Chiswick for Air, and now she is purely as my Friend Bob[2] said to the old woman.

I hope all your fears and apprehensions about Him are only signs of your feeling quicker and deeper than the generality of Parents, which you certainly do, and that His complaint is by this time, removed. I'll trust you for taking Him under your Eye the moment He ailes anything and I think you right, for a stitch in time spares nine says Bobby's Old Woman—

My dear Doctor I forgot entirely that you had a Copy of the little dutch Spire of my Hand, tis not worth a Farthing, so do what you please with it, hang it in your study at [Wood]house, where it may not be compared with the Original,[3] and I shall be easy; I'd give it to Mother Gibbon but she delights not in Wordly Prospects; I have a d—mned plague with Her when she comes to Town, to find out new Methodist Chapels enough for Her, for she Prays double Sides, and cares not a farthing for what Bishops can say, so that some Cobler swears that the whole work is already perform'd by promise

I beg my best respects to your
Family & am Dear Sir
Your ever Sincere & Obed
Servt
Tho Gainsborough

Pall Mall
24th June 1779

Tell Bob He will certainly find a use for His Gun for the French intend landing at Bristol—but don't you believe it yourself—

[*Addr.*] Doctor Charleton / at Wood house near / Bristol
[*Postmark*] 25 JU

1 William Heberden (1710–1801), one of the most eminent and learned physicians of his age.

2 'Bob', mentioned three times in this letter, was Dr Charlton's son, Robert, whom Gainsborough had painted as a youngster with his sister, Susannah, six or seven years before (Virginia Museum of Fine Arts, Richmond: Waterhouse, No.137, pl.149).

3 Gainsborough's copy of an Old Master, a work by Bout and Boudewijns, in Charlton's collection at Woodhouse, near Bristol (both the original and the copy were in Dr Charlton's sale, Christie's, 5 March 1790 (Lugt 4541), Lots 16 and 17 respectively).

In order to compensate for no longer having country on his doorstep, Gainsborough acquired (though when is not known) a retreat in the environs, on Richmond Hill, close to the house owned by Reynolds, where, so we are told, he was often visited from Kew by his royal patron, George III. He seems in addition to have had a cottage in Essex, possibly on Bate-Dudley's estate at Bradwell. Of summer tours he tells us in a letter written on a return visit to Bath in 1779 of hopes of sketching on the Devonshire coast; we also know of a tour he made to the West Country in about 1782 in the company of Gainsborough Dupont, and drawings survive of Tintern and Glastonbury. A tour of Wales is mentioned, and the guide to Cader Idris said that he had conducted not only Wilson but Gainsborough and other artists up the mountain in his time. The Lakes he visited in 1783.

84

TO WILLIAM JACKSON 8 JULY 1779

Untraced (transcribed by Mary Woodall from the original at that time owned by Major Norman Leith-Hay-Clark)

Dear Jackson,

The Gentleman who brings you this, is Mr Garvey an excellent Landskip Painter and particular Friend of mine, who lives in Bath[1]

He is no stranger to Mr Jackson's merit, tho' to his Person and wishes to be acquainted with one, so fond of Landskip, and so able a performer in his own branch of Painting—Pray shew him something of your doing, and get him a sight of whatever is worth his seeing in Exeter. I hope to see you in about a fortnight, as I purpose spending a month or six weeks at Tingmouth[2] or other places round Exeter—get your Chalks ready, for we must draw together—Excuse haste and believe me, Dear Sir yours most truly

Thos. Gainsborough

Bath July 8th 1779

1 Edmund Garvey (died 1813), a mediocre landscape painter who, 'for no fathomable reason' (Waterhouse), was elected a Royal Academician against Joseph Wright of Derby in 1783.

2 Teignmouth, a resort on the south Devonshire coast between Exmouth and Torquay noted as fashionable as early as 1803.

85

TO MARY DITCHER[1] 31 JULY 1779

Untraced (published in Reports of the Devonshire Association, 1878–87, vol.18, p.111, which also gives the address)

Madam,

I am very glad the Picture arrived safe, and meets with your approbation.[2] With regard to the Price of the Picture and Frame I must acknowledge myself over paid abundantly by my worthy Friend's attention to my Family while we lived at Bath, and which I shall ever remember with gratitude. If you can pardon my neglect in not paying the carriage, which I fully intended doing, but for the hurry I was in the day it went away, you may rest assured Madam that what remains unpaid is from us to you. My Family joins in best Respects,

and I remain your most obedient Servt.

Tho. Gainsborough

Bath July 31st 1779

[*Addr.*] Mrs. Ditcher / Lansdown Road / Bath

1 Mary Ditcher, a daughter of Samuel Richardson, married Dr Philip Ditcher, a Bath surgeon who attended Gainsborough's family.

2 The portrait of Philip Ditcher (Private Collection, England: Waterhouse, No. 196).

Gainsborough was unable to prevent the consummation of the attachment between Fischer and his daughter, Mary (Margaret had also been infatuated with him), and the wedding took place at St. Anne's, Soho, in February 1780. He so far relented in his feelings about his son-in-law that he painted him full length, and the result was one of his most exquisite and delicately coloured works. It was exhibited at the Academy of 1780, the first in the new premises at Somerset House, and for which Gainsborough painted a galaxy of masterpieces. But the marriage soon ran into difficulties, and the couple separated. After the death of their parents, Gainsborough's daughters lived together, first at Brook Green, then at Acton; Margaret died in 1820, and Mary, after pathetic years of insanity, in 1826.

86

TO MARY GIBBON 23 FEBRUARY 1780

Untraced (Fulcher 1856, pp.118–19)

Feb. 23rd, 1780

Dear Sister,

I imagine you are by this time no stranger to the alteration which has taken place in my family.[1] The notice I had of it was very sudden, as I had not the least suspicion of the attachment being so long and deeply settled; and as it was too late for me to alter anything, without being the cause of total unhappiness on both sides, my consent, which was a mere compliment to affect to ask, I needs must give, whether such a match was agreeable to me or not, I would not have the cause of unhappiness lay upon my conscience; and accordingly they were married last Monday, and are settled for the present in a ready furnished little house in Curzon Street, May Fair. I can't say I have any reason to doubt the man's honesty or goodness of heart, as I never heard any one speak anything amiss of him; and as to his oddities and temper, she must learn to like as she likes his person, for nothing can be altered now. I pray God she may be happy with him and have her health. Peggy has been very unhappy about it, but I endeavour to comfort her, in hope that she will have more pride and goodness than to do anything without first asking my advice and approbation. We shall see how they go on, and I shall write to you further upon the subject. I hope you are all well, and with best wishes,

I remain your affectionate Bro.,

Thos. Gainsborough

1 Mary Gainsborough's marriage to Johann Christian Fischer (see Biographical Register).

Johann Christian Fischer (1733–1800)
Canvas, 227.3 x 149.2. R.A. 1780
Royal Collection © Her Majesty Queen Elizabeth II

87

TO MARY GIBBON 21 OCTOBER 1780

MS. Yale Center for British Art, New Haven (Paul Mellon Collection)

My Dear Sister

I trouble you with this unknown to My Wife, and the reason will soon appear to you—Fischer has deceived me in his Circumstan<ces> and his Wife has been playing the devil to raise Money, and I want to learn out if `tis with or without his knowledge or Concent

She went to Mr Mendham's mercer in Bond Street[1] before she left Town, and bespoke 60 yards of White Sattin for a Bed, and at another Shop White Sarsenet to line it to the amount of 10 pounds more: and then wrote to George Coyte[2] to beg of him to sell <them> at any rate so that he could make money of them, and remit it immediatly to Her—I have stopt the Whole Scheme, but want sadly to know if these terrible undertakings are by his consent—could not you my dear send to speak with <u>Him</u> not Her, and tell him the nature of such proceedings, and that there is a Law lately pass'd which makes this matter Transportation,[3] to take up Goods at one shop and make money of them at another. She has convinced me that she would go to the Gallows to serve this Man—If he denies any knowledge of it, then (and not before) Send for Her and give her such a Lecture as may save her from distruction—do it in the most solemn Manner, for I am alarm'd at this appearance of dishonesty and quite unhappy—My Wife would smother it, but, I like truth and Day light—Excuse haste from

Dear Sister yours most Affectionatly

Tho Gainsborough

Saturday Eve.

give me a Line as quick as possible—

[*Addr.*] Mrs. Gibbon / No. 2 Circus / Bath.

[*Postmark*] 21 OC

1 Mr Mendham, who had previously run his business in the City, operating as Mendham Cass, silk mercers, moved to 24 Bond Street in or before 1778, when he was described as a silk and stuff weaver (*Kent's Directory for the Year 1778*). A Mr Mendham, along with Gainsborough and other Suffolk worthies, had subscribed to Joseph Gibbs's *Six Quartettos*, and it is possible that William Mendham was a relative and known to the Gainsboroughs as a Suffolk man.

My Dear Sister

I trouble you with this unknown to my Wife, and the reason will soon appear to you — Fischer has deceived me in his Circumstances and his Wife has been playing the devil to raise Money, and I want to learn out if 'tis with or without his knowledge or Consent. She went to Mr Mendham's mercer in Bond Street before she left Town, and bespoke 60 yards of White Sattin for a Bed, and at another Shop white sarsenet to line it to the amount of 10 pounds more; and then wrote to George Coyte to beg of him to sell them at any rate so that he could make money of them, and remit it immediately to Her — I have stopt the whole scheme, but want sadly to know if these terrible undertakings

Letter 87

2 George Coyte (born 1711/2–82), a Suffolk-born jeweller and silversmith then living in the Strand, possibly the silversmith with whom Gainsborough 'principally resided' on his first coming to London in 1740. Gainsborough's portrait of him is in the Philadelphia Museum of Art (John G. Johnson Collection) (Waterhouse, No.170).

3 Transportation as convict labour either to the American colonies (which were by then rapidly achieving independence) or to the West Indies. Botany Bay, Australia, became a penal settlement in 1788.

The Girl with Pigs
Canvas, 125.7 x 148.6. R.A. 1782
The Castle Howard Collection

In the 1780s Gainsborough enlarged the scope of his painting to include 'fancy' pictures, a kind of composition much favoured by Reynolds and which embraced a wide range of genre subjects of a broadly sentimental and domestic, everyday connotation. In Gainsborough's hands such pictures were to display 'that pathetic simplicity which is the most powerful appeal to the feelings' and provided an ampler vehicle even than his 'cottage door' subjects for the expression of that wistful sentiment which lay at the heart of his imagination. Unlike the majority of his landscapes, these works were also popular with the connoisseurs, and commanded increasingly high prices. The figures were drawn from the life: the models for many were a peasant girl and a boy named Jack Hill he encountered in Richmond—and even the pigs in 'The Girl with Pigs' (Castle Howard), which was bought by Reynolds after its exhibition at the Academy of 1782, were to be seen grunting around Gainsborough's studio.

88

TO SIR JOSHUA REYNOLDS[1] 1782

MS. Pierpont Morgan Library, New York (MA 2411)

Sir Joshua,

I think myself highly honor'd, & much Obliged to you for this singular mark of your favor; I may truly say that I have brought my Piggs[2] to a fine market[3]

Dear Sir

your Ever Obliged &

Obedient Servant

Tho Gainsborough

1 Sir Joshua Reynolds, President of the Royal Academy (see Biographical Register).

2 *The Girl with Pigs* (The Hon. Simon Howard, Castle Howard: Waterhouse, No.799, pl.245), for which Reynolds paid one hundred guineas.

3 As noted by Whitley (Whitley Papers, Dept. of Prints and Drawings, British Museum: Gainsborough box, Guard Book for 1781–1787, slip on fo.17), this phrase derives from Henry Fielding's *Tom Jones* (1903 ed., vol. 3, p. 319).

In 1781 Gainsborough painted full-lengths of George III and Queen Charlotte, which, appropriately, were shown at the Royal Academy. Apparently he was late with the portrait of the Queen for, so we are told by Northcote, 'the drapery was done in one night by Gainsborough and his nephew, Gainsborough Dupont; they sat up all night, and painted it by lamp-light.' Unlike Reynolds, whom the King disliked, Gainsborough was extremely popular with the royal family, and he became court painter in all but name. In September 1782 he was down at Windsor painting heads of the entire family—the King and Queen and their thirteen children—which he sent to the following year's Academy. Gainsborough accompanied his letter to the Secretary with a sketch of how he wished these small ovals to be hung, in rows of five and as a single block, the frames touching. A no doubt well-founded suspicion that the pictures might be placed above 'the line', a level equivalent to the height of the doorways which was the base-line for full-lengths, prompted a second, blistering note. The Hanging Committee acceded—the King was, after all, the Patron of the Academy—but the incident boded ill for the future.

George Dance (1741–1825)
Francis Milner Newton (1720–94)
Drawing, 25.2 x 19.1. Signed and dated 1793
Royal Academy of Arts, London

89

TO FRANCIS MILNER NEWTON [APRIL] 1783

MS. Royal Academy of Arts

Dear Newton,

I w.d beg to have them hung with the Frames touching each other, in this order, the Names are written behind each Picture[1] —

God bless you. hang my Dogs[2] & my Landskips[3] in the great Room.[4] The sea Piece you may fill the small Room with[5] —

y.ors sincerely in haste

T. Gainsborough

[*Addr.*] F. M: Newton Esq.re

1 The fifteen ovals of the Royal Family (H.M. The Queen, Windsor Castle: Waterhouse, Nos. 12, 22, 109 (pl.212), 132, 134, 175, 238, 310, 406 (pl.215), 471, 527, 625, 643, 703 (pl.213) and 726 (pl.214)).

2 *Two Shepherd Boys with Dogs Fighting* (The Iveagh Bequest, Kenwood House: Waterhouse, No.800).

3 Gainsborough only submitted one landscape to the 1783 Royal Academy exhibition, the large mountain landscape in the National Gallery of Scotland, Edinburgh (Waterhouse, No.966, pl.257).

4 The Great Room was the Royal Academy's principal exhibiting space at Somerset House.

5 The large coastal scene (156.2 x 190.5 cm.) in the National Gallery of Victoria, Melbourne (Waterhouse No.964, pl.244).

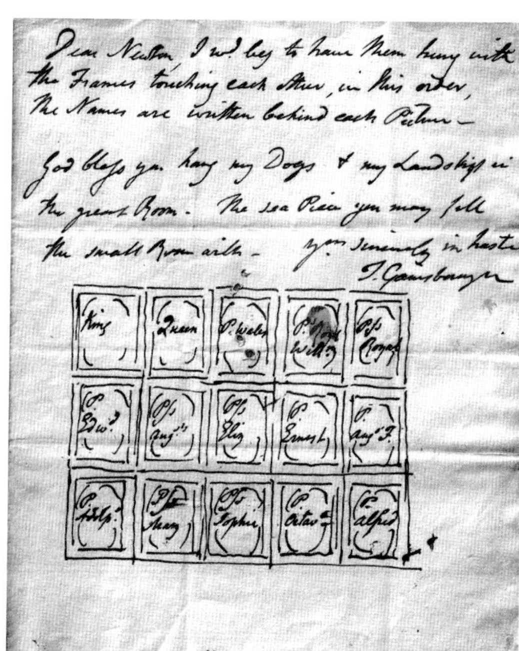

Dear Newton, I w.d beg to have them hung with the Frames touching each other, in this order, The Names are written behind each Picture —

God bless you hang my Dogs & my Landskips in the great Room. The sea Piece you may fill the small Room with — Yours sincerely in haste T. Gainsborough

Letter 89
Sketch of Gainsborough's instructions for the close hanging of his portraits of the King and Queen and their thirteen children
R.A. 1783

The Private View of the Royal Academy 1787
Engraving by P. Martini, 4 July 1787, after J.H. Ramberg

90

TO THE ROYAL ACADEMY HANGING COMMITTEE[1] [APRIL] 1783

MS. Royal Academy of Arts

Mr Gainsborough presents his Compliments to The Gentlemen appointed to hang the Pictures at the Royal Academy;[2] and begs leave to hint to Them, that if The Royal Family, which he has sent for this Exhibition, (being smaller than three quarters)[3] are hung above the line[4] along with full lengths, he never more, whilst he breaths, will [*word crossed out, perhaps* 'ever'] send another Picture to the Exhibition—

This he swears by God

Saturday Morn

[*Addr.*] To The Committee of Gentlemen / appointed to hang the Pictures / at the Royal Exhibition

1 As Rosenthal points out (p.105) it was 'a display of extraordinary presumption' to attempt to dictate where his pictures should be hung (see also Letter 89).

2 The annual exhibitions were selected, then as now, by the Council, a group of Academicians which rotated each year, and which appointed, from among its number, a Hanging Committee.

3 Three-quarters was a common description at the time for a standard 30 x 25 in. portrait, which was roughly three-quarters the size of a kit-cat, 36 x 28 in. The royal portraits were all about 23¼ x 17⅜ in.

4 The 'line' was a horizontal line eight feet from the floor, marked by a projecting ledge.

Gainsborough's Academy exhibits of the early 1780s demonstrate the width of his sympathies and determination to outdo Reynolds: 'Damn him', he declared, 'how various he is'. His 'Two Shepherd Boys with Dogs Fighting' (Iveagh Bequest, Kenwood), exhibited in 1783, one of the strangest and most untypically cruel of his paintings, was a work in which he tried to excel, in sheer observation of animal ferocity, the hunting scenes of Rubens and Snijders. In the late summer of the same year he visited the Lakes, by then the mecca of tourists in search of the picturesque, with the specific intention of achieving a grander style in his mountain landscapes, one that might prove to be acceptable as the eighteenth-century equivalent of Claude and Gaspard Poussin and evidence that he had turned 'a serious fellow'. His wash drawing of Langdale Pikes, one of the very few surviving sketches by Gainsborough of Lakeland scenery, was the basis for the landscape painted on his return, 'highly characteristic of that country', soon to be purchased by the Prince of Wales.

Sir William Chambers (1723–96)
Wedgwood medallion
Scottish National Portrait Gallery

91

TO SIR WILLIAM CHAMBERS[1] 27 APRIL 1783

Untraced. Whitley examined this letter when it was offered at Sotheby's in 1920, and the present text follows his transcription (Whitley Papers, Dept. of Prints and Drawings, British Museum: Gainsborough box, Guard Book for 1781–1787, pasted on fo.26). Most of the second paragraph, with some slight variations in the transcription, was published in the Charles Fairfax Murray sale, Sotheby's, 5–6 February 1920, lot 75 (purchaser unrecorded), and the W. Westley Manning sale, Sotheby's, 12 October 1954, lot 170, bt. Weiss-Hesse

Dear Sir,

You'l perceive the danger of writing polite, friendly letters to me, as I am already about to ask a favour of you. My wife has a poor relation from Scotland, a Joiner, who for want of work in his own country has been obliged to leave a handsome wife & his children behind him to seek employment in London. It has occurred to my good woman that as you must necessarily have a great number of hands at your *feet* that you might perhaps be so good as to think of him when convenient. He is a good workman about thirty years of age, an honest, sober, hardworking creature.

Two Shepherd Boys with Dogs Fighting
Canvas, 223.4 x 157.4. R.A. 1783
Iveagh Bequest, Kenwood

I hear poor Newton is better which I am honestly glad of; the world cannot supply his loss should he drop. I hope you had as cheerful a day yesterday as you could without him.[2] I sent my fighting dogs to divert you. I believe next exhibition I shall make the boys fighting & the dogs looking on – you know my cunning way of avoiding great subjects in painting & of concealing my ignorance by a flash in the pan. If I can do this while I pick pockets in the portrait way[3] two or three years longer I intend to sneak into a cot[4] & turn a serious fellow; but for the present I must affect a little madness. I know you think me right as a whole, & can look down upon Cock Sparrows as a great man ought to do with compassion.

Believe me, my dear Sir

Your always obedient Humble Servant

Thos. Gainsborough

Pall Mall, April 27th, 1783

1 Sir William Chambers (1723–96), the first Treasurer of the Royal Academy, was the architect of Somerset House.
2 Hanging the annual exhibition.
3 Since the transcription of this phrase in both the Sotheby's catalogues is 'in the Portraits', this is likely to be correct. It would be characteristic of Whitley to improve it.
4 Retire to a cottage.

William Pearce (c. 1751–1842)
Canvas, 63.5 x 53.3. c.1780
Private Collection, England

92

TO WILLIAM PEARCE[1] SUMMER 1783

MS. Gainsborough's House, Sudbury (1998.035)

Kew Green[2] Sunday Morn^g^
Church time

Dear Sir

I don't know if I told you that I'm going along with a Suffolk Friend[3] to visit the Lakes in Cumberland & Westmorland;[4] and purpose when I come back to show you that your Grays[5] and D^r^. Brownes[6] were tawdry fan-Painters. I purpose to mount all the Lakes at the next Exhibition, in the great Stile,[7] — and you know if the People don't like them, 'tis only jumping into one of the deepest of them from off a wooded Island, and my reputation will be fixed for ever —

I took the liberty of sending you a little Perry[8] out of Worstershire, and when the Weather settles in hot again, should be much obliged if you and M^rs^ [Pearce *scratched out*] would drink a little of <it> and fancy it Champaigne for my sake — I doubt whether I can shake you by the hand before I go, but when I come back, I'll shake you by the collar, if you'l <promise> to keep your hands still — [9]

Believe me Dear Sir most sincerely yours
Tho Gainsborough

Rocky Upland Landscape with Shepherd and Sheep and Distant Mountains
Canvas, 120 x 148.6. Autumn 1783
Bayerische Landesbank (on loan to the Neue Pinakothek, Munich)

[*Postmark*] Illegible
[*Stamped*] POST PAID

1 William Pearce (c.1751–1842), Chief Clerk of the Admiralty, was also an amateur writer and librettist of a number of comic operas.
2 Gainsborough was presumably staying with his old friend, Sarah Kirby, widowed since the death of her husband, Joshua (see Letter 37, note 1), in 1774. The Kirbys' house is now 61 Kew Green.
3 Samuel Kilderbee (see Biographical Register).
4 The trip, one fashionable among travellers in search of the picturesque, was evidently made in the summer, as Gainsborough refers later in the letter to his expectation of the weather settling in hot again.
5 Thomas Gray (1716–71), the poet, a lifelong devotee of mountain scenery.
6 Dr John Brown (1715–66), a close friend of the Gilpins, whose description of the lake of Keswick (Derwentwater) was published as a pamphlet posthumously in 1771, and described by Peter Bicknell as 'probably the earliest prose description of wild and mountainous scenery in Britain, in picturesque terms' (*Beauty, Horror and Immensity: Picturesque Landscape in Britain*, exhibition catalogue, Fitzwilliam Museum, Cambridge, July–August 1981 (1)).
7 That of Claude, Poussin or Gaspard Dughet.
8 A sparkling drink, similar to cider, but made from Worcestershire pear, rather than apple, juice.
9 An analogy from wrestling, in which the two opponents held each other by the collar.

John Gainsborough (1711–89)
Canvas, 72.4 x 59.7
c.1770–74
Private Collection

93

TO SARAH DUPONT[1] 29 SEPTEMBER 1783

Untraced (last recorded in Catalogue No.899, Maggs Bros., November 1965 (97)). Text transcribed from Anon. sale, Christie's, 11 June 1908, lot 203, where the letter is described as addressed from Pall Mall, September 29th, 1783.

I promised John[2] when he did me the honor of a visit in Town, to allow him half-a-crown a week; which with what his good cousin Gainsbro:[3] allows him, and sister Gibbon, I hope will (if applied properly to his own use) render the remainder of his old age tollerably comfortable; for villainously old he is indeed grown. I have herewith sent you 3 guineas, with which I beg the favour of you to supply him, for half a year, with 2^{s} 6^{d} p^{r} week, paying him on what Day of the week you judge most his good, I should think not on the same Days that either Sister Gibbon's two shillings is paid, nor on those Days which his Cousin do for him. And that he may not know but what you advance the money out of your own pocket, I have enclosed a letter[4] that you may show him, which may give you a better power to manage him, if troublesome to you [*second page not known*]

Mrs Philip Dupont, née Sarah Gainsborough (1715–95)
Canvas, 77.2 x 64.5
c.1777–79
The Art Institute of Chicago (Charles H. and Mary F.S. Worcester Collection)

1 Sarah (1715–95), Gainsborough's second sister, whom he called Sally, had married Philip Dupont, a carpenter in Sudbury; it was one of their sons, Gainsborough Dupont (see Biographical Register) who became Gainsborough's studio assistant.

2 John Gainsborough (1711–85), Gainsborough's eldest brother, then aged seventy-two, was known as 'Scheming Jack' on account of his many, but eccentric, inventions. Though he had a large family (seven daughters), any money he scraped together was immediately spent on brasswork for his inventions: hence Gainsborough's subterfuges and apparent lack of his customary generosity in the letter he sent to Sarah. In later years, Gainsborough's daughter, Margaret, made an allowance of twenty pounds a year to her uncle John's last surviving daughter, Ann.

3 John Gainsborough (1752–91), grandson of the artist's wealthy uncle, Thomas.

4 See Letter 94.

94

TO SARAH DUPONT 29 SEPTEMBER 1783

Untraced (Anon. sale, Christie's, 11 June 1908, lot 202)

I beg the favour of you to advance half-a-crown a week to Brother John, for his own use, from this Michaelmas, and I will pay you again the first oportunity. I thought what I gave him when in London sufficient to last 'till this time, which is the reason I did not trouble you with a line sooner [*remainder not known*]

William, 4th Earl of Essex (1732–99) presenting a silver cup to Thomas Clutterbuck
Canvas, 148.5 x 174. c.1784
The J. Paul Getty Museum, Los Angeles

95

TO WILLIAM, 4TH EARL OF ESSEX[1] 29 MARCH 1784

MS. J. Paul Getty Museum, Los Angeles (Department of Drawings)

Mr Gainsborough presents his humble service to Lord Essex; and acquaints His Lordship that the Exhibition opening very early this year, and the season having been so bad for finishing his Pictures, he finds it will be impossible to begin the Picture for Mr Clutterbuck,[2] without danger of spoiling it, before May; when if Lord Essex should be in Town, he will not undertake any work before he begins it, and will wait upon His Lordship or send to appoint a sitting—

Monday Eve—
29th March 1784

[*Addr.*] R^{t} Honble / The Earl of Essex

1 William, 4th Earl of Essex (1732–99), Lord of the Bedchamber to George II, 1755–60, and to George III,1782–99.

2 See Letter 51, note 1.

Having painted a variety of important and original landscapes and fancy pictures for the first three exhibitions at Somerset House, Gainsborough prepared a series of full-lengths for the Academy of 1784, including a ravishing group portrait of the three eldest daughters of George III which had been commissioned for Carlton House by the Prince of Wales. This obliged him to postpone other work. Once again, however, there was a row about hanging. Although his picture of the Princesses was at full-length, he insisted upon it being hung lower than the normal level because this was the height for which he had painted it. Perhaps understandably, and the more so in view of previous exchanges, the Hanging Committee was adamant. Gainsborough was as good as his word of the previous year, and never showed at the Academy again. Instead, he arranged his own annual exhibition of his pictures, the first of which was held at Schomberg House in July 1784.

96

TO THE ROYAL ACADEMY HANGING COMMITTEE [APRIL] 1784

MS. Royal Academy of Arts (mounted in Royal Academy Scrap-Book, p.2)

Portraits by T. Gainsborough the Frames sent
Princesses
Lady Buckingham
Lord Buckingham
Lord Rodney
Lord Rawdon
Two Boys with a Dog Master Tomkinsons
half length. Lord Hood
Family Picture Mr Bailey
NB—The Frame of the Princesses cannot be sent but with the Picture, as Their Majesties are to have a private View of the Picture at Buckingham house before it is sent to the Royal Academy

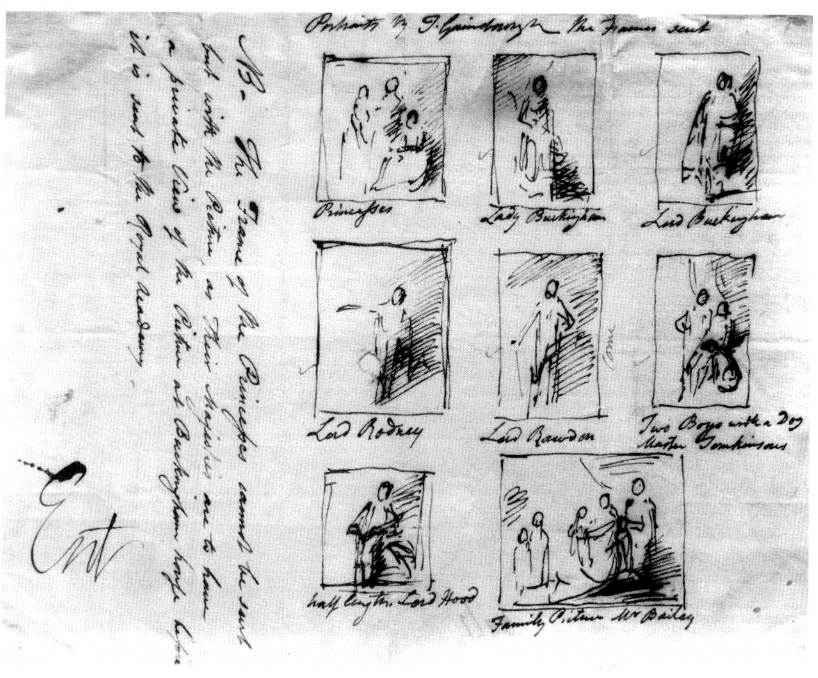

Letter 96
Thumbnail sketches of the portraits Gainsborough sent to the R.A. 1784.

The Three Princesses. Mezzotint by Gainsborough Dupont, 1793, after the Gainsborough painting in the Royal Collection, withheld from the R.A. 1784 and later cut down.

97

TO THE ROYAL ACADEMY HANGING COMMITTEE 10 APRIL 1784

Untraced (Minute Books of the Royal Academy Council Meetings: Vol.1., p.358, 10 April 1784)

Mr Gainsboroughs Compts to the Gentn of the Committee, & begs pardon for giving them so much trouble; but he has painted this Picture of the Princesses[1] in so tender a light, that notwithstanding he approves very much of the established Line for Strong Effects, he cannot possibly consent to have it placed higher than five feet & a half, because the likenesses & Work of the Picture will not be seen any higher; therefore at a Word, he will not trouble the Gentlemen against their Inclination, but will beg the rest of his Pictures back again—[2]
Saturday Evening

1 The full-length group portrait of the Princesses Charlotte, The Princess Royal (1766–1828), Augusta (1768–1840) and Elizabeth (1770–1840), cut down to fit as an overdoor in the early part of Queen Victoria's reign (H.M. The Queen, Windsor Castle: Waterhouse, No.135, colour plate facing p.44).

2 After this letter had been read to the Council, it was 'Resolved That the following Letter be sent him. Sir In compliance with your request the Council have ordered Your Pictures to be taken down & to be delivered to your order, when ever Send for them. I am &c Saturday Evening 9 oClo: FM. Newton Secy'

98

TO JOHN, 4TH EARL OF SANDWICH[1] 29 NOVEMBER 1784

MS. The Earl of Sandwich, Mapperton, Dorset

My Lord,

Dash'd entirely out of countenance this Evening by the receipt of your Lordship's Letter, I have nothing left but to hope and pray that the Assembly may not happen til the latter End of the week; the dampness of the weather having been such, that the confounded Paint would not dry so as to bear rolling up before saturday night; on Sunday Morning my Servant saw the Case put into the Waggon; so that I hope the Picture will be at Huntingdon near as soon as your Lordship will receive this Letter. I have not a word to say in favor of the young Man's Performance;[2] but hope that if your Lordship should not think it well enough for the intend-

John, 4th Earl of Sandwich (1718–92)
Canvas, 233.7 x 152.4
R.A. 1783
National Maritime Museum, London (detail)

ed purpose, that your Lordship's cook maid will hang it up as her own Portrait in the Kitchen and get some sign-post Gentleman to rub out the Crown & Sceptre, and put her on a blue apron, and say it was painted by G— who was very near being King's Painter only Reynolds's Friends stood in the way.[3]

I am

Your Lordship's

most Obedient and very humble

Servant

Tho Gainsborough

Monday Nov.r 29.th
1784

1 Lord Sandwich (1718–92) was for long a political associate of John, 4th Duke of Bedford (see Biographical Register), and spent much of his ministerial career at the Admiralty, a practical administrator set on overhauling a deteriorating fleet; his private enthusiasms included cricket, sailing and music: he was the prime mover behind the great Handel commemoration of 1784. In retirement Sandwich lived mainly at Hinchingbrooke, his country seat just outside Huntingdon.

Gilbert Stuart (1755–1828)
Sir Joshua Reynolds (1723–92)
Canvas, 107.9 x 93.3
1784
National Gallery of Art, Washington, DC
Andrew Mellon Collection

2 Gainsborough had been commissioned to paint a copy of Thomas Hudson's state portrait of George II's consort, Queen Caroline, for Huntingdon Town Hall, and deputed the task to his assistant, Gainsborough Dupont.

3 In August 1784 Allan Ramsay died. As a friend of the Royal Family, Gainsborough may legitimately have hoped that he would be appointed to succeed him as Principal Portrait Painter to the King. But Reynolds was equally determined to secure this prestigious, if financially unrewarding, job for himself; and Gainsborough's defection from that year's Academy was ill-timed. That the issue was far from clear-cut is shown by the fact that it was a full fortnight before Reynolds was notified of his appointment.

Gainsborough does not figure a great deal in the memoirs and letters of the period, so that it is difficult to form an impression of his position in society. But he was a recognized wit. Johnson spoke of him to Garrick as 'your sprightly friend', and one writer remarked that 'his gaiety enlivened every group. He knew everybody and everybody knew him', adding that James Christie, the auctioneer, often declared that the presence in the rooms of Gainsborough and Garrick, with their banter and good humour, added fifteen percent to his commisssion on a sale. Abel's death in 1787 was the end of an era as far as Gainsborough was concerned: he and J.C. Bach, who had died five years

Richard Cosway (1740–1821)
Self-Portrait
Pencil and wash drawing (oval)
c.1785–90
National Portrait Gallery, London

before, had been among his closest friends for a quarter of a century, and the sudden blow seems to have given the artist a premonition of his own mortality.

99

TO RICHARD COSWAY[1] [c.1784–88]

Untraced. Whitley examined this letter when it was in the possession of W. Westley Manning, 20 December 1915, and again after it was purchased by Francis Wellesley, Sotheby's, 29 June 1916, lot 173 (Whitley Papers, Dept. of Prints and Drawings, British Museum: Gainsborough box, Guard Book for 1745–1780, transcription pasted on fo.54)

Mr. Gainsborough presents his compliments to Mr. and Mrs. Cosway; & will do himself the honor ['u' *crossed out*] of waiting on them on Monday evening, ['on condition' *crossed out*] if they do not expect <any> other company

1 Richard Cosway (1742–1821), a brilliant miniature painter, and his wife, Maria (1760–1838), artist, musician and renowned hostess, were Gainsborough's neighbours from 1784, occupying the centre part of Schomberg House. This almost certainly provides a *terminus post quem* for Gainsborough's note.

100

TO RICHARD COSWAY [C.1784–88]

Untraced (transcribed by Mary Woodall (No.14) from the original in the possession of Messrs. Myers, 1945)

Mr. Gainsborough presents his Compliments to Mr. Cosway; and as he finds there has been a loss of Iron betwixt us,[1] he begs in case it must be repaired with Gold or Silver, that he may be permitted to share the expense with Mr. Cosway.

1 Jacob Simon has very plausibly suggested to me that this refers to a domestic incident at Schomberg House which involved damaged or collapsed ironwork.

101

[TO THE REVD HENRY BATE-DUDLEY][1] 20 JUNE 1787

Untraced (Whitley, p.282)

Poor Abel died about one o'clock to-day, without pain, after three days sleep. Your regret, I am sure, will follow this loss. We love a genius for what he leaves and we mourn him for what he takes away. If Abel was not so great a man as Handel it was because caprice had ruined music before he ever took up the pen.[2] For my part I shall never cease looking up to heaven—the little while I have to stay behind—in hopes of getting one more glance of the man I loved from the moment I heard him touch the string. Poor Abel!— 'tis not a week since we were gay together, and that he wrote the sweetest air I have in my collection of his happiest thoughts. My heart is too full to say more.

1 The Revd Henry Bate-Dudley (see Biographical Register).

2 Gainsborough is referring to the performing of the galant style which had permeated music from Germany in the mid-eighteenth century. Thurston Dart concluded his analysis of the embellishments of the adagio for flute and continuo printed in a treatise published in 1752 by the virtuoso flautist Johann Joachim Quantz (1697–1773), who was in the service of Frederick the Great: 'The final result is exactly comparable to the contemporary taste for rococo ornament; all is artificial, sentimental, and highly mannered' (*The Interpretation of Music*, London, 4th impression (revised), 1960, p.98). The reverence for Handel had recently reached an apogee in the great Handel Commemoration of 1784.

Carl Friedrich Abel (1725–87)
Canvas, 223.5 x 147.3. R.A. 1777
Henry E. Huntington Art Gallery, San Marino, California

Gainsborough raised the prices of his portraits, for the last time, in 1787. The new scale was forty guineas for a head, eighty for a half-length, and one hundred and sixty for a full-length, closer to Reynolds's fees, which, since 1782, had been fifty, one hundred and two hundred guineas respectively, for these sizes. He also made an attempt at reconciliation with the Academy, offering to paint an overmantel for the Council Room; but this was never executed. He remained absorbed by family affairs—although the cause of the dispute involving his sister, Elizabeth Bird, is unknown—and critical of slipshod work.

102

TO MARY GIBBON 31 JULY 1787

MS. Gainsborough's House, Sudbury (1992.079)

My Dear Sister,

I was extremely sorry to find by your last Letter, that you could suppose me offended in the least degree by what you said in your former; I hope My dear we have more Affection for each other, if not more sense, than to suffer what may be said in Joke to make any material difference in our good wishes towards each other; I assure you what I said was without the least intention of offending, I only meant <u>in my own manner</u> to urge all parties to claim their Right; and to set all Joking aside, I do think that Poor Betsey[1] should be allowed somthing besides her share in other respects to reward her giving up what she might so reasonably expect to recover by Law—I meant no more than to express my warm wishes for her advantage. But I am contented that they should judge for Themselves; and have now only one wish remaining in the Affair which is that no misunderstanding betwixt you and I may take place, after we have been 60 Years Friends—I have in truth every good wish at Heart for your Happiness here and here[af]ter; and so we will let Jokes alone [*word obliterated, probably* 'till'] we meet which I hope will not be long fu[rther]

We are all well, & join in best Affections to you, and all Relations at Bath—

I remain

Dear Sister

most truly your loving Bro:

Tho Gainsborough

July 31 –

William Petty, 1st Marquess of Lansdowne (1737–1805)
Engraving 1787 by Bartolozzi after the portrait painted by Gainsborough the same year.

[*Addr.*] M^{rs}. Gibbon N°. 2 / Circus / Bath
[*Postmark*] [31] JY 87

1 Elizabeth (born 1723), Gainsborough's third sister, who had married John Bird, a currier in Sudbury.

103

TO WILLIAM PETTY, 1ST MARQUESS OF LANSDOWNE 8 DECEMBER 1787

MS. The Marquess of Lansdowne, Bowood

My Lord,

Mr Bartolozzi has this Day favor'd me with the Print of your Lordship; and I could wish He had favor'd me a little more in preserving your Lordships chearful Countenance. It wants (in my humble opinion, <u>a full Bottle of Champaigne</u> to give even the Vigour that is in the Picture; and <u>That</u> falls as short ['G' *crossed out*] as dead Small = Beer of the Original — I beg pardon my Lord, but

I'm in a damn'd passion about it, because I have ever been so partial to Bartolozzi's Work—He has mounted your Lordship's figure up to about Lord Stormont's height,[1] and sloped the shoulders like my Layman stuff'd with straw; which he need not have done in order to bring into that size Oval, as he might have taken the Head larger: But what hurts me most is that the Head is long instead of round—Why will Bartolozzi, my Lord, spend his last precious moments in f—g a young Woman, instead of out doing all the World with a Graver; when perhaps all the World can out do Him at the former Work?

Pray My Lord apply these private hints as from your own Eyes, lest I should have my throat cut for my honesty—

your Lordships most Obedient
humble servant
Tho Gainsborough

Dec[r] 8th 1787

1 Gainsborough's remark implies the existence of a Bartolozzi engraving of Lord Stormont (later 2nd Earl of Mansfield, 1727–96) which would have been known to Lord Lansdowne, but none is recorded. His other comments do not seem very fair, although the sitter's right side is certainly unduly sloped.

104

TO THE REVD HENRY BATE-DUDLEY 11 MARCH 1788

Untraced (*The Morning Herald*, day and month unknown, 1789: *Press Cuttings from English Newspapers on Matters of Artistic Interest, 1686 / 1835*, 6 vols., vol.2, fo.503, Victoria and Albert Museum Library)

My Dear Sir,

You have thanked me handsomely, for what has not been handsomely done;[1]—but I intend you shall have something better soon.

Mr. Boydell bought the large Landscip you speak of, for seventy-five guineas, last week, at Greenwood's:[2]—It is in some respects a little in the schoolboy stile—but I do not reflect on this without a secret gratification; for—as an early instance how strong my inclination stood for Landskip, this picture was actually painted at Sudbury, in the year 1748:[3] it was begun before I left school;—and was the means of my Father's sending me to London.

It may be worth remark, that though there is very little idea of composition in the picture, the touch and closeness to nature in the study of the parts and minutiae, are equal to any of my later productions.—In this explana-

Cornard Wood
Canvas, 122 x 155. 1748
National Gallery, London

tion, I wish not to seem vain or ridiculous, but do not look on the Landskip as one of my riper performances

It is full forty years since it was first delivered by me to go in search of those who had taste enough to admire it! Within that time, it has been in the hands of twenty picture dealers, and I once bought it myself during that interval for Nineteen Guineas: — Is that not curious?

Your's, my dear Sir,

Most sincerely,

Thomas Gainsborough

Pall-Mall, March 11, 1788

1 'Some drawings which Mr. Gainsborough sent as a present' (note to the letter published in *The Morning Herald*).

2 *Cornard Wood, near Sudbury, Suffolk* (National Gallery, London (925): (Waterhouse, No.828, pl.22).

3 Hugh Belsey has identified the viewpoint (see Judy Egerton, *National Gallery Catalogues: The British School*, London, 1998, p.72).

In April 1788 Gainsborough made the first mention of a growth in his neck of which he had been conscious for three years past, though hitherto without alarm. He made his will, which he signed on 5 May. At the end of that month he was taken down to his house at Richmond for rest and quiet, and Bate-Dudley reported that he was 'perfectly recovered'. But after two or three weeks it became obvious that this was not true. He was obliged to be brought back to town, and, in spite of the constant ministrations of William Heberden and John Hunter, two of the most eminent medical men of their day, his condition grew steadily worse. Only a few days before the end he scrawled a pathetic note to Reynolds, urging him to call. 'The Woodman', which the King had requested him to bring to Buckingham House for him to examine earlier in the year (and which was bought by Lord Gainsborough for five hundred guineas shortly after the painter's death, but subsequently destroyed by fire), was the picture Gainsborough regarded as his greatest work, and among the canvases brought to his bedside for Reynolds to inspect. 'If any little jealousies had subsisted between us', Reynolds said afterwards, 'they were forgotten, in those moments of sincerity; and he turned towards me as one, who was engrossed by the same pursuits. … Without entering into a detail of what passed at this last interview, the impression of it upon my mind was, that his regret at losing life, was principally the regret of losing his art'.

105

[TO AN UNKNOWN RECIPIENT] 1788 [PROBABLY APRIL]

MS. Wellcome Institute, London (MS.5610/2)[1]

Sir,

Your extreem kind Letter is more than I should think I deserved from any intimate Acquaintance, but from a Gentleman to whom I have not the honor of being the least known, I must ever think it proceeding from the best of Hearts — What this painful swelling in my Neck will turn out, I am at a loss at present to guess, Mr John Hunter[2] found it nothing but a swell'd Gland, and has been most comfortable in pesuading me that it will disperse by the continued application of a Sea:water poultice. My Neighbour Dr Heberden[3] has no other notion of it — It has been 3 years coming on gradually,[4] and having no pain 'til lately, I paid very little regard to it; now it is painful enough indeed, as I can find no position upon my pillow to admit of getting rest in Bed — I would fain see what turn it will take before I alarm myself too

Sir William Beechey (1753–1839)
Dr William Heberden the Elder (1710–1801)
Canvas, 76.2 x 63.5, c.1796
Royal College of Physicians of London

much – In the mean time Sir, as I am always at Home, if you will be kind enough to drop in for a moment [(]giving your Name to my Servant) You will afford much comfort & do great honor to

Sir your ever Obedient & most
grateful humb[le] Servant
Tho Gainsborough

N° 87 Pall Mall –
Monday Afternoon

1 Dr Chris Fletcher, of the Department of Manuscripts, British Library, kindly informed me of the whereabouts of this letter.

2 John Hunter, the distinguished surgeon (see Biographical Register).

3 Dr Heberden (see Letter 83, note 1) had lived since 1771 in a house (now destroyed) which James Paine had built for him on the site of what is now 79 Pall Mall.

4 Maggs Bros., who sold the letter to the Wellcome (Catalogue No.899, 1965 (94)), pointed out the inconsistency between this remark and the announcement in the *Morning Herald* on 5 May that Gainsborough's 'indisposition proceeds from a violent cold caught in Westminster Hall [attending the trial of Warren Hastings]; the glands of his neck have been in consequence so much inflamed as to require the aid of Mr. John Hunter and Dr Heberden'.

Catherine Andras (1775–1860)
Robert Bowyer (1758–1834)
Wax medallion
Private Collection, England

106

TO ROBERT BOWYER[1] 1 MAY 1788

MS. Wellcome Institute, London (MS.5610/3/1)[2]

Sir,

I am extreemly Obliged to you for your kind Anxiety for my recovery: But as I have reason and every assurance from D^r. Heberden (who has known many Swellings dispersed like mine, and no mischief come) I shall not on any account interfere in what Mr Hunter is about.—

I am[3]

Tho Gainsborough

May 1st. 1788

[*Addr.*] R. Bowyer Esqre

1 Robert Bowyer (1758–1834), who succeeded Jeremiah Meyer as miniature painter to the King in 1789, occupied Gainsborough's house in Pall Mall, 1793–1803, after Mrs Gainsborough moved out in 1792. He used the premises for an Historic Gallery.

2 As in the case of Letter 105, Dr Chris Fletcher kindly informed me of the whereabouts of this letter.

3 The valediction and signature have been cut away; when this letter was neatly repaired only these two words and the signature were replaced.

Sir Joshua Reynolds (1723–92)
John Hunter (1728–93)
Canvas, 140 x 113
RA 1786
Royal College of Surgeons of England

107

TO WILLIAM PEARCE 1788

Untraced (Fulcher, pp.147–48)

Wed. Morning

My dear Pearce,

I am extremely obliged to you and Mrs. Pearce for your kind enquiries; I hope I am now getting better, as the swelling is considerably increased and more painful. We have just received some cheeses from Bath, and beg the favor of you to accept two of them.

My dear Pearce,

Ever yours sincerely,

Thos. Gainsborough

108

TO THOMAS HARVEY[1] 22 MAY 1788

MS. Witt Collection 4599, Courtauld Galleries, Courtauld Institute of Art

Dear Sir,

Your very obliging Letter inclosing a Norwich Bank Bill, Value seventy three Pounds, on Mess$^{r.s}$ Vere & Williams, I acknowledge (when p$^{d.}$) to be in full for the Landscape with Cows[2] & all demands.

I am glad Sir, that the Picture got no damage; if ever you should find anything of a Chill come upon the Varnish of my Pictures, owing to its being a Spirit of Wine Varnish, take a rag, or little bit of sponge with Nut oil, and rub it 'til the mist clears away, and then wipe as much of it off as a few Strokes with a clean Cloth <will Effect> — this done once or twice a year after damp weather you will find convenient —

My Swelled Neck is got very painful indeed, but I hope is the near coming to a Cure — How happy should I be to set out for Yarmouth and after recruiting my poor Crazy Frame,[3] enjoy the coasting along til I reach'd Norwich and give you a call — God only knows what is for me, but hope is the Pallat of Colors we all paint with in sickness —

'tis odd how all the Childish passions hang about one in sickness, I feel such a fondness for my first imatations of little Dutch Landskips that I can't keep from working an hour or two of a Day, though with a great mixture of bodily Pain — I am so childish that I could make a Kite, catch Gold Finches, or build little Ships —

Believe me Dear Sir
with the greatest Sincerity
Your ever Obliged & Obedient
Servant
Tho Gainsborough

Pall Mall
May 22$^{d.}$ 1788 –

P.S. I have recollected that a Stamp Re$^{\underline{ct}}$ may be proper.

[*Addr.*] Thomas Harvey Esq$^{\underline{re}}$ / at Catton near / Norwich

1 Thomas Harvey (1748–1819), of Catton Hall, near Norwich, an amateur artist, collector and patron, notably of John Crome.

2 This landscape has not been identified. Harvey had bought the celebrated *The Cottage Door* now in the Huntington Art Gallery, San Marino, California, in 1786 (Hayes *Landscape Paintings*, No.123).

Francesco Bartolozzi (1727–1815)
Thomas Gainsborough
Pencil drawing after the self-portrait for the authorized posthumous engraving, 21 x 16.5
c.1788
National Portrait Gallery, London

3 Jackson remarked shortly after his death that his was 'a Life where Nature is kept upon the Stretch' (letter to Thomas Jackson, 6 September 1788: published in Amal Asfour and Paul Williamson, 'William Jackson of Exeter: New documents', *Gainsborough's House Review* 1996/97, p.125).

109

[TO AN UNKNOWN RECIPIENT] 15 JUNE 1788

MS. British Library Add MS.70951, fo.20 (The Charnwood Autograph Collection, Vol.4)[1]

June 15th, 1788

It is my strict charge that after my decease no plaister cast, model, or likeness whatever be permitted to be taken: But that if M [*two letters above the line indecipherable, presumably a clumsily written* 'r'] Sharp,[2] who engraved Mr Hunter's Print, should chuse to make a print from the ¾ sketch which I intended for Mr Abel painted by myself,[3] I give free consent.

Tho. Gainsborough

1 This letter was recently rediscovered by Dr Chris Fletcher (see also Letter 105, note 1, and Letter 106, note 2).
2 William Sharp (1749–1824), a highly sophisticated line-engraver with a European reputation.
3 The self-portrait now owned by the Royal Academy (Waterhouse, No.292, pl.208). In the event, it was Bartolozzi who made the posthumous engraving.

The Woodman
Engraving by Peter Simon, 1791, after the work painted in the summer of 1787, which Gainsborough regarded it as his chef d'oeuvre. Purchased for 500 guineas at the studio sale held at Schomberg House in 1789 by the Earl of Gainsborough, it was destroyed, along with other Gainsboroughs, when one wing of the family home, Exton Park, Rutland, was burnt down in 1810.

110

TO SIR JOSHUA REYNOLDS JULY 1788

MS. Royal Academy of Arts

Dear Sir Joshua

I am Just to write what I fear you will not read, after lying in <a> dying state for 6 month The extreem affection which ['Sir Joshua' *crossed out*] I am informed of by a Friend which <Sir Josha has expresd> induces me to beg a last favor, which is <to> come once under my Roof and look at my things, my Woodman you never saw, if what I ask more is not [*a second* 'not' *crossed out*] disagreable to your feeling that I may have the honor to speak to you. I can from a sincere Heart say that I always admired <and sincerely loved> Sir Joshua Reynolds.

Tho Gainsborough

On 2 August Gainsborough died at Schomberg House. He was sixty-one. At his own request the funeral was private (Reynolds's funeral at St. Paul's was a state occasion), and he was buried in Kew Churchyard next to the grave of his Suffolk friend, Joshua Kirby. The pall-bearers were six artists: Bartolozzi, Chambers, Cotes (the miniaturist), Reynolds, Sandby and West. Gainsborough's pictures and drawings, and the collection he had formed, were offered for sale at his house in 1789; subsequent sales were held by Christie's, in 1792, in 1797 after the death of Dupont, and in 1799 after Mrs. Gainsborough died.

LETTERS CONCERNING PAYMENTS AND RECEIPTS

A number of Gainsborough's instructions to his bankers, some for payments of surprisingly large amounts, happen to survive from the 1750s, mainly for the years 1757–59. Bertie Burgh and James Unwin, who were partners, are those who are known to have acted as his bankers in the early part of his life; Unwin was still acting in this capacity in 1763 (see Letter 9). From 1762 to 1785 Gainsborough kept an account with Hoare's Bank, chiefly in connection with his wife's annuity, and from 1782 until his death in 1788 one with Drummond's; in both cases, happily, the ledgers are still preserved.

III

TO JAMES UNWIN 3 JUNE [1754]

Untraced (transcribed from NPG Ref. Neg. 5990)

3rd June

Sir

Please to pay to Mr. Allen Catchpool[1] or Order one month after the Date hereof, the sum of Twelve pounds Nine Shillings & place it to the Acct. of

Sir your most humbe Servt.

£12=9 Tho: Gainsborough

[*Addr.*] To Mr. James Unwin / In Castle yard Holborn / London

1 Allen Catchpool (born 1721), the son of John and Martha Catchpool, was baptised at St. Andrew's, Mickfield. Mrs Catherine Catchpool, perhaps his wife or widow, is described as a milliner in Ipswich in 1764.

112

TO JAMES UNWIN 19 MARCH 1755

Untraced (Harrison 1922, p.5, where the address is also given)

March 19th 1755

Sir,

Please to pay Mich^{l} Thirkle[1] Esqr or order two months after the date hereof the sum of one hundred pounds and place it to the account of

Sir your most hum^{le} Servt

£100 Thomas Gainsborough

[*Addr.*] To Mr. James Unwin in Castle Yard, Holborn, London

1 Michael Thirkle (c.1713–66), son of Michael Thirkle, an Ipswich merchant, married Elizabeth Sparrow at St. Matthew's, Ipswich, on 10 January 1731. A man of some wealth, he was deeply involved in Ipswich politics, and was joint Mayor in 1747, 1749, 1751 and 1753. Either he or his father was a subscriber to Joshua Kirby's *Twelve Prints and Monasteries, Castles* etc., 1748 and Dr Brook Taylor's *Method of Perspective Made Easy*, 1754.

113

TO JAMES UNWIN 10 NOVEMBER 1757

Untraced (listed Harrison 1922, p.5)

Payment dated Nov. 10th, 1757 to Mich^{le} Thirkle[1] £10–10–0

1 See Letter 112, note 1 above.

114

TO JAMES UNWIN 13 NOVEMBER 1757

Untraced (transcribed from part of the account between Gainsborough and Unwin, 1757, repr. Harrison 1922, p.7)

Novr 13th 1757

Rec^{d} of Mr James Unwin the above Ballance of thirty seven pounds two shillings & ten pence in full of all Demands[1]

Tho: Gainsborough

1 Gainsborough's receipt in Unwin's account with him for the second half of 1757 for the balance of two years' annuity from the Duke of Beaufort (£400) after paying off a loan from Edward Fowler of £300 and other debts.

115

TO JAMES UNWIN 16 NOVEMBER 1757

Untraced (listed Harrison 1922, p.5)

Payment dated Nov. 16th, 1757 to John Leggatt[1] £26–12–10

1 John Leggatt has not been identified.

116

TO BERTIE BURGH[1] 28 JANUARY 1758

MS. British Library Add. MS.48964, fo. 1r

Sir

Jan: 28th 1758

Please to pay to Mrs. Ann Christian[2] or order a Month after the Date hereof the sum of forty nine pounds ten shillings, and place it to the Acct. of Sir your most Obedt hume. Servt.

£49 " 10 Tho Gainsborough

[*Addr.*] To Bertie Burgh Esqre. in Castle yard Holborn Londn

1 Bertie Burgh, with whom James Unwin entered into partnership, was Gainsborough's banker before he moved to Bath (see Biographical Register).

2 Ann Christian may have been the wife of the Revd Humphrey Christian (d. 1773), Rector of St. Peter's, Palgrave, near Eye, in Suffolk, 1755–57; he was also Rector of St. Mary's, Burnham Deepdale, 1749–66, and St. Peter and St. Paul, Knapton, 1759–73, and Vicar of St. Mary's, Docking, 1766–73, all in Norfolk.

117

TO JAMES UNWIN 28 JANUARY 1758

Untraced (listed Harrison 1922, p.5)

Payment dated Jan. 28th, 1758 to William Stanton[1] £40

1 William Stanton was a linen draper at 61 Cheapside.

118

TO JAMES UNWIN 27 JUNE 1758

MS. British Library Add. MS.48964, fo.2r

June 27th. 1758

Sir

Please to pay to Mich^{l}. Thirkle Esqre. or Order six weeks after the Date hereof the sum of Ten Pounds and place it to the Acc^{t}. of Sir

your most hum^{e} Servt.

£10 Tho Gainsborough

[*Addr.*] To M^{r}. James Unwin in Castle yard Holborn. London

119

TO JAMES UNWIN 3 JULY 1758

MS. British Library Add. MS.48964, fo.3r

July 3^{d}. 1758

Sir

Please to pay to M^{r}. Nath^{el}. Burrough[1] or order a Month after the Date hereof the sum of Ten pounds and place it to the Account

of Sir your most Obed^{t}. Servt.

£10 Tho Gainsborough

[*Addr.*] To Mr James Unwin in Castle yard Holborn Lond.

1 Nathaniel Burrough (1723/4–94) was the second son of the Revd Humphrey Burrough, master of Sudbury Grammar School, 1723–55, where Gainsborough was a pupil. He had a business in Threadneedle Street (*A Complete Guide*, London trade directory for 1758).

120

TO JAMES UNWIN 10 JULY 1758

MS. British Library Add. MS.48964, fo.4r

July 10th. 1758

Sir

Please to pay to M^{r}. John Fowler[1] or order twenty Days after Date, the sum of sixty seven Pounds sixteen Shils and place it to the Acc^{t}. of

Sir your most humb^e. Servt.
£67"16 Tho Gainsborough

[*Addr.*] To Mr James Unwin in Castle yard Holborn London

1 John Fowler has not been identified.

121

TO DANIEL WAYTH 1 AUGUST 1758

Untraced (Waterhouse, No.715)

[*A signed and dated receipt, 1 August 1758, now lost, for 15 guineas for a half-length of Daniel Wayth*[1] *was found in a lawyer's office in Bury St. Edmunds in April 1928.*]

1 David Wayth (1729–85) was the brother-in-law of Gainsborough's close friend, Samuel Kilderbee. The portrait (Waterhouse, No.715) is no longer extant. This receipt is the only evidence for Gainsborough's charge for a half-length (a 50 x 40 in. canvas) at this period.

122

TO JAMES UNWIN 4 FEBRUARY 1759

Untraced (transcribed from NPG Ref. Neg. 5990)

Sir Feb: 4th. 1759

Please to pay to Mich^l. Thirkle Esqr. or order ten Days after the Date hereof, the sum of Eighty pounds, as p^r. advise, and place it to the account of

Sir your most hum^e Servt.
£80 Tho Gainsborough

[*Addr.*] To Mr James Unwin Attorney at Law in Castle yard / Holborn London

William Lee (d. 1778)
Canvas, 76.2 x 63.5. 1759
Private Collection, England

123

TO WILLIAM LEE[1] 19 APRIL 1759

MS. National Gallery Library

April 19 1759

Rec^{d} of Willm Lee Esq^{e} The sum of sixteen guineas in full for a portrait of Mrs Lee and another of himself

£16 „ 16 Tho Gainsborough

1 William Lee (died 1778), of Hartwell House, Buckinghamshire, then being remodelled in the rococo style by Henry Keene. The portraits of Lee and his wife, Philadelphia (died 1799), (last recorded in the Heathcote Art Foundation sale, Sotheby's, New York, 15 January 1987, lot 140 (repr.col.) and in the Lord Doverdale sale, Sotheby's, 8 November 1950, lot 108, bt. Bellesi: Waterhouse, Nos. 434 and 435) were both head-and-shoulders (30 x 25 in.) canvases. This, and the receipts sent to George Lucy (Nos.127–28), provide the evidence for Gainsborough's charge of eight guineas for portraits of this basic size in 1759–60. Thicknesse (p.17) asserted that he raised his price from five to eight guineas soon after his initial success in Bath, where he arrived to spend a season in October 1758. He presumably increased his charge for a half-length from fifteen to twenty guineas at the same time (see Letter 132, note 2). The price for a full-length is unknown.

124

TO BERTIE BURGH 22 JULY 1759

MS. British Library Add. MS.48964, fo.5r

Sir July 22^{d}. 1759

Please to pay to M^{r}. Sam^{el}. Kilderbee or Order ten Days after the Date hereof the Sum of fifty pounds, and place it to the Account of

Sir your most humb^{e}. Servt.

£50 Tho Gainsborough

[*Addr.*] To Bertie Burgh Esqre. in Castle yard Holborn / London

125

TO JAMES UNWIN 31 DECEMBER 1759

Untraced (listed Harrison 1922, p.5)

Payment dated Dec. 31st, 1759 to Hanbury Pettingal[1] £70

1 Hanbury Pettingal was a well-known silk retailer in Bath, and Susan Sloman has suggested that the payment of £70 (a considerable sum) may have been in connection with lodgings taken by Gainsborough before he moved in to Abbey Street (letter to the compiler, 25 November 1999).

126

TO JAMES UNWIN 31 DECEMBER 1759

MS. British Library Add. MS.48964, fo.6r

Sir Bath Decemb^{r}. 31st. 1759

Please to pay to Mrs Ann Christian or Order three weeks after the Date hereof the sum of Thirty pounds, and place it to the Account

of Sir your most Obed. hum^{e}

Servt.

Tho Gainsborough

[*Addr.*] To M^{r}. James Unwin / Castle yard Holborn Lond—

George Lucy (1714–86)
Canvas, 76.2 x 63.5. 1760
National Trust,
Charlecote Park

127

TO GEORGE LUCY[1] 27 FEBRUARY 1760

MS. Warwickshire County Record Office (L6/1684, fo.132)

Feb: 27th 1760 Recd of George Lucy Esqr the sum of Eight Guineas in full for a portrait of himself

£8.8 Tho Gainsborough

1 George Lucy (d. 1786), of Charlecote Park, Warwickshire. Lucy commissioned two head-and-shoulders portraits of himself in 1760 (National Trust and Lucy Collection, Charlecote Park: Waterhouse, Nos.462 and 463) for which the charge was eight guineas apiece (see also under Letter 128). As Lucy's correspondence and the two receipts show, the second portrait—from separate sittings and in a different suit—was painted soon after the first (see Susan Sloman, 'Sitting to Gainsborough in 1760', *Burlington Magazine*, vol.139, May 1997, pp.325–28).

128

TO GEORGE LUCY 25 APRIL 1760

Untraced (Mary Elizabeth Lucy, *Biography of the Lucy Family*, 1862, p.112)

Apr: 25th 1760 Recd of George Lucy Esqr the sum of Eight Guineas in full for a portrait of himself

£8.8 Tho Gainsborough

129

TO GEORGE LUCY 27 APRIL 1762

MS. Warwickshire County Record Office (L6/1312)

April 27th 1762

Received of George Lucy Esqr. the sum of three Guineas and a half for a three quarter Frame Burnished Gold, and seven shillings for a Case

£4.0.6 Tho Gainsborough

130

TO RICHARD STEVENS 13 APRIL 1762

MS. (fragment of letter) Koriyama City Museum of Art, Japan

I have put it into the sort of Frame which you was pleasd to order, which comes to two Guineas; the picture ten Guineas;[1] and the ['Frame' *crossed out*] Case seven Shillings, in all twelve pounds nineteen shillings.

I am

Sir your most Obedient humble

Servant

Tho. Gainsborough

Bath April 13th. 1762

1 The picture was a head-and-shoulders (Mrs Naylor sale, Christie's, 3 July 1951, lot 72, bt. Davidge: Waterhouse, No.634), but the price was two guineas higher than usual: the reason for this is unexplained.

131

[TO AN UNKNOWN RECIPIENT] [ABOUT 1763–70][1]

MS. British Library Add. MS.19197, fo.34 (David Elisha Davy (1769–1851): Papers Relating to Suffolk, Add. MS.19077–19247)[2]

For a Cough

Take two Calfs feet, two quarts of Spring water, two ounces of sugar candy, one ounce of Hartshorn shavings, and one quart of Milk; put them into an Earthern pan, and send them to the Oven to be baked after the Bread is taken out, and to remain all night in the Oven: When Cold, take off all the fat; and if the Jelly proves to heavy for the Stomach, lower it with water: It must be taken warm, about a quarter of a pint at a time, three or four times a Day.[3]

This Cured M[r] Gainsbro: of a galloping
Consumption witness my Hand
TG. [*in monogram*]
Riding is included![4]

1 This dating is suggested by the handwriting, which is not inconsistent with Letter 12, dated 30 December 1763, on the one hand, and Letter 45, dated 9 June 1770, on the other.

2 This document was recently discovered among the Davy Papers by Dr Chris Fletcher, of the Department of Manuscripts, British Library, and has been published by him in *Gainsborough's House Review*, 1999–2000.

3 As Fletcher points out, 'The ingredients are fairly typical of culinary and medicinal receits of the period. Nevertheless, there remains the intriguing possibility that this particular preparation was Gainsborough's own.' Letter 8 refers to his recipe for varnish, Letter 64 to his complicated formula for making varnished drawings.

4 The pun on 'galloping' may have arisen from Gainsborough's reliance on riding as healthy exercise (see Letters 10 and 12).

132

TO JOHN, 3RD EARL OF BREADALBANE[1] 13 APRIL 1763

MS. Scottish Record Office (GD 112/21/251/32)

April 13th 1763 Received of the R[t] Hon[ble] Earl of Breadalbane twenty one pounds seven shillings in full for a half length Portrait of Lord Glanorchy[2] & a Case

£21. 7 Tho Gainsborough

After Allan Ramsay (1713–84).
John, 3rd Earl of Breadalbane (1696–1782).
Canvas, 76.2 x 63.5. c.1750s.
Private Collection, Scotland

1 John, 3rd Earl of Breadalbane (1696–1782) was Member of Parliament for Suffolk, 1727–41, and Orford, 1741–48. After succeeding to the title in 1752, he was a representative peer for Scotland, 1752–68 and 1774–80. His daughter, Jemima, married Philip, 2nd Earl of Hardwicke (see Letter 7, note 1), whom Gainsborough painted in the same year as her half-brother John, Lord Glenorchy.

2 John, Lord Glenorchy (1738–71), younger but, in 1763 only surviving, son of Lord Breadalbane by his second wife, Arabella. The portrait is in a private collection in Essex, but is not listed in Waterhouse; a head-and-shoulders portrait of his wife, Willielma, was last recorded in an Anon. Sale, Christie's, 20 November 1987, lot 94 (repr.col.)(Waterhouse, No.316). The receipt provides the evidence for Gainsborough's charge for a half-length at this time (from probably 1758 to 1763 or 1764).

133

TO JOHN, 4TH DUKE OF BEDFORD 5 NOVEMBER 1764

MS. Marquis of Tavistock and the Trustees of the Bedford Estate, Woburn MSS

Novr 5th 1764 Rec.^d of His Grace The Duke of Bedford sixty three Pounds, in full for Three Portraits £63[1]

Tho. Gainsborough

1 A head-and-shoulders of the Duke of Bedford and two repetitions (Waterhouse, No.54) (see Letter 19 concerning the delivery of the original). The price of twenty guineas each shows that Gainsborough had raised his scale of charges once again since 1763.

134

TO RICHARD STEVENS 28 JANUARY 1768

MS. (first paragraph of Letter 29) Koriyama City Museum of Art, Japan

Sir

I have rec^{d}. the favor of your inclosing a Bill Value £15 Which when p^{d}. I acknowledge to be in full for M^{rs}. Awses Picture & Frame & all Demands.[1]

[*Addr.*] To / Rich^{d}. Stevens Esqre / at Winscott near Torrington / Devonshire: / M:P:

[*Postmark*] BATH

1 Mrs Awse was Richard Stevens's sister (see Letter 27, note 1). This head-and-shoulders had been commissioned long since (see Letter 27); nonetheless, the receipt does not correspond to Gainsborough's scale of fees either before or after 1763, neither does it represent a half-payment.

135

TO JOHN, 4TH DUKE OF BEDFORD 28 APRIL 1768

MS. Marquis of Tavistock and the Trustees of the Bedford Estate, Woburn MSS

April 28th 1768 Rec^{d}. of His Grace The Duke of Bedford twenty one pounds, for a three quarter Portrait of his Grace,[1] sent to Mrs. Fortescue in Dublin

£21 Thos. Gainsborough

1 A head-and-shoulders, size 30 x 25 inches (whereabouts unknown: Waterhouse, No.57). The Duke of Bedford was elected Chancellor of Trinity College, Dublin, in 1765. For the term 'three quarter' see Letter 90, note 3.

136

TO JOHN, 4TH DUKE OF BEDFORD [15 NOVEMBER 1768]

MS. Marquis of Tavistock and the Trustees of the Bedford Estate, Woburn MSS

November 15th 1768 Recd. of His Grace The Duke of Bedford sixty

Guineas, in full for a whole length Portrait of His Grace[1] By me
Thos. Gainsborough

1 This full-length was presented to Trinity College, Dublin, in 1768 (Waterhouse, No.53), presumably at the time of the Duke's installation as Chancellor, 9 September. Sixty guineas was Gainsborough's price for a full-length from 1763 or 1764 to between 1770 and 1772.

137

TO THE CORPORATION OF STRATFORD-UPON-AVON
[1769]

MS. Whereabouts unknown. A copy is contained in *The Jubilee Volume*, a scrap-book compiled by George Daniel, bound 1836 (fo. 130, pasted in on p. 54) (British Library)

Rec^{d}. of the Corporation of Stratford upon Avon, by the hands of David Garrick Esqr sixty three pounds in full for a whole length Portrait of that Gentleman

£63.[1] Tho. Gainsborough

1 The full-length Gainsborough provided for the Shakespeare Bicentenary celebrations at Stratford-upon-Avon in 1769 was a re-working of the full-length of Garrick he had exhibited at the Society of Artists in 1766 (Waterhouse, No.304, pl.86). It was destroyed during a fire at the Town Hall in 1946.

138

TO WILLIAM, 2ND EARL OF DARTMOUTH 25 MAY 1769

MS. Staffordshire Record Office, Stafford (D(W)1778/III/257)

May 25th. 1769

Rec^{d}. of the R^{t}. Honb^{le} Earl of Dartmouth, one hundred & twenty six pounds, in full for two half length Portraits[1]

£126 Tho Gainsborough

1 The half-lengths of the 2nd Earl and his wife, Frances, remain in the ownership of the family (Waterhouse, Nos.185 and 186). The price of sixty guineas each is inexplicable, since forty guineas for a half-length and sixty for a full-length was still Gainsborough's scale in 1769 (see Letters 140 and 137).

Henry, 3rd Duke of Buccleuch (1746–1812)
Canvas, 123.2 x 96.5
1770
Duke of Buccleuch and Queensberry KT, Bowhill

139

TO THE REVD NICHOLAS BACON 5 AUGUST 1769

MS. Pierpont Morgan Library, New York (MA 2411)

Augst. 5th 1769

Rec^{d}. of The Rev^{d} M^{r}. Nicholas Bacon five Guineas which I paid for a Fruit-piece[1]

£5.5 Tho Gainsborough

1 This is the only documentation of Gainsborough having acted on someone's behalf in a picture purchase (probably in the sale-room). The Revd. Nicholas Bacon (d.1795), a member of the Bacon family of Shrubland Park, near Woodbridge, in Suffolk, was Vicar of St. Mary's, Coddenham, Curate of All Saints, Hawstead, and Rector of St. Mary's, Barham, all in Suffolk.

140

TO JOHN, 4TH DUKE OF BEDFORD 23 NOVEMBER 1769

MS. Marquis of Tavistock and the Trustees of the Bedford Estate, Woburn MSS

Bath Novr. 23rd 1769 Recd. of His Grace The Duke of Bedford forty

Guineas for a half length Portrait of His Grace,[1] and ten shillings for a Case, in full of all Demands

£42–10 Thos. Gainsborough

1 Woburn Abbey, Bedfordshire (Waterhouse, No.55).

141

TO HENRY, 3RD DUKE OF BUCCLEUCH[1] 21 NOVEMBER 1770

MS. The Duke of Buccleuch and Queensberry KT, Drumlanrig

Mr Gainsborough presents his humble service to the Duke of Buccleugh, and thanks His Grace for having leave to Draw for a hundred Pounds, which he has now done and made payable to M^{r}. Stanton of Cheapside,[2] and which he acknowledges to be more than in full of all demands.

Bath Novr. 21st. 1770

M^{r}. G— will take the first Opportunity of restoring the Drawing of the Duke of Montague,[3] and of sending it to His Grace.

1 Henry, 3rd Duke of Buccleuch (1746–1812). The portrait is at Bowhill, the family's seat in the Scottish Borders (Waterhouse, No.88, pl.120).

2 Either William Stanton, linen draper at 61 Cheapside (see also Letter 117, note 1), or John Stanton, haberdasher at 111 Cheapside (*Baldwin's New Complete Guide*, 1770). Presumably Gainsborough was owing one of them money, though the figure is substantial.

3 Presumably the pastel which he had done a few years previously, in about 1768 (John Hayes, *The Drawings of Thomas Gainsborough*, London, 1970, No.41, pl.116).

142

TO CLEMENT TUDWAY[1] 2 JULY 1773

MS. Tudway MSS, Somerset Record Office, Taunton (DD/TD/2/72–74)

Bath July 2^{d}. 1773 Rec^{d}. of Clem: Tudway Esq. the sum of seventy Pounds sixteen Shillings, in full for two I Portraits (Viz. Himself & Mrs. Tudway) and two Frames Burnish'd Gold, Case & ec.—

Thos Gainsborough £70:16

1 Clement Tudway (1734–1815), who was Member of Parliament for Wells, 1761–90, and became the Father of the House of Commons, managed the family's extensive sugar

Clement Tudway (1734–1815)
Canvas, 76.2 x 63.5
Early 1770s
North Carolina Museum of Art, Raleigh

plantations in Antigua. His portrait is in the North Carolina Museum of Art, Raleigh (Waterhouse, no.678); that of his wife is in the Philadelphia Museum of Art (Waterhouse, No.679). Both portraits are head-and-shoulders, and evidently cost thirty guineas each, Gainsborough's new price for this size.

143

TO ALDERMAN THOMAS HARLEY[1] 17 FEBRUARY 1778

MS. Gainsborough's House, Sudbury (1990.042)

Feb: 17th. 1778

Recd. of The Honble. Mr Harley, ninety Guineas, being half payment for three half-length Portraits of Miss Harley's
£94–10 Tho Gainsborough

1 Alderman Thomas Harley (1730–1804) was a wealthy banker and army contractor who was Lord Mayor of London in 1767 and Member of Parliament for the City of London, 1761–74, then for Hereford, 1776–1802. Harley built a new house, Berrington Hall, to the designs of Henry Holland, on his Herefordshire estate, 1778–81, and the portraits of his three elder daughters were intended to decorate the drawing-room

Alderman Thomas Harley (1730–1804)
Stipple engraving after Henry Edridge (1769–1821)
National Portrait Gallery (Archive Engravings Collection)

there. The portrait of Martha (1756–88), who married the banker, George Drummond, in 1779, was last recorded in an Anon. sale, Sotheby's, 16 November 1988, lot 57 (repr.col.), bt. Lady Abdy (Waterhouse, No.212); that of Anne (1759–1840), who married George, eldest son of Admiral Lord Rodney in 1781, is in the Philadelphia Museum of Art (Waterhouse, No.584); and that of Sarah, who married Robert, 10th Earl of Kinnoull, also in 1781, was last recorded in the Keck Collection sale, Sotheby's, 13 November 1991, lot 49 (repr.col.) (Waterhouse, No.415). Gainsborough's price for a half-length had presumably increased to sixty guineas in or before 1773 at the same time as his price for a head-and-shoulders to thirty (see Nos.144 and 142).

144

TO SIR THOMAS CLARGES, 3RD BT.[1] 7 AUGUST 1778

MS. (last recorded with Kenneth W. Rendell Gallery, New York,1999)

Augs^{t}. 7th. 1778

Rec^{d}. of Sir Thomas Clarges Sixty five Guineas in full for a Portrait of Lady Clarges and a Frame
68.5 Tho Gainsborough

1 Sir Thomas Clarges, 3rd Bt. (1751–82), of Aston, near Stevenage, in Hertfordshire, was Member of Parliament for Lincoln, 1780–82. A lover and patron of music, Clarges married in 1777 a harpist, Louisa Skrine (c. 1755–1809), who was later to achieve eminence; Lady Clarges travelled frequently in Italy after she was widowed and attracted many admirers, notably Sir William Hamilton. The half-length portrait of Louisa is in the Holburne of Menstrie Museum, Bath (Waterhouse, No.149).

145

TO SIR JOSHUA REYNOLDS 20 APRIL 1782

Untraced (transcribed from the Whitley Papers, Dept. of Prints and Drawings, British Museum: Gainsborough box, Guard Book for 1781–1787, slip on fo.16 with the note 'This is taken from the earlier Artist's Magazine').

April 20th 1782—

Received of Sir Joshua Reynolds One hundred guineas in full for a picture of 'A Girl with Piggs' & all demands.[1]

£105. Thomas Gainsborough

1 See Letter 88 and note 2.

146

TO JOHN, 3RD DUKE OF DORSET 15 JUNE 1784

MS. Sackville MSS, Knole

Recd of His Grace the Duke of Dorset one hundred Guineas in full for two ¾ Portraits of his Grace, one full length of Madlle Baccelli, two Landskips and one sketch of Begger Boy and Girl £105[1]

June 15 1784 Tho. Gainsborough

1 Receipt for a payment, presumably the final one, for a group of pictures painted over the previous few years. A head-and-shoulders of the Duke was intended for the Royal Academy exhibition of 1782, but was not sent (still in the family collection at Knole, near Sevenoaks, Kent: Waterhouse, No.203, pl.251); the whereabouts of the second version is unknown. The full-length of the Duke's mistress, Giovanni Baccelli (died 1801), depicted in her role in *Les Amans Surpris*, which she danced with great success in the 1781–82 season at the King's Theatre, Haymarket, was exhibited at the 1782 Academy (now Tate Gallery, London: Waterhouse, No.29, pl.235). The Duke bought three landscapes in 1778, for which he paid eighty guineas each; none of them survives. The sketch of a beggar boy and girl (now Sterling and Francine Art Institute, Williamstown: Waterhouse, No.801) has been known since at least 1817 as a portrait of Miss Linley and her brother and may have been cut down from the larger portrait of the two Linleys upon which Gainsborough was engaged in 1768.

Ozias Humphry (1742–1810)
Charles, 3rd Earl Stanhope (1753–1816)
Canvas, cut down from 127 x 101.6 to 76.2 x 63.5.
1796. Unfinished
Private Collection, England

147

TO CHARLES, 3RD EARL STANHOPE[1] 3 MARCH 1787

MS. Chevening MSS (No.748) (kindly communicated to me by John Harris)

March 3rd 1787 Rec[d] of the R[t] Hon[bl] Earl Stanhope thirty Guineas, being half payment for a Portrait of His Lordship
£31.10 Tho Gainsborough

1 Charles, 3rd Earl Stanhope (1753–1816). The portrait (Private Collection, England: Waterhouse, No.632) was left unfinished at the artist's death, and was later cut down from 50 x 40 in. to 30 x 25 in.

APPENDIX I

CONCORDANCE

The following table refers to the second edition of Mary Woodall's *The Letters of Thomas Gainsborough*, published in 1963, which included the additional numbers 101-108. NI: not included; NK: not known to Woodall

WOODALL NO.	THIS EDITION	WOODALL NO.	THIS EDITION
1	90	30	50
2	89	31	34
3	96, 97	32	62
4	101	33	51
5	104	34	63
6	NI	35	74
7	17	36	76
8	19	37	77
9	32	38	78
10	106	39	81
11	91	40	86
12	83	41	102
13	72	42	15
14	100	43	108
15	138	44	68
16	52	45	69
17	53	46	65
18	54	47	16
19	85	48	33
20	71	49	22
21	26	50	23
22	93	51	24
23	94	52	41
24	4	53	42
25	5	54	30
26	21	55	39
27	35	56	40
28	36	57	43
29	137	58	44

WOODALL NO.	THIS EDITION	WOODALL NO.	THIS EDITION
59	38	104	1
60	79	105	NI
61	45	106	103
62	84	107	NI
63	37	108	NI
64	92	NK	2
65	107	NK	3
66	58	NK	25
67	110	NK	47
68	88	NK	55
69	145	NK	56
70	7	NK	57
71	98	NK	61
72	75	NK	67
73	27	NK	80
74	28	NK	82
75	29, 134	NK	87
76	130	NK	95
77	59	NI	99
78	60	NI	105
79	49	NI	111
80	6	NI	112
81	70	NI	113
82	9	NI	114
83	11	NI	115
84	10	NI	117
85	13	NI	121
86	14	NI	122
87	12	NI	123
88	18	NI	125
89	20	NI	127
90	31	NI	128
91	46	NI	129
92	48	NI	132
93	126	NI	133
94	118	NI	135
95	116	NI	136
96	120	NI	139
97	119	NI	140
98	124	NI	141
99	109	NI	142
100	8	NI	143
101	66	NI	144
102	73	NI	146
103	64	NI	147

APPENDIX II

RECIPIENTS OF LETTERS

Bate-Dudley, the Revd. Sir Henry, Bt.	101, 104
Beaumont, Percival	17, 19
Bedford, John, 4th Duke of	32
Bowyer, Robert	106
Chambers, Sir William, R.A.	91
Charlton, Dr. Rice	83
Cipriani, Giovanni Battista, R.A.	72
Cosway, Richard, R.A.	99, 100
Dartmouth, William, 2nd Earl of	52, 53, 54
Ditcher, Mrs. Mary	85
Dodd, the Revd. William	71
Dodsley, James	25, 26
Dupont, Mrs. Sarah	93, 94
Essex, William, 4th Earl of	95
Garrick, David	21, 34, 35, 36, 50, 51, 62, 63, 66, 73
Gibbon, Mrs. Mary	74, 76, 77, 78, 80, 81, 86, 87, 102
Hardwicke, Philip, 2nd Earl of	15
(when Viscount Royston)	7
Harris, Mr, possibly Charles or Josiah	2
Harvey, Thomas	108
Hatley, James	3
Henderson, John	68, 69
Hoare, William, R.A.	65
Humphry, Ozias, R.A.	16
Jackson, William	22, 23, 24, 30, 33, 38, 39, 40, 41, 42, 43, 44, 45, 64, 79, 84
Kirby, Joshua	37
Lansdowne, William Petty, 1st Marquess of	103
Lowther, the Revd. Sir William, 1st Bt.	82
Mayhew, William	4, 5
Newton, Francis Milner, R.A.	89
Pearce, William	92, 107
Phipps, the Hon. Constantine, M.P., later 2nd Baron Mulgrave	55, 56, 57, 61
Pulteney, William Johnstone,	58
Rasse, Mrs. Elizabeth	1

APPENDIX III

BIOGRAPHICAL REGISTER

CARL FRIEDRICH ABEL (1725-87), a member of the court band at Dresden for ten years, came to London in 1759, and later became one of Queen Charlotte's court musicians. He and Johann Christian Bach organized series of subscription concerts in London, most famously at the Hanover Square Rooms. Gainsborough came to know him in the early 1760s and painted him twice with his viola da gamba, which Abel called 'the king of instruments' (National Portrait Gallery, London (5947): Waterhouse, No.3; and Henry E. Huntington Art Gallery, San Marino, exhibited R.A. 1777: Waterhouse, No.1, pl.171). Abel's apartments were covered with the artist's drawings and the two were close friends and boon companions for a quarter of a century, Gainsborough deeply mourning his death in 1787 (see no.101).

EDWARD STRATFORD, 2ND EARL OF ALDBOROUGH (died 1801 aged about 60), of Irish descent, was Member of Parliament for Taunton, 1774-5, then represented Baltinglass in the Irish Parliament until he succeeded his father in 1777. A member of the Royal Society, he was both able and eccentric. He built Stratford Place and Aldborough (later Derby) House, north of Oxford Street, shortly after his correspondence with Gainsborough; he built a mansion for himself next door to Aldborough House after his marriage to his rich second wife in 1787.

THE REVD. HENRY BATE-DUDLEY (1745-1824), rector of St. Thomas's, Bradwell, in Essex, and later a Prebendary of Ely Cathedral, was known as 'the fighting parson' because of his fast despatch of bullies and malefactors. Joint proprietor and editor of the Morning Post, 1772-80, and sole proprietor and editor of the Morning Herald, 1780-1824, he was a close friend and admirer of Gainsborough and reported his work in detail in the columns of his newspapers. Gainsborough's cottage in Essex, drawn by Rowlandson, may possibly have been on land inherited by Bate-Dudley. Bate-Dudley, a Foxite, was eventually created a baronet in 1813.

JOHN, 4TH DUKE OF BEDFORD (1710-71), who played an active part in the management of his huge estates, had an influential following in politics largely due to this vast wealth. He was a reforming First Lord of the Admiralty, 1744-8, and a successful and popular Lord Lieutenant of Ireland, 1755-61; in 1762 he went as Ambassador to Paris to negotiate peace with France, ending the Seven Years War. Proud and hot-tempered, he was also honest and warm-hearted. The Duke, who was much involved with the arts from the 1740s, commissioned two landscapes from Gainsborough in 1755, and several portraits, 1764-8; the two were clearly on cordial terms.

BERTIE BURGH came of a Monmouthshire family and succeeded his father as Receiver General to the Dukes of Beaufort. Unfortunately, the Beauforts' trust was misplaced in the son since, after the 4th Duke's death in 1756, it was found that no proper accounts had been kept since 1748; Burgh was pursued, but was found to be bankrupt. Burgh practised as a lawyer and a banker from Castle Yard, Holborn, where Gainsborough had an account with him in the 1750s, though only two transactions survive (more survive with Burgh's partner, James Unwin, q.v.).

DR RICE CHARLETON (1723-88), with Dr Moysey a Physician to the General Hospital, 1757-81, frequently attended Gainsborough and his family. A man of considerable wealth, he was a friend of William Shenstone and an enthusiast for landscape gardening, and owned a splendid art collection, mostly hung at his country seat overlooking the Severn, Woodhouse, near Almondsbury, just north of Bristol (no longer extant). Gainsborough presented him with a fine, large landscape, painted c.1762/3 (Hayes Landscape Paintings, No.77), after recovering from his serious illness, and painted him at full length at the beginning of 1764 (exhibited Society of Artists, 1766 (51): Holburne Museum of Art, Bath: Waterhouse, No.136, pl.87), probably also as a gift in lieu of medical fees.

WILLIAM, 2ND EARL OF DARTMOUTH (1731-1801), step-brother of Lord North, held office in the latter's administration, 1772-82, first as Secretary of State for the Colonies and President of the Board of Trade and Foreign Plantations, then as Lord Privy Seal; conciliatory towards the American colonists, unfortunately he lacked resolution or indeed adminstrative capacity. Intensely pious, he had close affiliations with methodism. Dartmouth commissioned twelve finished drawings of Rome by Richard Wilson during his Grand Tour with his step-brother, 1752-4, and sat to Batoni and Reynolds (several times) as well as Gainsborough. Dartmouth's wife, Frances (c.1733-1805), whom he married in 1755, and the style of whose portrait was the cause of some contention between Gainsborough and his clients, was the only daughter and heiress of Sir Charles Gunter Nicoll.

GAINSBOROUGH DUPONT (1754-97), the second son of Gainsborough's second eldest sister, Sarah, and Philip Dupont, a carpenter in Sudbury, was apprenticed to Gainsborough in 1772 and entered the Royal Academy Schools in 1775, soon after the Gainsboroughs moved to London. He remained Gainsborough's (only) studio assistant until the latter's death and then took over the studio, making a respectable living as a portraitist and also painting landscapes. Overshadowed by the young Lawrence, however, and lacking the genius of his late uncle, he failed three times to become an Associate of the Royal Academy, and died young.

JOHANN CHRISTIAN FISCHER (1733-1800), the great oboeist, was, like his friend, C. F. Abel (q.v.), a member of the court band at Dresden and, after settling in London (1768), of Queen Charlotte's band (1780). He had a virtuoso performing technique, and his sophisticated new instrument, the two-key oboe, is seen on the pianoforte in Gainsborough's full-length of him (exhibited R.A. 1780 (222): Royal Collection, Buckingham Palace: Waterhouse, No.252, pl.216). Fischer seems to have courted both Gainsborough's daughters, and in 1780 married Mary; the marriage, of which Gainsborough disapproved (see Nos. 86 and 87), was, however, unhappy and short-lived.

MRS JOHANN CHRISTIAN FISCHER, née Mary Gainsborough (1750-1826), was Gainsborough's elder surviving daughter (his first died in infancy in 1748). She married the virtuoso oboeist, Johann Christian Fischer (q.v.), at St. Anne's, Soho, on 21 February 1780 (see Nos. 86 and 87), but the relationship soon foundered. After her mother's death she lived with her sister, Margaret (q.v.), first in Brompton and Brook Green, finally in Acton; she had early shown signs of mental instability - Farington described her in 1799 as 'not like her Sister but of a melancholy aspect' - and died insane (it is noteworthy that it was her younger sister who was named both her father's and her mother's executor). Gainsborough painted her many times, often with her sister, the best-known being the enchanting canvas of the two youngsters chasing a butterfly (National Gallery, London: Waterhouse, No. 285, pl.52); the double portrait of them as teenagers, with pencil and portfolio, in the Worcester Art Museum, Mass. (Waterhouse, No.287, pl.90) illustrates Gainsborough's intention to teach them to paint landscapes in case they should ever be forced to earn a living (see No.13).

THE REVD. HUMPHRY GAINSBOROUGH (1718-76) was Gainsborough's second eldest brother. In the latter part of his life he was minister of the Independent chapel in South Street, Henley-on-Thames. A man of considerable mechanical and inventive abilities, he was also, from 1773, collector of the tolls on the locks between Hambleden and Sonning.

MARGARET GAINSBOROUGH (1751-1820) was Gainsborough's younger daughter. She was executrix of her mother's will, 1798, and died unmarried. See also her elder sister, Mrs J. C. Fischer.

MRS THOMAS GAINSBOROUGH, née Margaret Burr (1728-98), was the illegitimate daughter of Henry, 3rd Duke of Beaufort, who settled an annuity of £200 upon her from the date of his death (1745). In July 1746, when she married Gainsborough at Dr Keith's celebrated Mayfair Chapel, she was resident in Duke Street, a shopping street north of Grosvenor Square not far from the Beauforts' palatial town mansion (later Grosvenor House), and may have been placed in employment there by her father. Nothing is known of her mother. Of the several surviving portraits of her by her husband, the most moving is that in the Courtauld Institute Galleries, painted when she was about fifty (Waterhouse, No.299, pl.209). The couple were devoted to each other, but, as the letters reveal, they were in many ways incompatible.

DAVID GARRICK (1717-79) was the greatest actor of his age and managed the Theatre Royal, Drury Lane, from 1747 until his retirement from the stage in 1776. A vain man, he was much portrayed. Gainsborough came to know him in the early 1760s, and the two became close friends; in later years their wit was to enliven Christie's auction room. A full-length exhibited at the Society of Artists in 1766 was destroyed by fire at Stratford Town Hall in 1946 (Waterhouse, No.304, pl.86); the head-and-shoulders exhibited at the Royal Academy in 1770 (see No.63) is now in the National Portrait Gallery (Waterhouse, No.305).

FELICE DE' GIARDINI (1716-96), invited to England in 1749 or 1750 by Frederick, Prince of Wales, was the first great virtuoso violinist to perform in London. Although he is said to have hated Handel and the modern German composers, he led the band at the King's Theatre, Haymarket, for over thirty years, and came to know Gainsborough in Ipswich (see No.34), when he embarked on a long series of concert tours in the provinces in the late 1750s. The two became close friends and boon companions (see no.72). Gainsborough painted a replica of his first 'Cottage Door' composition for him c.1773; a half-length portrait, probably painted in the early 1760s, was bought by the Duke of Dorset in 1778 (Waterhouse, no.311).

JOHN HENDERSON (1747-85), an actor who was regarded by the public as inferior only to Garrick, started his stage career in Bath, where he was engaged by John Palmer (q.v.). Owing to lack of support in the profession, he did not perform in London until 1777, when he played Shylock at the Haymarket Theatre. Small and ill-favoured, he was 'the soul of intelligence' (Sarah Siddons) and an excellent mimic. Gainsborough befriended the young actor during the latter's first season in Bath, but his warnings against over-indulgence went unheeded and Henderson died young. A half-length of him which Gainsborough exhibited at the Royal Academy in 1780 (194) is on long-term loan to Gainsborough's House, Sudbury, from the National Portrait Gallery (Waterhouse, No.360).

JOHN HUNTER (1728-93), the distinguished surgeon, skilled in dissection, was first and foremost an experimental scientist, making important discoveries in geology and natural history as well as in surgery and comparative anatomy. His celebrated museum (acquired after his death by the Royal College of Surgeons) was formed to illustrate life in its entirety, whether healthy or diseased (he commissioned several pictures of animals from Stubbs). Hunter took no fees from authors or artists, but Gainsborough never painted his portrait: the great surgeon was unsociable,and the two may never have met until Gainsborough's last illness.

WILLIAM JACKSON (1730-1803) was a composer of church music and popular songs and, later, two operas, of which The Lord of the Manor (1780) was a lasting success. Of modest abilities, he had resorted to teaching music in his native Exeter when, in 1777, he was appointed organist of Exeter Cathedral. Jackson took up landscape painting as a hobby in 1757, and became acquainted with Gainsborough in the early 1760s through Samuel Collins, the miniature painter. The two men, sharing similar pleasures, soon became intimate friends, and settled into a correspondence; advice (and admonishment) on painting was exchanged for instruction in music. Gainsborough painted a half-length of Jackson which he exhibited at the Royal Academy in 1770 (Private Collection, Scotland: unknown to Waterhouse). Jackson's odd, indeed malicious, account of Gainsborough's musical abilities in his book The Four Ages (1798) is hard to explain, and has been refuted.

SAMUEL KILDERBEE (1725-1813) was an attorney from Framlingham who served as Ipswich Town Clerk, 1755-67. Brought in in a year of local political squabbling, Gainsborough soon painted a vigorous three-quarter-length of him (San Francisco Museums: Waterhouse, No.407, pl.44). The two became lifelong friends; they travelled to the Lake District together in 1783 (see No.92), and Gainsborough requested Kilderbee to act as overseer of his will and assist his wife and younger daughter, Margaret, who were named as executors. Gainsborough's letters to his old friend, described by William Jackson (q.v.) as 'brilliant but eccentric, and too licentious to be published' have never been traced, and may have been destroyed in a more squeamish age.

DR ABEL MOYSEY (1715-80) was one of the best known Bath physicians, holding the prestigious appointment of Physician to the General Hospital; he was a wealthy man, with a fine house in Queen Square and an extensive property at Hinton Charterhouse (presumably Hinton House, the only grand house with a large estate in the area), about six miles south of Bath. Moysey attended Gainsborough and his family, and it was he who pronounced of Mary Gainsborough's illness in 1771, much to Gainsborough's distress, that 'it was a family complaint and he did not suppose she would ever recover her senses again'. Gainsborough painted a three-quarter-length of him, c.1764 and a full-length of his son, c.1771, both as gifts in lieu of fees (Private Collection, England, the former on long-term loan to the Holburne Museum of Art, Bath, the latter on long-term loan to Gainsborough's House, Sudbury: Waterhouse, Nos.505 and 506, pls.91 and 137).

CONSTANTINE PHIPPS, 2ND BARON MULGRAVE (1744-92), was an intrepid sailor who served in the West Indies as a youngster in the last years of the Seven Years War, and in the American War of Independence, when he was also one of the lords of the Admiralty. He was Member of Parliament for Lincoln, 1768-77, Huntingdon, 1777-84, and Newark-upon-Trent, 1784-90. An antiquary and bibliophile, his library of works concerned with nautical affairs was unsurpassed. Gainsborough taught him to make drawings in his sophisticated technique of the early 1770s (see No.64). Gainsborough exhibited a head-and-shoulders of Phipps at the Royal Academy in 1772 (97) (Marquess of Normanby, Mulgrave Castle: Waterhouse, No.508), and later supplied two full-lengths of him in 1785 and 1786 (Marquess of Normanby, Mulgrave Castle and Smithsonian Institution, Washington: Waterhouse, Nos.509 and 510). Gainsborough also painted for him a swashbuckling full-length of his uncle and first commanding officer, Augustus Hervey, 3rd Earl of Bristol, which was exhibited at the Society of Artists in 1768 (60) (National Trust, Ickworth: Waterhouse, No.82, pl.105).

FRANCIS MILNER NEWTON (1720-94), although a portraitist of limited ability, played a leading role in the movement for establishing an academy and exhibiting body in the 1750s, and was elected the first Secretary of the Royal Academy in 1768, retiring in 1788; Farington described him as 'pettish, with troublesome Office Pomp'. It was probably he who introduced Gainsborough to his cousin, Goodenough Earle, of Barton Grange, near Taunton, Somerset, the recipient of some of the artist's finest drawings. Newton inherited Barton Grange in 1789, and died there.

JOHN PALMER (c.1720-88), a prosperous brewer and tallow-chandler in Bath, became the proprietor of a new theatre in the city in 1750, and opened another in 1767, in Orchard Street. In 1768 this became the first Theatre Royal in the provinces, when Palmer was granted a virtual monopoly of theatrical property in Bath by Act of Parliament. His son, John (1742-1818), who helped in these endeavours as his agent in London, took over management of the theatres, and another in Bristol, in the second half of the 1770s, and was later celebrated as the entrepreneur who, supported by William Pitt, transformed Britain's postal services, becoming Comptroller-General of the Post Office in 1786. Gainsborough knew both the Palmers well, and painted a half-length of the son, c.1775 (Philadelphia Museum of Art: Waterhouse, No.533).

SIR JOSHUA REYNOLDS (1723-92), the first President of the Royal Academy, was Gainsborough's principal rival as a portrait painter. He was able to command much higher prices - 200 guineas for a full-length in 1782 compared to Gainsborough's 100 - and Gainsborough acknowledged the range of his achievement: 'Damn him, how various he is'. Opposite in so many ways, their relations were strained; a final reconciliation took place during Gainsborough's last illness, and a few months later Reynolds delivered his memorable, and conspicuously generous, Discourse devoted to Gainsborough's art.

GEORGE PITT, 1ST BARON RIVERS (1721-1803), was Member of Parliament for Shaftesbury, 1742-7, and for Dorset, 1747-74, before he was created Baron Rivers of Stratfieldsaye in 1776. He served as envoy in Turin, 1761-8, but declined taking up his appointment as ambassador in Madrid, 1770-1, 'as he cannot have his peerage'. Gainsborugh described him as 'a staunch Friend' (see No.46) and it was a full-length of George Pitt that he sent as an example of his male portraiture to the first Royal Academy exhibition of 1769 (Private Collection, England: Waterhouse, No.577, pl.110).

RICHARD STEVENS, of Winscott, near Great Torrington, Devonshire, was the chief agent for Lady Orford's estates in Devon and Cornwall. He served on her interest as Member of Parliament for Callington, 1761-8. Gainsborough painted a head-and-shoulders portrait of him, completed in April 1762 (last recorded in the Mrs Naylor sale, Christie's, 3 July 1951, lot 72, bt. Davidge: Waterhouse, No.634).

PHILIP THICKNESSE (1719-92) was an increasingly quarrelsome and malicious character who had befriended Gainsborough, and given him a commission for a decorative landscape, soon after his arrival as Lieutenant-Governor of Landguard Fort, opposite Harwich, in 1753. Shortly after Gainsborough's death he wrote a brief biographical sketch of him the purpose of which, as Robert Wark has noted, was to present the author as a benefactor of the arts who had discovered and promoted Gainsborough and was an important influence thoughout his career; the memoir gives a good impression of Gainsborough's mercurial temperament and generosity of spirit, but is hastily written and little more than a series of personal anecdotes, much of it unreliable, centring on the artist's failure to proceed with his portrait. Gainsborough's full-length of his beautiful third wife, Ann Ford, painted in 1760, two years before her marriage (Cincinnati Art Museum: Waterhouse, No.660, pl.62) is one of the painter's most original masterpieces.

JAMES UNWIN (1717-76) was an attorney with a connection with the Admiralty Prize Courts who acted as an agent for successive Dukes of Beaufort and other grandees and was, by the 1750s, a partner of Bertie Burgh (q.v.) in Castle Yard, Holborn. Until 1762 he was responsible for the payment of Margaret Gainsborough's annuity of £200 from Henry, 3rd Duke of Beaufort, and he became Gainsborough's banker and attorney and an intimate friend; the letters he received from Gainsborough, 1763-70, are the most extensive in the artist's surviving correspondence save those to William Jackson (q.v.). Gainsborough painted a half-length of him in the late 1750s (last recorded in an Anon. (= Unwin) sale, Sotheby's, 26 July 1950, lot 173, bt. Bellesi: Waterhouse, No.687) and also completed in 1771 a three-quarter-length of his wife, Frances, née Stephenson (Private Collection, Canada: Waterhouse, No.688), formerly a friend of Captain Edward Wheeler, who died in 1761 bequeathing his considerable estates to Unwin.

WALTER WILTSHIRE (1719-99) of Shockerwick, near Bath, whose father was the proprietor of one of the two lower Assembly Rooms, was a wealthy Bath merchant, and Mayor of the city in 1772, 1780 and 1791. Amongst other enterprises he ran a carrier's service between Bath and London. In Gainsborough's time at Bath, before he built the present Shockerwick House on his estate, c.1778-85, he lived nearby, at Bathford. Wiltshire had a fine collection of pictures, including Gainsborough's celebrated The Harvest Wagon (Barber Institute of Fine Arts, Birmingham: Hayes Landscape Paintings, No.88), which the artist gave him in 1774, when he left Bath, reputedly in return for a grey horse he had been accustomed to ride on his visits. There is no record of Gainsborough having painted Wiltshire.

INDEX

excluding recipients of letters (see pp. 199–200)